ABOUT AUTHOR

Born in Dublin in 1946, I spent my early years on a farm in Ireland with my grandmother and took on responsibilities way beyond my age. These years shaped my future national identity. In 1960 I emigrated to London, just in time to join the social and cultural changes that were sweeping away post war austerity. I had the good fortune to stay beyond the school leaving age and gain a place at London University, becoming the first in my immediate family to do so.

At university I participated in anti-war demonstrations, became President of the London University Debating Society and met my future Norwegian wife. After teaching in grammar schools, I joined the comprehensive education movement and became Head of Science and later Deputy Headteacher in three different comprehensive schools. A growing family, politics and sport were now central to my life. My wife's contacts as a language teacher coupled to my marathon running across the world served as a link to the global family.

After early retirement in 1999 from state schools, I started a new career teaching in some of England's elite private schools, had a heart bypass, kept on running and completed my first 100 mile Olympic Legacy Bike Ride for Cystic Fibrosis in 2015.

LIFE'S LESSONS
LEARNT

FROM IRISH BOHAREENS TO LONDON STREETS TO THE TEMPLES OF LEARNING

SEAN A O'REILLY

authorHOUSE®

AuthorHouse™ UK
1663 Liberty Drive
Bloomington, IN 47403 USA
www.authorhouse.co.uk
Phone: 0800.197.4150

Published by AuthorHouse 05/12/2016

ISBN: 978-1-5246-3042-3 (sc)
ISBN: 978-1-5246-3043-0 (hc)
ISBN: 978-1-5246-3044-7 (e)

Print information available on the last page.

This book is printed on acid-free paper.

A MEMOIR

Dedicated to the memories of family who have completed their earthly journey and prepared me for mine

Dedicated to my immediate family, wider family, friends and former pupils who shared my life's journey with me

Dedicated to the family of the future in the hope that this memoir will provide them with some signposts to help them on their way

CONTENTS

INTRODUCTION

Writing this memoir has allowed me to reflect with both joy and sadness on events that have influenced my life and my good fortune in reaching the biblical three score years and ten. Four overwhelming themes have governed my life: family and all that entails; the quest for knowledge, scientific truth and intellectual betterment and the lifelong effort to pass on my learning to others; the effort in a small way to try to alleviate the suffering of those less fortunate than I have been; the joy coupled to the physical and emotional challenge of sport as both participant and spectator.

Every person has an interesting life story to tell and I do not claim that my story is unique or better. I do believe that I have been fortunate to have a wonderful close and wider family and to have an education than encompassed several disciplines to tertiary level and beyond. It is a privilege to share a wonderful marriage with my Norwegian wife for nearly fifty years who has also opened doors for me into the wider European family.

My early years on a farm with my grandmother in Ireland were formative and shaped my national and cultural identity. I was given the opportunity and privilege – even if born out of necessity – to take on responsibilities way beyond my years and would not be allowed in the health, safety and politically correct driven world of today.

I was very fortunate to emigrate to England in 1960 to rejoin my family in time for the "wind of change" that was sweeping through Britain, freeing up that country from post war austerity and entering into a dawn of new educational, employment and cultural opportunities for young people. I was the first in my family to go to university and engage directly in the political and social changes of the 1960s.

The first time I entered a grammar school was to teach in one. In the 1970s I played my part in establishing comprehensive education for all, irrespective of social and economic status and the provision of a science and technology curriculum that embodied the spirit of discovery by experiment and the move away from Victorian didactic teaching methods.

My life was not shaped by the playing fields of Eton; but it was enriched by the Gaelic football, soccer and rugby pitches that I played on as well as on the tennis and squash court. Underpinning all my physical activities has been my ability to keep on running throughout most of my life. The most testing form of this activity was the completion of nearly sixty marathons in thirty countries. Even more satisfying was the amount of funding raised for different charities ranging from a children's hospice to medical research.

CHAPTER 1

THE EARLY YEARS – IRELAND – LAND OF MY BIRTH

At two years old, I had curly fair hair and a cherubic chubbiness. My mother was holding me in her arms whilst expertly balancing a cigarette from the side of her mouth. My father, thin and gaunt, age 34 years, was standing to her right, cigarette in hand. Mother gave me a few nice squeezes and got in a couple of puffs on her cigarette as my father looked on. I could see the lovely colours of the cultivated flowerbed in the background.

The scene was a public park in Dun Laoghaire, Dublin, Ireland in 1948. The cinematographer was my mother's uncle, Father John McKeever visiting from America.

This silent colour film represents for me the beginning of my existence on this earth, as I cannot remember anything from the first 3 years of my life and time in Dublin before we moved as a family to Co Wicklow. I was the only one of my siblings to be born in a hospital maternity ward and my father – the ever romantic- came to collect my mother and me in a fancy horse and carriage to take us home. He was delighted to have a son after two daughters, so much, so that he called me John after himself. My arrival provided my sister Dorothy – three years older than me- with her first childhood memory. She remembers our mother coming in the side door up the stairs to the sitting room above the shop holding her newborn baby brother wrapped in a white blanket. No doubt her memory was enhanced even more when she was given the job of keeping an eye on me in my carriage pram outside the shop. My mother was a great believer in fresh air and it appears I got plenty of that outside the family shop on the windswept street of 1 Lower George Street. My mother managed to get me a very distinguished Godfather, Professor Conway who she worked for as cook and general housekeeper using her qualifications gained in a residential vocational school before she got married. Professor Conway was a great friend and adviser to her uncle J C Fitzsimons when he set up the first lager brewery in the Republic of Ireland at Kells.

The fruit and vegetable shop that my parents operated did well during the years of the Second World War. Although the Irish Free State was neutral, they served as the breadbasket for a Britain cut off from its commonwealth food supply. My father's cattle dealing business in the 1930s was badly interrupted by the British 'Economic War' with Ireland when they refused to import Irish goods – mostly foodstuff. This action was a consequence of De Valera refusing to pay reparations to Britain resulting from the foundation of The Free State in 1921. It was only when German ships arrived in the Port of Dublin to buy Irish cattle and surplus foodstuff that Britain lifted the blockade.

My parents were able to get supplies of vegetables from my Granny's farm in Kells and her brother's farm in Ardee in Louth. Relatives worked in the shop from time to time and this caused problems especially when my father thought some of them were dipping their hands into the till. The links between the shop and the farm in Ardee brought my granny's brother Father John to Dublin with his colour film camera. The years of the war were good times for our family and my father always regretted having to leave the shop in 1950. He could not accept that the economic isolation of Ireland after the war was the main reason for the shop's demise. Recently in 2015 in Hertford, UK, I met an 89-year-old man, Mr Brennan, who remembers my father's shop well and who followed my father to England in 1956. I recognised him because he taught my daughter Astrid to swim in the 1990s in Hertford – small world.

I was the third born of four siblings: my sister Dorothy was born in 1943, Avril in 1944 and Vincent, born in Baltinglass, Co Wicklow in 1954.

BALLYJAMESDUFF, COUNTY CAVAN IN THE PROVINCE OF ULSTER, HOME OF MY FATHER.

I was aware as a young boy that my father came from Ballyjamesduff in County Cavan and that the O'Reilly (O' Raghallaigh in Irish) was a well-established name in and around Cavan. My loyalty to Cavan was established when I was about 8 years old when my dad took me to see Cavan play Meath in the Fitzsimons Cup in Kells. I remember the blue shirts of the Cavan team in contrast to the green and gold of Meath. My father told me that (in 1952) Cavan beat Meath in a replay to win the All Ireland final in Croak Park, Dublin and had to endure some local Meath displeasure on their way back to Cavan through Meath. I did not know then that Cavan had beaten Kerry in The Polo Grounds, New York in 1947 in the only all Ireland final played outside of Ireland. The final was staged in New York to commemorate the 100th anniversary of the worst year of the great Irish famine. Therefore, this was a very strong Cavan team but I still cannot remember who won and how my father would have reacted given the fact that the Fitzsimons Cup competition was set up by my mother's uncle who owned the bakery and brewery in the town of Kells. I suspect he would have been very keen on a Cavan win to get one up on the Fitzsimons family. Cavan's fortunes were soon to take a downward dip as the county suffered a drop in population in the 1950s/60s due to emigration and have not won the all Ireland since in contrast to Meath winning it on several occasions. At least the Cavan women did win an all

Ireland in 1977. Fathers have a great influence on which teams their children support in later life. My daughter and sons are great supporters of Arsenal and the London Irish and Ireland rugby teams. I like to think that I may have had an influence. They in turn have spread the Arsenal gospel further afield to their Norwegian relatives.

A year or so later I got a very special Christmas present, made even more so as I never got too many when I was living with my Granny in Kells. I went to bed on a moon lit Christmas Eve and could not get to sleep for ages thinking of what Santa might bring me. I woke up early on Christmas morning to find my present at the end of the bed – a brand new full size Gaelic football. I was to practise with that ball for many years until it fell apart. It was my ticket to playing to junior county level Gaelic football. It was a great pity that my dad never saw me play mainly because he was living and working in England at the time.

I had to wait until 1981 to visit Cavan when my wife, sons, and I toured Ireland in our caravan. We arrived in Ballyjamesduff – the O'Reilly heartland – in great anticipation of seeing the name on many shops and pubs. We were to be disappointed. All we saw was one run down pub with the name 'Reilly'. There were bars called 'Joe's, Pat's Watering Hole and Mick's Bar and Grocery. We parked up in the town square and went across to Joe's Bar. After ordering drinks I asked the barman" where were all the O'Reilly names in the town?". He looked at me as if I had taken leave of my senses and blurted out 'Sure Jasus I am an O'Reilly and if we used the name who the feck would know who was who'. Well I felt like a complete eejit but I could see my wife and sons knew they were at last in the O'Reilly homeland. On the way back to the car we noticed a bronze statue of a man sitting on a bench with some music sheets in his hand. On taking a closer look at the music sheet I saw a song titled "Come back Paddy Reilly to Ballyjamesduff" and the bronze statue was of Percy French.,

Lyrics go:

The Garden of Eden has vanished, they say
But I know the lie of it still;
Just turn to the left at the bridge of Finea
And stop when half way to Cootehill.
'Tis there I will find it,
I know sure enough
When fortune has come to me call,
Oh the grass it is green around Ballyjamesduff
And the blue sky is over it all.
And tones that are tender and tones that are gruff
Are whispered over the sea,
'Come back, Paddy Reilly to Ballyjamesduff
Come home, Paddy Reilly to me'

Before we left on our Irish tour I had asked my father, where exactly the farm was where he was born. He was surprisingly vague or even evasive. He mentioned the area was Farragh but they were many townships in and around Ballyjamesduff. I had already sensed that his early years in Ireland were not too happy. He was the youngest of eight sons and one daughter. His father was several years older than his wife was and died at 77 years old leaving the eldest son Patrick to inherit the farm. The farmhouse was two story with a slated roof with three bedrooms upstairs and had to accommodate Pat, his mother, sister and my father – the other siblings had moved out. The problem became acute when Pat met his wife to be – a man with a farm at that time in Ireland was a good catch for a young woman seeking a husband. Mrs Bennett, in trying to marry off her daughter Elizabeth, in Jane Austin's "Pride and Prejudice", comes to mind here. My father was very close to his brother Benny a few years older than he was. Benny had been working in London, sometimes for his brother Michael who had acquired a pub on the Isle of Dogs, The Angel Hotel in Ilford East London and a third pub in Epping. Benny and my father rented a shop in Summerhill, County Meath and had enough rooms to take their mother and sister from the farm to live with them. One of my first cousins, Ann O'Reilly from Virginia in Cavan, told me that Benny employed her brother Pat in the shop. One day the Weights and Measures inspectors arrived and found out that the scales were displaying weights greater than they should be. Benny contested their claim and a court case ensued. The court found Benny guilty but Pat took the rap and spent a short time in prison for the offence. Ann's family were not very pleased with Benny. Later big brother Michael in London bought a house in the seaside resort of Bray for their mother and sister where their mother- my paternal granny – died at the age of 85 years. Their sister Anna Maria sadly died of cancer there in 1960s – she never married but her mother did her best to find a rich farmer for her. My father used to send some money to them and in one letter – surprisingly without too much emotion – she tells him about a farmer showing some interest in her daughter.

We had a breakthrough in finding my father's birthplace on a second caravan tour of Ireland in 1992. Prior to this trip my second cousin Clare O'Reilly from Epping in Essex had visited my father and managed to get some more detailed information. She also got the address of my first cousin Ann O'Reilly – Perry who lived in Virginia, County Cavan. We found a nice rural basic campsite along the lake in Virginia and called in on Ann. This was the first time I ever met a first cousin on my father's side of the family and there are many of them. Ann was one of the daughters of Michael who had inherited the farm. She had visited my parents in Swiss Cottage in the early 1960s and was photographed by the iconic London photographer David Bailey. She was a good-looking young woman with lovely glossy long hair.

Luck was on our side. The farm was now in the ownership of her brother John, who was unmarried and had let the farm run down. John was to die only a few years later and Ann managed to secure the farm for her son Robert; but some of her siblings were not too happy with this outcome but at least the farm stayed in the family. We went with Ann to visit the farm, which was up a long gravel lane that ran past my father's small national school. I was quite impressed with the farmhouse and out buildings and found it difficult to understand why none of my family, including my mother, had ever been there. My father could be a bit touchy but he had nothing to be ashamed of from his past. Yes, my mother's farm was much bigger and she did see herself above most people in Cavan. It was not until 2003 just after my father died that she visited her husband's place of birth, and that after 61 years of marriage. Their birthplaces were only about 40 miles apart – a long bicycle ride. My father did have a scar on the side of his face that allegedly was the result of being struck with a hot poker when he was young. There again it could have been an accident as open coal and turf fires were very common in Ireland at that time. We do not know who might have done this to him on the farm but he was very sensitive about it. I have to conclude his early childhood on the farm was a hard experience and that he was glad to be out of it. He left the local school at 11 years old and could read and write to a high standard and there is a school class photograph from the early 1920s, in which he appears with two of his older brothers. Before he left the farm, he did have a favourite uncle back from America who he worked for as a cattle drover and dealer and who made the not uncommon promises of leaving his farm to him...

CHAPTER 2

BALTINGLASS, WICKLOW – BROTHER VINCENT'S BIRTHPLACE

We left Dublin around 1950 and settled in Baltinglass, County Wicklow about 40 miles to the south of the city. My parents rented a house in Ballyhacket but did not stay there long after the rat incident. This is probably my earliest childhood memory. After a Christmas visit to my granny's farm in Meath, we returned home and upon entering the front door of the house we saw scores of rats scampering in all directions. They had the Christmas party feast of their lives on the food specially prepared by my mother for our return. My parents decided on the spot to find another place to live.

The Baltinglass house was a two story stone one with separate stables and a good-sized garden. In front, there were lovely views of hills and a few hundred yards to the back the Slaney River provided the opportunity for some fishing. Unfortunately there was no running fresh water so every day we kids had to go to the well a few hundred yards away to fetch pales of water. We were only in the house a year or so when the government installed electric lighting – no more dirty smelly oil lamps. I used to love looking at the glowing clear electric bulb filaments and I was astonished with how much light came from the bulbs compared to the oil lamps. We were also able to use mains electricity to run our radio and could now get rid of the big lead batteries that needed regular recharging.

ACCIDENTS WILL HAPPEN – DANGEROUS LIVING.

The stable area was the scene of my first encounter with near death. A neighbour stabled a couple of ponies that were given the freedom of the yard. I was in the habit of crawling around when I got too close to the rear hoofs of one of the ponies. I can remember the pony kicking out backwards with both hoofs missing me on the way up put striking the back of my head on the way down. I was out cold. After a time I came round with a great pain in the back of my head and ringing in my ears. My mother found me, eventually, and poured cold water on the back of my head. I am not sure she realised how close I came to being killed, especially if the pony had caught me first with the upward kick.

A little later on a frosty night I ran up some stone steps leading out of the front garden and duly slipped and gashed the underside of my chin. Then it was a question of applying pressure to stem the flow of blood followed by plenty of salt water and when the blood had congealed, the iodine was applied that felt like putting a flame to the wound. No one thought of going to the hospital for minor accidents in the 1950s Ireland and I still have a nice scar to remind me of this accident.

My baby brother Vincent was next in line to be scarred. Our mother was a keen gardener – we needed to grow our own produce to survive. My sisters and I were enlisted to help with the digging and weeding duties. Unfortunately, as Vincent crawled around the vegetable plot one of my sisters caught him across the bridge of his nose with her spade. As with my chin, Vincent received the Iodine treatment to screams that could be heard by most of our neighbours. Our mother was in her early thirties and as her younger brother told me much later at her funeral, she could be a feisty woman. This we already knew in Baltinglass. My offending sister's turn to scream came later when our mother selected a thin branch from the side hedge that made a good 'Swish' and gave her a lashing. We always knew what was coming when she made her way to that hedge.

Our canine friends were also prone to accidents. We had a mongrel dog called Crab who had the freedom of the surrounding area but he liked to be with us when we were playing on the road outside our house. A rare car passed by with poorly inflated tyres. Crab ran to our side of the road but under the car. I can still see in slow motion the look in Crab's eyes as the rare car wheel ran over him. The wheel went straight over the middle of his body but Crab managed to roll with the wheel as it went over him. The flat tyre had spread the load and coupled with Crab's rolling action, meant he lived to see another day. Sometimes Crab took a liking to one of our chickens; he too got the swish treatment from my mother.

Compared to children in England where polio and other child diseases were common, my only encounter with illness other than colds was when I went blind for a few days and when the inside of my hand ballooned up. I developed a love for Lilac and its lovely scent very early on in life. I was in the habit of collecting some Lilac to bring indoors. On one occasion and a few days after my Lilac collecting my eyes swelled up so much so that I could not see. I was put to bed and when the doctor arrived he was not sure what was wrong with me. He suspected I might have had an allergic reaction to Lilac. The outcome was to do nothing but stay in bed for a few days to see if the swelling would subside. Luckily for me after about three days I began to see again. I am still not sure what caused it because I have had no problem with Lilac these days and still love that lilac smell in spring. Another strange ailment was the swelling on one of my hands. This time the Doctor cut into the swelling with a pair of sharp scissors and blood and mucous gushed out. It seemed to solve the problem but I never did find out the cause.

In contrast to my simple childhood health problems, my sister Avril had hearing and nasal problems that required hospital outpatient treatment. In the 1950s radiation treatment was very popular and was pioneered by The John Hopkins Hospital in the US. The medics believed that radium applied by specially designed applicators up the nasal cavity could cure middle ear infections and deafness. Deafness was a big problem in the US air force due to the new highflying pressurised jet aircraft. After applying the new radium method to several thousand military personal, it was deemed suitable for treating children with middle ear infections. In the US, many thousands of children received radiation treatment and it was not long before the practice spread to Ireland and other European countries. Avril visited Dublin for her radium treatment and she has never forgotten the time that she was in a ward on her own when a doctor arrived carrying a large wooden box and carefully took out the radium dial with long tongs. He then put the applicator holding the radium up her nose, taped it into position, and left the room for several minutes. To an eight-year-old child and one as sensitive and shy as Avril this must have been a great ordeal. I can remember my dad designing a balloon like contraption to act as a decongestor to help the treatment. Our father was very creative and practical – he would have made a great engineer if he had had the chance. Avril's problems were alleviated but there was a sting in the tail. People were coming slowly to realise that this radioactive element could have damaging as well as beneficial effects. Radium was in paint form to put on the hands of watches so that they would glow in the dark. The workers – mostly women – painting the dials used to lick the tip of the brushes to get a fine point. Some years later, some of them developed cancer of the tongue and or mouth. Therefore, it seemed strange that radium was used on children with hearing problems. It is now known that it can take years for cancers to develop after exposure to radiation. Only recently, Avril had a hard lump in her lower inside jaw and was worried if it could be something sinister from her childhood radiation treatment. Surgery revealed the lump was not malignant and she got the all clear.

Of course some of our neighbours had their problems. As kids we visited the Kelly family – they made good tea and there was a chance that one might get a nice rich tea biscuit as well. Old Ned Kelly liked to listen to the radio and always made sure that the big liquid lead accumulator was charged and the wick and oil for the oil lamp were regularly trimmed and filled. We would join him to listen to the Gaelic football commentaries from Croak Park in Dublin. One day we found out that Ned was in hospital – no tea and biscuits this time. Later we heard that Ned was back so we went to see him. We were in for a shock. Ned had an eye removed and was lying on a kitchen bench groaning in great pain. This went on for days before Ned died. I can still feel the helplessness of those around Ned to alleviate his pain. Did they use morphine in the early 1950s I wonder?

It was not long after that I saw my first corpse when I was about six years of age. The O'Neills had a farm and Mrs O'Neill's father was well on in years and died at about 90 years of age. Ireland is famous for its wakes and burials normally take place within a few days of death. Traditionally the body 'lies in state' for a night in the house and is then taken to the church to spend a second night before morning mass and burial. Most of the local community will come to pay their respects and members of the family will take it in turn to stay with the deceased throughout the night. The second night is party time – drinking and telling tales about the life of the deceased. I was too young to be at the second night but I can remember seeing a rigid figure with silver grey hair lying on a bed dressed in a sombre brown gown with crucifix in hand -an image that has remained with me ever since. It was over fifty years before I attended another wake. This time for my Aunt Phyllis Fitzsimons who died in her mid eighties. I celebrated Phyllis's life for both wake nights, the second night was a whole night drink- in and at the funeral mass the next morning I really did feel like a corpse myself. A couple of years later I attended a wake in the same house for the husband of my first cousin who died suddenly from a heart attack aged only 58 years old.

This was a much sadder experience but it convinced me of the great benefit of a wake for everybody including the closest relatives of the deceased.

The O'Neill farm was a regular place for me to visit. I was encouraged by the fact that Mrs O'Neill would always offer me some bread and bacon – I can remember always being slightly hungry and my mother was not into second helpings. We collected our daily evening milk from this farm and sometimes we might arrive during the rosary and we duly got down on our knees for the rest of the Hail Marys and Lord's Prayers. Our reward was a slice of brown bread with a lump of bacon as the O'Neill family sat down for their tea. Each year they slaughtered a pig on the farm and the pig's screams were heard for miles around. They hung suitable salted bits of the pig from the kitchen ceiling and in time were cured by the heat from the open fireplace. Sometimes I would go out with one of the sons to collect cocks of hay from the fields. A chain was put round the base of the haycock and then it was levered up the tilted slope of the cart. On one occasion, I was away at the O'Neills for several hours – a five or six-year-old boy is not the best judge of time. When I got home, my mother gave me the 'swish' treatment and put me to bed. Later she told my father about my absence and wound him up so much that he came up to the bedroom and gave me a few almighty slaps. He wanted to know what I had told the O'Neill's about the family. Whenever I met the neighbours I was instructed to say 'I don't know' to any questions. My parents were terrified of the neighbours knowing anything about the family business. In retrospect, I can understand their position as some of the neighbours were very nosey and gossipy. Even in England my mother was always obsessed with what people might think of her and would say 'Don't disgrace yourself in front of people'. I am sure that she found her own advice useful at her London Mill Hill Golf Club but as for me, I never let what people might think be a primary factor in my decision making.

MY FIRST SCHOOL.

I have a hazy memory of my first days at school but I have never forgotten the walk to and from school. I had my two sisters to walk with me but that did not make the walk any shorter. The school walk was about a mile and a half each way. These days it would be 'the school run' with the 4X4 BMW taking the strain rather than my little legs. Yes, it is hard for modern parents driving their children all over the place. I can still remember each house, clumps of trees, the Gaelic football ground, the church, the garage, the sweet shop, the nationalist memorial and the uphill final turn that led to my school.

The only time that I had a problem getting to school was my very first day. My older sister was responsible for dropping me off at the school but on the way, I needed to go to the toilet so she helped me over the wall and I headed off for some distant bushes. That was the last she saw of me. As I had not returned she thought that I may have ran back home. She returned to our house to find I was not there. My mother was not pleased and she vowed to give her a thrashing if she did not go back and find me. At the place where I crossed over the wall, there was still no sign of me. She carried on into the town to find me already in the classroom. To this day, how I ended up at the school on my own is a mystery. Conjecture is that maybe somebody passed by and gave me a lift on their bike.

The toilet stop on the way to and from school became a regular occurrence. I had clearly inherited my father's weak bladder. Years later, my father told me the story how a London police officer tried to arrest him for urinating in public. He had just left the pub on a cold frosty night. Pub Landlords only allowed customers ten minutes to drink up after last orders – even if you still had two pints to drink. They would shout at you that you were 'breaking the law'. Someway down the road, my father now desperate for a pee walked into a front garden and relieved himself behind the garden wall. Unfortunately, for him the garden was sloped towards the pavement resulting in a stream of steaming urine going across the pavement towards the road. As my father got back on the pavement, he met a police officer coming towards him who immediately accused him of urinating on the pavement. My father denied it was his and challenged the Officer to prove it. The officer thinking he had an easy arrest if my father had admitted the offence now realised there could be trouble so he told my father to 'f*** off you lying Paddy'. From then on, my father's advice was to make sure to use the toilet before you leave the pub.

The school building consisted of a four room stone building with slate roof and still exists but now as a community centre. Discipline was strict and there was more than one-year group in the same room so we often had to alternate between the front and backbenches. The windows were high up so all that you could see was the sky and treetops. Chalk, slates, Irish, Religion – with prayers, Maths, Reading and Writing and Irish History were our daily diet. I cannot remember getting a beating at this first school, which was certainly not the case in my later schools. My sisters attended the nearby girls' convent school. My sister Dorothy was not so lucky up at the Convent. According to my other sister Avril, one nun took a particular dislike to one of Dorothy's 'mistakes' and decided to stand her on a stool with a dunce's hat on at the entrance to the classroom. Children could see her as they walked past including Avril to her eternal embarrassment. On checking this out with Dorothy she told me that she has no memory of this punishment and had a great time at the Convent. (No comment from me on this one).

I always like to look forward to Christmas and would get excited if I saw even an advert with a sprig of holly in the local paper. On a day when the paper included a Santa, I was excited. Always Christmas was a long time coming. There were no advent calendars with a little window and hidden chocolate to look forward to in those days. The one Christmas present that I have never forgotten – thanks Santa – was the metal red steamroller. With that steamroller, I smoothed many imaginary tarmac roads around the floors of the house. The day came, on the way up to O'Neills, I decided to give it a work out on a real tarmac road. After about a hundred yards, I decided to hide the steamroller in the roadside hedge for collection on the way home. Unfortunately, I could not find it on the way home and my efforts to find it several times later failed. I was heartbroken. The sense of loss is still with me.

Time was running out for us for our stay in Baltinglass. Ireland was becoming an economic backwater. The economic decline after the war that forced my father out of Dublin to seek work in Wicklow had not abated. Ireland was isolated economically from Europe and the British Commonwealth. My father tried several activities to keep bread on the table. I remember going with him on his logging adventures. To take a tree down he would use a hatchet to chop out one side of the tree trunk and a handsaw cut made to allow steel wedges to be sledge hammered in so that the tree would fall down in the right direction. A two-man handsaw was used to cut through the tree trunk. He then hammered extra wedges into the saw cut to stop the weight of the tree resting on the saw. Soon we would start to hear the wood cracking and it was time to run – hopefully in the right direction. The branches were cut off and the tree trunk sawn into log sections and these would be lifted using a pulley up onto the lorry. After several large logs were loaded, the lorry would hopefully be driven out of the forest to the sawmill. I believed the logs were used for making coffins. Most of the trees came from the grounds of local convents and the idea was to use the trees to make coffins and this fact helped my father to get a good purchase price. Another venture my father tried was making concrete posts. I can remember laying out the steel wires in the moulds before pouring in the concrete. There was another job that he tried and this was to do with buying and selling chickens and eggs. My mother and father worked as a team and my mother was the head chicken plucker. Many of the customers used to pay by cheque and I had great fun playing with the piles of cheque stubs pinned on nails along the shed wall. I thought my parents were very rich – unknown to me many of the cheques bounced.

Our main mode of transport was a green Bedford van with dodgy breaks and a battery that was always going flat. Sometimes we drove the eighty miles, going through the centre of Dublin, on our way to my Granny's farm in Kells, County Meath but we nearly always had a breakdown. I cannot remember if we kids had proper seating in the back of the van. The van was also our home when we stopped at pubs – sometimes for what appeared to small children to be an eternity.

The day arrived in 1954 when my father had to leave to catch 'the boat to England'. My last memory of him was putting a sack with his belongings into the van and giving us all a big hug. He had tried everything to stay economically afloat but there was a big post war-building programme going on in Britain supported by US Marshall Aid and jobs on building sites were available. We headed for the town of Kells to stay with my Granny.

CHAPTER 3

LIFE ON THE FARM, KELLS, COUNTY MEATH 1954-1960 – THE MAKING OF ME

My time on my Granny's farm was a very formative period in my life. My Granny – Mrs Theresa Fitzsimons – was herself from a farm in Richardstown, Ardee, County Louth – about thirty miles from Cookstown. She was one of many siblings from a proud close family called the McKeevers. They were all intelligent, some became priests and nuns, and others emigrated. My granny got a job in a haberdasher in Cross Street, Kells and there she met her future husband Patrick Fitzsimons who owned a baker's shop in the same street. The Fitzsimons family had done well for themselves since their father had walked many miles from a mill in Nobber to seek work in one of the town's bakeries. Eventually he ended up owning the only bakery left in the town along with two shops. His two sons Patrick and James inherited the business from their father. James continued with the bakery and Brewery. My grandfather Patrick built his own farmhouse on land acquired by his father in Cookstown just outside Kells. Patrick had some success with his race horses and dairy farming but died of long term asthma problems in 1940 leaving a wife and 8 children – my mother being the eldest age 19 years and Philip the youngest aged 3 years. He died intestate which meant that none his six sons could afford to buy out the others. My granny managed to run the farm through the war years and by 1954, only two sons were left on the farm. The older brother Tom had served in the Irish Free State army, but suffered from mental health issues. The youngest suffered from rheumatic fever at 14 years and spent months in a local hospital and missed a year of schooling at the Christian Brothers in Kells. He had the chance to go to London and stay with his older brother Peter where he got a job in accounts with the Galbani Italian cheese company and started evening classes. At 18 years old he had a severe bout of tonsillitis and ended up in The Royal Free Hospital who managed to also sort out his other medical ailments. He came back to Cookstown for a few months when he was nineteen years old and made a singular contribution to my school essay on "Our Garden". We did not have much of a garden but my Granny did have a lot of nice Geranium pots and some wallflowers and rosebushes. Under Philip's guidance my essay converted our motley garden into the Garden of Eden coupled with a touch of the Hanging Gardens of Babylon. The schoolmaster Peter Smith was impressed with my essay but told me that my uncle had developed and honed his writing skills since he last taught him in Cortown.

When my mother and her four children arrived at Cookstown in 1954 we were very welcome as my Granny needed company and there was plenty of work to be done – the cows could not milk themselves. The intention was that my mother would join my father in London and bring the eldest and youngest of her children and this happened a year later in 1955. In the meanwhile, my mother made herself useful making butter and sorting the house out. As for me I started at the local national school in Cortown about a mile walk from the farm on 7th Sept 1954 and registered in Irish as Sean O'Rahaille. The school had two classrooms for boys and girls with separate entrances. Mr Peter Smith supervised the main classroom and his sister looked after the junior classroom. Miss Smith made a big stir one day when she turned up in a brand new Morris Minor.

Each day she drove out from Kells past our farm to Cortown at a maximum speed of about 20 MPH sitting bolt upright in the driver's seat.

Peter Smith was a kindly man and a great Irish patriot. Our Irish history lessons were epic tales of the nation's struggles with 'the English'. We seemed to win great battles even if the history books recorded that we lost them. Perfidious Albion always seemed to have a nasty trick up her sleeve to thwart and undermine our brave patriots. Two of his children attended the school and it was not long before the older boys set me up for a fight with the teacher's son. I was keen to establish myself in our playground and in the fight landed a few punches on a gentle reluctant opponent. The outcome was that he ran inside to his father with a bloody noise. Peter Smith did not give me the strap – which I deserved – but a gentle telling off. He probably reasoned that he could not show favouritism towards his son and besides he as a scholarly boy could do with a bit of toughening up. My attitude to his daughter Helen was very different. She was a real beauty but older than me so forbidden fruit but she did appear in my dreams as the untouchable beauty. It was not long before a more realistic proposition came into my fancies – Mary Coyne. Mary was a Gaeltacht who were native Irish speakers that De Valera brought from the poor lands of the west and south west of Ireland to small farms made up from the large estates in Meath vacated by Irish Landlords after the War of Independence. For years, cattle were droved from the west of Ireland to the rich pastures of County Meath:

To Meath of the pastures I lead my cattle and me
Through Leitrim and Longford I name the byways which
they are to pass without heed
To Meath of the pastures where there is grass to the knee
and salt by the sea. Anon

Mary had lovely carrot colour hair which was particularly noticeable at Sunday Mass in Cortown when sunlight streamed through the church windows. Again, Mary remained only in my dreams and it was her brother Joe Coyne – two years older than I was that became a close friend. The girl that I had the most contact with was another red head: Sheila Rennicks who lived in a cottage opposite our farm. Her father was a stonemason and she had a sister Nancy and two brothers Billy and Sean that I knew.

Sheila was a couple of years younger than I was and we played together in the haystacks, barns and fields. In our innocence, Sheila gave me my first simple lessons in female anatomy. I can remember a rhyme we use to find worth reciting without fully understanding it :' Uncle Tom had a thing long, Uncle Tom stuck his thing long into Aunt Mary's hairy thing, What was it? A brush of course!' Another rhyme that we liked went like this:

'Where are you going Bob? Down the road to see a little girlieo. Can I go Bob? No Bob, Why Bob, because you will steal all the Rhubarb.'

Sheila was to marry a local lad and together they have a son who became a famous flat racing jockey – Johnny Murtagh. Johnny won many top races including the English and Irish Derbies and Europe's biggest race the Prix de l'Arc de Triomphe. Through my friend Johnny Ward in Cookstown I nearly met up with Sheila a few years ago at Stanstead Airport; but Sheila I think had a few too many drinks on board to contact me.

Billy Rennicks Sheila's oldest brother led the way in teaching us to swim. Our swimming pool was the local river; but first we had to build a stone dam to make it deep enough to swim in. Billy had been to England where he learnt to swim – a powerful breaststroke. He impressed us with his power and elegance. Most of us had to start with a dog paddle not possessing Billy's powerful arms; but after a couple of summers, we progressed to a basic breaststroke. The local river was the scene of a much sadder event years later when in 2013 Billy's wife walked down to the stream early one morning and managed to drown herself under the bridge in quite shallow water.

I had a lot more contact with Sean Rennicks who was three years older than I was. Sean was great at catching rabbits by snaring and by dog hunting. I retain the ability to skin a rabbit in a few minutes and get a supply of them from local lads in my retirement years here in Hertford. He was expert at finding the rabbit trails to set the snares up. Occasionally he used ferrets or his favourite terrier dog to flush them out of their burrows and sometimes he had to dig his stuck terrier out of the burrow. My Granny made the odd rabbit stew which had a strong gamey taste. Much later, I learned to get rid of the gamey taste by soaking the skinned rabbits overnight in diluted white wine vinegar. Some of Sean's age group was engaged in rural activities that were not appreciated by our fire and brimstone parish priest Father O'Keefe. Other rural areas of Britain and Ireland may have preferred sheep but young cows were popular in our area with the wilder lads. Luckily I was sexually too immature to fully understand what was going on. In retrospect, the hell fire sermons of the visiting missionaries did not make much impact on the activities of the older boys in the parish. In 2014 I met Sean for the first time in 64 years. He was living alone in the family cottage but still a very strong and fit man at 72 years old. He had spent a short time working in England and many years working in the nearby Tara mines. Married and now divorced he seemed content enough with his lot in life.

Father O'Keefe's method of extracting money from his parishioners was very blunt. He would read out the Easter dues from the pulpit giving a lot more emphasis and time to those who contributed the most money and short shrift to those who gave only a few shillings – in most cases more than they could afford. There were not many activities that escaped Father O'Keefe's ever watchful eye. He was the celebrant for my parent's marriage and according to my mother advised her not to marry my father – she deserved someone better!

She brought this up repeatedly – but my father took it in good humour. Funerals were a good source of funds for the parish. Nearly all in the parish would attend a funeral and at the end of the funeral mass a table was placed close to the coffin and the congregation would file pass and place their cash contribution to the parish on the table under the keen eye of Father O'Keefe.

My Uncle Tom had a crush on Father O'Keefe's housekeeper and it was my task to deliver his love letters to the Presbytery. Maybe the housekeeper welcomed my uncle's advances but Father O'Keefe did not and made it know that the letters must cease – I still wonder if he opened them before they got to his housekeeper. Father O'Keefe died a few years later and was succeeded by a more gentle and humane priest called Father Conway who was instrumental in setting up a new all conquering parish Gaelic football team that was the making of me and the housekeeper got her freedom to marry – but alas too late for my Uncle.

GAELIC FOOTBALL

One present that I got from Father Christmas – my father was back from England for a few days – was a real leather football that over several years became my love, joy and a way to my dreams of being a great Gaelic footballer. Winter and summer I practised against the wall of our house and developed very good kicking and catching skills. Every lunchtime at my local school we played football and at times I had to overcome severe chilblains to do so. In wintertime my feet would get cold and wet in the wellingtons I wore to bring the cows in for milking. When playing football my feet got hot and sweaty – a real recipe for developing chilblains. This was further compounded by my granny's hot water bottle that she used regularly throughout the winter months. I slept at the end of her bed and my feet were warmed by the hot water bottle but unfortunately this set off my chilblains. The itchiness was almost unbearable. My toes and heels were swollen and the skin was red with cracked blisters. I used paraffin oil to soften the cracked skin but it was only when summer arrived that I got relief.

The new parish priest recognising that we had football potential and a lot of energy to expend set up evening practice matches at Bohermeen. Some of the senior players were also training in the park and I can remember being impressed with how high they could kick a ball. At 69 years of age, I can still kick a ball very high thanks to their example. I used my granny's bike to cycle the six mile round trip from our farm. On long summer evenings we would practise until dusk and granny would be worried and start calling for me. Her call would be relayed by neighbours along the 3-mile route and on the way back I would be told at regular intervals that my granny wanted me home. On one occasion in a rush I fell into a ditch full of nettles and got badly stung. I tried rubbing the stings with green dockets but to no avail. That night in bed I suffered much worse than even my most severe chilblain attack.

With all the training and support from the parish it was not long before we began to gel as a team and started to win matches. Eventually we reached the county under 14 final and played Duleek at the county ground in Navan. It was a very close game and we came out on top by just one point. Towards the end of the game Duleek went for a goal trying to win the game and I managed to save a shot that was bound for the back of our net. I came out of defence ball toe to hand and kicked it up field. The referee blew his whistle and Bohermeen had won their first county championship at any age group for decades. I can remember being carried shoulder high by one of the parents off the field. My final save was singled out in The Meath Chronicle report of the match. Later we went on to win The Curran Cup and defeat the Louth County under 14 champions at Drogheda. We also played the Gaelic speaking Gordonstown Boarding School in a friendly that felt like playing in a foreign country and we won that game as well ending the season undefeated. In October 1960 the farm was sold, we emigrated to England and my Gaelic football career was over. I was not able to attend the medal presentations but Father Conway made sure that my medals arrived to our new home address in London. He was a priest that did a lot more for the community than most.

In 2010 I got a surprise phone call from my old school friend Johnny Ward inquiring if I could attend a 50 year reunion for the 1960 Bohermeen (St Ultans) team at The Headfort Arms hotel in Kells in December. It turned out to be one of the coldest Decembers in decades with part of the lake of Virginia in Cavan frozen and snow and hard ice on the roads but the trip was well worth it. In the 50 years since I played Gaelic football, Bohermeen have had many successes from junior to senior level and they had another county cup win in 2010 – Bohermeen Senior Women's team. The evening was graced by the winning women team looking resplendent in their evening dress and we older lads in our best suits. It was quite an experience to meet people that I had not seen for 50 years. What was even more surprising was how many of my fellow players still had the same personality traits that I remembered from when they were 14 years old. The main organiser of the reunion was Tommy Rogers. Tommy was a great reader of the game, with a real turn of speed and no surprise that he was our leading scorer. I could see that he still had his businesslike approach to life. Our captain Jim Flanagan was mature for his age and had a great rapport with the players. He still displayed these qualities at the reunion. Sadly he had cancer and died only a few months later. Joe English was a tall talented footballer but slow to get him up and going, mainly because he thought too much about even the simplest of instructions. He still had this trait when he quizzed me about which branch of the Kells two Fitzsimons families I came from. Was it the blacksmith Fitzsimons with the actor Maureen O'Hara (died age 95 in 2015) as one of their offspring or the Fitzsimons of Bakery fame. It took me about twenty minutes to convince him that it was the later. To paraphrase Socrates (and The Jesuits) give me the boy and I will give you the man. He would need to start before they were twelve because by fourteen in my view many future personality traits are already well established.

One member of the team and near neighbour was not present – Tommy Ward. Tommy was the youngest member of the team and sadly was the first to die at only 48 years old. Happily, his daughter and her husband were present to receive his anniversary certificate. They have a son Tom Mulligan who is keeping the sporting tradition going in 2015. Tom is one of the top young European golfers in his age group. Over the years I have managed to visit Tommy's older brother Johnny at his home near Dublin. His mother still lives in Cookstown and always provides the best tea, brown soda and homemade jam when we visit her. She was still going strong when I last met up with her in 2015.

LIFE ON THE FARM

My sister Avril- two years older than me – stayed on the farm for about two years before rejoining our family in London. She was painfully shy but was brave enough to seek out a position high up a chestnut tree that gave her a great panoramic view over the local countryside and especially our immediate neighbours the Rennicks family. Sometimes she saw things that she should not have and often the Rennicks children would shout from across the road that they knew that she was up there. Avril remained silent, still and unseen at all times.I would follow her later on and climb the same tree but never was as discrete as Avril. In fact Sheila Rennicks- a couple of years younger than me- was quite happy to leg it up the tree to join me.

Avril went to the convent school in Kells and managed to avoid the beatings common in schools in Ireland at that time.

My earliest memory of life on the farm at Cookstown was the annual visit of The Thresher. Our ten-acre field was used for wheat and combine harvesters had not yet arrived. The sheafs of wheat would be brought in from the field and put into a big stack ready for the arrival of the Thresher. I managed to make tunnels using the thrashed straw and then like a mole worked my way through them. I was not alone. After being bit several times by field mice, I gave up my straw mining activities. The threshing was a great local and social occasion with neighbours joining in to help.

My Granny gave up on tillage and concentrated only on hay making when most of her sons had gone to England. Hay making was hard work but was the making of me in farm labouring. The cut grass was laid out and it was necessary to turn the rows every few days to help dry the grass out. It was then necessary to rake the dried grass – now hay – into long rows in order to put it into cocks. To do this we used a metal rake on wheels with saddle and release mechanism pulled by our horse 'Jacksypanama'. Astonishingly I was allowed to use this dangerous machine even though my legs were barley long enough to press down on the pedal to lift the rake to release the collected hay. Tony Brady was our main worker, supported by my Uncle Tom when he was not ill. We forked the hay into cocks and then made hay ropes to tie the tops down to the base to keep them protected from the wind. Hay had to be pulled out from around the bottom of the cock to allow the rain to run off and stop the hay from rotting at the bottom as the cocks could be in the field for several weeks before taken into the farmyard to be put into big stacks to feed the cows and cattle in winter. Putting the hay into cocks was hard thirsty work and Granny would bring out to the field a great pot of tea with bread and jam. The tea tasted wonderful along with the homemade jam and all augmented by that lovely smell of fresh hay. If one thinks that haymaking is hard work in Ireland, then the Norwegians had to work even harder. There they had to make special fences in order to hang the hay to dry it vertically as it would be very difficult to dry by leaving and turning it on the ground.

My Granny encouraged me and allowed me to do jobs way beyond my age. Her praise was never ending and I responded with unfettered enthusiasm even driving our Morris Minor Eight series car to take her into town when twelve years old and just about able to reach down on the pedals and still see through the front windscreen.

One of my jobs I had was to bring the cocks of hay in from the field and Tony Brady and some hired help would fork them into a stack up to 8 yards high. I would harness our horse up, collect a large chain twenty feet long and ride him bare back out to the hay field. When I reached a cock, I would dismount and run the chain carefully around the base of the cock and connect the ends to the horses halter. I would then sit on top of the cock and tell Jacksypanama to "giddy up" and he headed for home without fail. I did have reins but rarely had to use them except for one occasion. I fell forward from the top of the cock and could see the cock about to be pulled over me. I managed to grab a side chain and pull on the reins. Jacksypanama stopped and I lived to tell the tale. He was an obedient horse but all horses can be difficult to stop when they start heading for home. If the haycocks were several fields from the farmyard a special cart with a pulley would be used to lift the cock onto the cart.

Sometimes the stacks of hay would start to smoke because the hay was still damp and the only solution was to undo the stack and find the hotspot and spread it out to dry again – very hard work.

FROGS GALORE

Once I discovered a wealth making opportunity in the collection of frogs. The cutting of the luscious meadow for the hay crop disturbed the frogs from their very comfortable habitat. There was a man in the town that paid one Irish old penny for each suitable sized frog. The rumour was that the he sold the frogs on for making shoe polish. On a good day, I could collect up to fifty suitable sized frogs and store them in a large concrete tank near the cow shed. Sometimes at night I would dream that the frogs escaped and that I was running around trying to catch them as they jumped and hoped to freedom. After a few weeks I had up to 500 frogs in store and would put them in old sacks and take them into the town. Even after the frog's departure, I still had dreams that they had escaped but when I woke up I realised that I had a pile of pennies for my troubles.

It was years later when camping in France that I got my first taste of cooked frog legs in garlic flavoured butter sauce – delicious that was far better than using the frogs as shoe polish! Upon reflection we also had many large snails around the farm that maybe could have been collected and exported to France; but alas too late for me now.

The thistle maybe the national symbol of Scotland but on our farm they were a nuisance taking up valuable space and nutrients needed for grass growing. My Granny ever the motivator and delegator got me to go out to the meadow fields in late spring to cut the thistles using a scythe before they seeded.. This was a very thankless task that seemed never ending as the thistles could regrow quickly and it was a bit like King Canute trying to hold back the tide. My Granny did give me some extra pennies for this task that were saved and added to my increasing collection of half-crowns, which she generously gave me from my child allowance from my mother in England. A further source of income was from a daily two mile round trip to O'Connell's shop to get my Granny's twenty full strength non-tipped Gold Flake cigarettes. She gave me an extra penny which was sometimes used to buy a rock hard stick of butterscotch toffee. This I duly sucked on the way home. Some years later in London my dentist did not react too kindly to the state of my teeth and in time I needed two front teeth to be crowned.

As well as losing some of my teeth my arrival in England in 1960 coincided with the loss or theft of my half-crown collection. I stored some of my cash in an old range which was removed when I was at school as part of a kitchen refurbishment.

OH MY LOVELY COWS

I developed my lasting love affair with cattle and cows on the farm in Cookstown. We had about twenty cows and up to thirty bullocks and calves. On a recent visit in 2015 to Cookstown I heard that the new owner Cassidy had a 300 dairy heard -how things have changed in Ireland since 1960.

Our milkman Tony Brady milked the cows twice a day. The milk was cooled by passing it over a steel grill that was kept cold by water flowing under gravity. Then it was poured into steel churns and submerged in a concrete water tank. The milk lorry arrived daily in summer and the churns had to be strapped to the booth of our Morris Eight car and taken a half mile to the crossroads and put on a raised platform for collection. On some particular hot days the milk would arrive at the dairy and deemed to be sour – not surprisingly with all the shaking around in the lorry – and returned to us the next day. This was not good for business – but good for buttermilk to drink, especially with freshly boiled potatoes. An added problem could arise when Tony had difficulty getting out of bed and we would miss the delivery collection. I soon learned to milk cows and Granny would lend a hand and sometimes we would have completed the milking before Tony arrived.

Unlike the Nordic and Alpine countries we could allow the cows out at night for most of the year. My main job would be to round up the cows and lead them in for the milking. I quickly learnt that there was a lead cow to help me. I also was able to ride on her back, which made life even easier. Some cosy winter evenings in the barn Tony would tell me stories whilst he milked and I managed to create a nice armchair to hear about great

Irish battles and of Napoleon's adventures across Europe. My armchair consisted of two cows standing close together whilst munching their hay. I was able to straddle between their two stomachs with an arm across each of the cow's back. If they moved apart, a quick command would cause them to push back together so that I did not fall through.

Sometimes we took the cows to the local farmer's bull for covering but more often, we relied on artificial insemination. With only a small herd of cows we tried to keep them milking throughout the year and could expect two or three cows to calve each month. It normally takes nine months after insemination with the cow not milked for a couple of months before calving. Granny – a great worrier – got me to check up on a cow that she thought was due to calve but she was not a good predictor and often I would be checking on a cow for two or three weeks before she calved. In summer time the cows were out in the field and Granny would wake me up during the night to see if a due cow was ok. Armed with torch I would set off across the fields trying to find the relevant cow. Shadows, mists and dark weird shaped objects were everywhere. It was very scary work especially when I heard strange noises distorted by the mists and landscape – Banshees perhaps! The worry was that the cow could be lying down in a ditch or hollow trying to calve or that if calving it was a breach and a helping pull would be necessary. Wintertime we kept the due cows in the cowshed and things were a lot easier. In extreme cases I had to run to Tony Brady's house to get him out of bed to help. I hoped that Tony had not been on the booze the night before.

It was always a very sad time when we had to sell some of our cattle. I had seen them grow up from birth and became very attached to them all. Some cattle were sold individually when Granny needed some ready cash and the local auctioneer would arrive and a long bargaining session would ensue. Normally several cattle would be sold as a lot and walked the three miles into town to the cattle market. When sold a sticker would be put on their back. Buyers and sellers took the opportunity to enjoy a few pints in the pubs and occasionally we would find some of our sold cattle back at our farm next day. They had taken the opportunity run to freedom from their new inebriated owner.

In 2013 I visited a farm in western Norway where the cows were housed in a multimillion dollar specially built milking parlour. They never saw the light of day or many humans. They were milked by robots and even had their backs scratched by mechanised brushes. This was not my idea of a diary farm.

GRANNY GOES TO LONDON

My Granny had nine children – my mother was the eldest. She lost a son at the age of four from what I think was diphtheria, a child killer before a suitable vaccine was discovered. She also lost a second son Billy who died in London in his early thirties in the mid 1950s. Billy had a splendid singing voice, dark curly hair and good looking. He gave great renderings of Slim Whitman songs like My China Doll and On Top of Old Smokey. In time, Billy emigrated to England where he died in mysterious circumstances. He may have suffered from mental depression compounded by drink. All I can remember was Granny going to London – the first time that she had left Ireland – for his funeral. Avril and I stayed with a new neighbour in Cookstown Mrs McGarr who lived in the house and small farm rented by my father and his brother Benny in the late 1930s. Mrs McGarr was a trained horticulturist from Cork whose husband was a vet and she was a larger than life character. We loved our weeklong stay at the McGarr's house and the little luxuries provided by Mrs McGarr.

One of Mr McGarrs side jobs was to buy calves in the poorer regions of the west of Ireland and fatten them up on the rich grasslands of Meath. Every day he would have a bottle of Guinness with his lunch but surprisingly died only after a few years in Cookstown; but he was quite a few years older than his wife was. His only son Christopher, a few years younger than me, followed his father's example and became a vet enriched by a spell in Canada where he gained a masters degree. Mrs McGarr was a great supporter of Fine Gael – the pro treaty party- and was on good terms with Bruton the local Dail member who became Taoiseach. She was a very out spoken women on all political and religious issues and a great conversationalist. She was the only person I knew who held the local priests in tow. When I went back to Ireland over the years I always made a point of visiting Mrs McGarr. Sadly, she died in 2014 in her 90s.

Soon it was time to leave the happy environs of Cortown School and head into Kells to the Christian Brothers' School. I had to take a primary leaving school examination. Most of the children in my class left school at 14 years of age so I had to go up to Bohermeen to take the exam. Peter Smith gave the few pupils in Cortown taking the exam some extra lessons and to my surprise I passed despite my difficulties with the Gaelic language.

FIRST TRIP TO LONDON

That summer I had a big surprise when my mother came back from London to take me over for a few weeks holiday. My Granny never wanting to be alone had my first cousin – 3 years younger than me as a stand in. The trip to London by Ferry and Steam Train from Holyhead to Euston was a great adventure for me. On the ferry people were seasick and others drank their way through the journey despite glasses falling off the bar and smashing on the floor – great excitement for me. I really did love the train journey especially sleeping in the upper bunk bed, hearing the new noises, and flashing lights as we chugged our way to London. Euston and the underground with its wooden escalators was another astonishing experience for me as a young boy straight from the farm. At Swiss Cottage we stayed in the top two floors of a six storey Estate Agents – my mother was the caretaker and cleaner for The Agents. I went to bed to rest after the long journey but could not sleep on that hot August afternoon. The new noises from the street below – rising up in the heat – were overwhelming.

One memorable experience of my short stay in London was the chance to swim in an indoor pool near Baker Street instead of my local river, which we had to dam to get the water level to about three feet deep. The swimming pool was in great demand during school holidays and a colour band system allowed one to have a maximum of 90 minutes in the pool. I could have stayed there all day despite the heavily chlorinated water. Polio was still a major risk and there were times when they closed the pool because of an outbreak of this dreadful disease. My sister Avril's friend had polio but was lucky to end up with only a withered leg.

THE CHRISTIAN BROTHER'S SCHOOL – BAPTISM OF FIRE

I loved my stay in London but had to go back to Ireland to start life at The Christian Brothers' School. My glamorous Aunt Phylis who had her own hairdressing business in London was delegated the task of taking me back and collect her son Patrick who was staying with my Granny. Phylis liked to travel in style and avoided overcrowded ferries and dirty steam trains. We flew to Dublin with Air Lingus, a completely new and unexpected adventure for me. My Granny got Phylis to take me to my new school and meet the Head teacher, Brother O'Halloran. Even as a young boy I could sense that he was very impressed by the actor type glamour that exuded from Phylis. He must have wondered what a women of such style and glamour was doing with a toe rag like me. During my stay at The Brothers, I noticed that whenever Brother O'Halloran had to use the leather strap on me he did not go full out and I still owe Phylis for that restraint.

The Brothers' School was a big step up for me. I had to study Latin, Religious Studies, Geography and Science for the first time. Regular homework came as a big shock as well as the need to attend school on Saturday morning. A welcome surprise was school games on Wednesday afternoons with a lay teacher Mr Brunnock from Cork. He introduced the boys to rugby which most of us enjoyed but did not fully understand. I still have difficulty understand rugby rules but it does not stop my enjoyment of watching London Irish and the Ireland national team play. Mr Brunnock seemed a lot more relaxed than the brothers who seemed to be a little frustrated with their teaching role. I still remember Mr Brunnock praising the English for their litter free cities and towns. He would tell us about the time he saw an Englishman pick up the discarded butt of a cigarette off the street. I think Kells CBS was his first and only teaching post. He retired in the late 1990s and wrote a book about the history of the school. I often wonder if he had any success with his anti litter campaign in Kells.

Latin was taught by rote learning. On occasions, I did not find time to do my homework or learn my Latin declensions. The farm cows and cattle took priority. Unable to recite my Latin verbs I would get a few stokes of the strap and then sent back to the end of the line of boys to learn them immediately. A second failure resulted in another belting. I noticed early on that the townies did their homework and were belted less than we country lads. One boy never got the strap but he was the son of the local GP Dr Brannigan and he ended up a GP like his father..

Kids can be nasty if they sense a weakness in the teacher's discipline or if the teacher has special traits. One such teacher had a hard time- Ducky O'Mahony. I did not recognise it then but Mr O'Mahony was probably Gay and a little effeminate to go with it. He always seemed to have some rouge make-up on. We could hear the boys almost rioting when he was teaching in a classroom directly above our heads and we took advantage when he came down to teach us. Now and again the Head

Brother would arrive and extract some boys for a strapping. Things would calm down until the next lesson with Ducky. I felt a little bit sorry for him because it was not in his nature to beat boys and he clearly was a very intelligent and gifted individual. Later on when I became a teacher I was surprised just how much punishment weaker teachers would put up with before they eventually left the profession.

I had a very close friend – Joe Coyne – two years older than me at the school. Joe was a member of The Gaeltacht and fluent in Irish. His younger sister Mary as I mentioned earlier was my fantasy girlfriend. The Gaeltacht tilled and farmed the land given to them by De Valera well. They were hard working and helped each other on their farms and that caused resentment from the locals at their success. Joe helped me with my Irish homework and I acted as a punch bag for him at the local crossroads on the way home from school. Joe loved boxing and we both would re-enact the boxing bouts that we heard on BBC radio- British champions like Joe Erskine, Brian London and others were given an extra work out unknown to them by Joe and me. Joe liked to go for the solar plexus and a straight left hand jab was my speciality. How we found the energy to box after a long school day and only a few sandwiches and a bottle of milk/water to sustain us was a minor miracle. Cycling home our conversation turned to what we might get for our evening meal. I knew that Granny would nearly always cook steak, cabbage and potatoes – never a dessert. I used to envy our neighbours the Rennicks family who had custard and jelly but they did not have steak too often. It was Joe who decided that we should mitch off school on occasions especially in the early autumn. We would meet up near one of the big estate house and supplement our sandwiches with the fruits from the walled orchard near to the big house. As the day progressed into afternoon, we would plan our letters of absence for the next day and I would do my best to copy my Granny's handwriting in the knowledge that her absence notes for me were always just a line or two.

Joe finished his leaving certificate not long after I immigrated to England. We kept in contact by letter for more than a decade. Joe went to Baltimore USA and completed a Masters in Aeronautical Engineering. He was conscripted into the army and sent to Vietnam. As Joe liked real action, he chose to join the infantry but unfortunately got more action than expected. He fought in the Mekong Delta against an unseen enemy in dense jungle. When I went to Vietnam in January 2014 I visited some of the tunnels dug by the Vietcong and saw the terrible camouflaged pit traps set up for the unsuspecting GIs. Joe was affected badly affected by his warfare experience in Vietnam. I lost contact with him but knew that he visited Ireland occasionally to see his family. He was still alive in the US in 2015.

Many farms today in the UK are lifeless; nothing but hundreds of acres of cornfields and rapeseed, where the hedges have been removed. Ireland is still primarily grasslands with livestock. At our farm in Cookstown as well as cattle we had chickens, a work horse and a mongrel dog called Crab. Before Crab, we had a sheep dog called 'Shot' that died of old age. We found Crab as a stray in Wicklow and brought him to Cookstown when we moved house. After Crab's car accident in Wicklow he had an accident free existence at Cookstown. He was very attached to my Granny and delighted in going for walks with her. Our hens had the freedom of the farm and laid their eggs all over the place but would come from all corners when called for feeding. I was surprised that we did not lose many hens to foxes probably because they were so scattered and not in a hencoop.

Our horse, Jacksipanama, was the love of my life. One could say he was a Jack of all tasks. My pride and joy was to ride him bare back at full gallop across the fields and steering him by tapping his right or left cheek. I held on to his main for dear life. Sometimes we even used him to pull our Morris Eight car to give it a kick-start. Sadly the time came when we had to leave for England and sell Jacksiepanama. When farm animals died or were put down they were often sold to the local Hunts.

Healthy livestock, including horses were exported. Ireland in the 1950s had a poorly developed meat factory industry so the real value added was gained by the countries importing the livestock. There was great resistance, unlike the continent, to eating horsemeat in the UK. The popular press often ridiculed Ireland for exporting horses to Belgium. They choose to forget that many horses were sent to England during the Second World War and no doubt formed part of their meat rations. When I first went to Norway in 1967 I had horse salami and very tasty it was indeed. In 2009 I ran a marathon in Slovenia and saw fresh horse burgers advertised for 5 Euro but I never got round to buying one.

We had the Farrell family as near neighbours. Jimmy Farrell (1903-1979) was a great friend of my grandfather Patrick Fitzsimons. They both loved and trained racehorses but Jimmy was also a great rugby union player who played for Ireland and The British Lions. He did two tours for The Lions to Argentina, where he played in two of the four Tests in 1927 and to Australia/ New Zealand. In 2012, I had tea with one of his daughters in Virginia County Cavan and she showed me some of his rugby photographs. I remember one in particular of Jimmy on deck looking splendid in his Lions blazer and flannel trousers on his way to Australia. Jimmy also has a talented scientist son who is Emeritus Professor of Nutrition in Australia and quite a famous artist son Michel who died in 2000. Micheal did most of his work in France but used Irish historical events including Bloody Sunday as inspiration for his art. His ashes were placed in the family grave in Cortown Cemetry.

Jimmy married a woman from Britain who liked the high social life and their farmhouse with its swimming pool was the venue for many a raucous party. However, the bills mounted and the Farrell family had to sell their farm in the late 1950s and move to England. I can remember going to the open auction at the farm and saw valuable furniture, pictures and ornaments sold for ridiculous low prices by modern standards.

Me in Wicklow 1952

O'Reilly Bros Shop
1940s
1 Lower George St,
Dunlaire, Dublin
Birthplace of Dorothy,
Avril and Sean

BARGAINWEAR

My Birthplace Dublin 1946

Mae and John at
home,circa1952
Baltinglass,Wicklow

Mum and Dad Baltinglass 1951

Dorothy, Avril and me Baltinglass with parents 1952

Group 1923
Front Row L to R: Mattie Dowd, Frank Coleman, John Francis Smith, Sheila Dowd, Benny Boylan, James Coleman, Matty Reilly.
2nd Row L to R: Annie Reilly, Mary Galligan, Jim Lee, Annie Rudden, Benny Reilly, Julia Fitzpatrick, Benny Reilly, Mary Fay, John Lee, Maggie Rudden, Lizzie Lee.
3rd Row L to R: Mrs. Mary Brady N.T., Sissy Kimmons, Jimmy Rudden, Kathy Smith, Pat Galligan, Ellie Fay, John Joe Smith, Bridget Reilly, Tommy Kimmons, Susie Galligan.
4th Row L to R: Eileen Smith, John Francis Reilly, Cis Lee, Tommy Galligan, Ba Kimmons, Tommy Reilly, Maggie McGivern, Bonnie Galligan.

My Dad top row 2nd from left and his brothers
Benny and Tommy, Ballyjamesduff

Dorothy Avril Vincent and me with Pauline
McKeever Ireland circa 1955

Uncle Tom Mum Granny and we four

Granny 1st cousins Patrick and Glenda
with dog crab and Morris 8 car

Cookstown House built by my Grandfather 1920s

Bohermeen winning County Team Meath
1960 I am 4th from right FRow

Me with Curran Cup Meath 1960

CHAPTER 4

EMIGRATION – THE LEAVING OF IRELAND 1960

S oon it was our turn to sell up and leave for London. Unlike the Farrell family, my Granny was not broke. My grandfather had not left a will so Granny was entitled to a third of the farm and her nine children to the rest divided equally between them. This was one reason why it was difficult to leave the farm to any one sibling. Besides most of them had already left and were happy to receive their inheritance. When the farm was sold my Granny was able to buy a house and live with her youngest son Philip in London.

Like the Farrell family we had an open auction and saw some lovely furniture and ornaments sold for next to nothing. One of our oak dining tables and two paintings are still in our ex-farmhouse in Cookstown today. As for me, Granny let me keep the money from the sale of my favourite white cow that I had fed as a calf. This money was to come in useful to me in London. Our Morris Eight car was given to the Rennicks family and the new owner agreed to keep our dog Crab.

My mother came over to Cookstown along with Philip (if memory serves me right) to finalise the departure. My emotions were very mixed – excited by a new life and opportunities in London and sadness at leaving neighbours, the farm and its animals and not being able to play my beloved Gaelic football again. I cannot imagine what it must have been like for my

Granny emigrating at the age of 70 years and leaving a house and farm established by her husband. She never returned to Ireland and died in London in 1972 aged 82 years. Her body was returned to Ireland and she was laid to rest with her husband in the Fitzsimons family grave in Kells.

As the taxi moved out the front gate and headed for Kells, Crab came running after us. We speeded up so did Crab. Eventually he could not keep up and as we turned a corner that was the last I ever saw of Crab and my cattle and cows. It still gives me pain to reflect on our final departure from Cookstown and the Ireland of my youth.

LONDON 1960-1965 AND MY TEENAGE YEARS

Buckland Crescent, Swiss Cottage, contained fine five storey Georgian fronted houses. We occupied the top two floors of one house that was converted into offices owned by Match and Co. We were the caretakers and offered the Company security by our presence in the building especially out of office hours. My mother was contracted to clean the offices and provide morning and afternoon tea. It was not long before we children were part of her work force – a lot of hoovering of offices and staircases had to be done each day including Saturdays. It was quite a change for me from milking cows and cutting thistles. The immediate benefit for me that winter was that I had no chilblains – warm dry feet at last.

After eight years, we were again reunited as a family. My sisters shared a bedroom on the fourth floor where my parents also had a bedroom and access to a separate toilet. Another room was an office occupied by a Mr Cohen, a Greek Jew, and there was a storage room. I remember Mr Cohen telling my sister Aril when she was thinking of going to Canada, that there was no place better than Europe. The top floor had a low ceiling but we had a good size lounge, a big kitchen where we could all eat and a separate toilet and bathroom. My brother and I shared a small bedroom on this floor and my parents had done well to acquire this accommodation especially in view of the shortage of housing in a city that still had many bombsites as late as 1960. We had a great panoramic view of London from our top floor. We could see from St Paul's Cathedral to the Houses of Parliament and Swiss Cottage was only 3 miles from the West End of London. There were no one-way streets and roundabouts to worry about in London in 1960.

The great luxury that we had was our very own black and white television with two channels – ITV and the BBC. We also had an oil heater which although a bit smelly was a great help in winter. The offices down stairs had central heating and as heat rises, we were never too cold.

I still missed my Granny and managed to find a cheap bike and cycle about 4 miles to Haringey to see her regularly. It was not an easy ride for a lad used to quiet country lanes with all the traffic and buses going through Chalk Farm, Camden Town, pass Holloway prison to Finsbury Park, then Manor House and finally up Green Lanes to her house in Seymour Road. Granny settled in well with her son Philip and his wife Agnes and of course she still had her twenty Gold Flake cigarettes each day. She also got to see more of her sons and daughters than she did back in Ireland. I must admit that I missed her kindness and praise and my bike journeys to visit her were a great comfort to me.

TIME TO GO TO SCHOOL IN HER MAJESTY'S REALM

I arrived in October and the autumn school term had already started in early September. Which type of school still had places available for me? The Grammar schools were full and at 14 years of age I was way too old to sit the 11plus. The only choice for me was no choice. I was to join the 80% who had failed the 11plus even though I never had the opportunity to sit the selection test. This applied to nearly all foreign children coming to the UK. Even if they had the opportunity to sit the test they would have probably failed it not because they were unintelligent but because of language issues and the test was culturally biased and many of the indigenous pupils were specially coached for it in the more middle class primary schools. My sister Avril also missed out on the 11plus but was lucky to find a Catholic secondary modern school, St Richard of Chichester, in Kentish Town that had a Head teacher –Mr O'Connell – who was ambitious for his school and made every effort to encourage pupils with ambition to take some GCE exams at 16 years. The school leaving age was then 15 years so an extra year at school was required. Those taking GCE would be competing with Grammar and Private school pupils with far superior facilities and more highly-qualified teachers – it was not a level playing field – in fact, St Richards had no playing fields at all. Avril did well to gain a few GCEs passes and got a job in a bank when she left school at 16. Therefore, it was going to be St Richards for me as well.

I will never forget my first day at school. It was brilliant! The journey on the top deck of the 31 buss from Swiss Cottage to Camden Town with my free bus pass was a separate experience. It was like a roller coaster in the smoked filled upper deck as the bus with its open staircase swayed from side to side around corners. The centre of gravity of the London double decker is so low they can lean 60 degrees or more without flipping over. When I arrived at the school a prefect took me to the school library – what would the Christian Brothers have thought of having a library in a school? I was told that free milk was issued at 11 am and a two course cooked lunch would be served at 1pm. Was this a hotel rather than a school that I was in? My first lesson was English Literature with a woman teacher called Miss Villa – my first ever with a female teacher. She had no cane or leather strap – was there something wrong here? Another lesson was History with Mrs Mary Jones – Welsh and an amazing attractive young blond women – she also had no strap or cane. I cannot remember much of the rest of the day except the lovely apple and custard pudding. OK my granny always made a great Christmas pudding that lasted for weeks. My Irish school lunch of a brown bottle of fresh milk, milked that morning, and my four slices of white Fitzsimons loaf with some cheese, no butter, was now only memory.

Getting rid of The School Certificate exam in the early 1950s was a great help to non-grammar school pupils because you did not have to pass five or six subjects all in one sitting but could take as few or as many separate General Certificate of Education (GCE) subjects over several sittings. My target was to try to pass five: Mathematics, English Literature, History, Art and Religious Studies at one sitting at 16 years old. It meant that I had only 18 months to do it having arrived in the school so late. In 1962 five GCEs could get you a good job in banking, accountancy, insurance or as a technician. Nowadays you might need a Masters degree to get into these professions.

To get into the top set I did alter a mark from my Christian Brother's report. My mathematics report mark was recorded as Algebra 70%, Geometry 80% and Arithmetic 30%. On the day of the test I was not fully tuned in for the Arithmetic exam and felt the mark did not reflect my true ability. I changed the 30 to 80, easily done in the same ink colour. I was quite pleased with my creativity – I felt I had enough disadvantages as it was without having to start in a lower maths set. As it turned out I was the best student in the top set and went on to get top A grades in mathematics at GCE A' level and a distinction in the scholarship paper.

We had one science lab situated on the roof of the Victorian building that still had separate boys' and girls' entrances and tarmac playgrounds. The lab was essentially a biology lab and could draw on sunlight for growing plants. As for Physics and Chemistry we had normal classrooms with cupboards containing some chemicals, magnets, batteries and a few electric meters. We were taught General Science and not the separate science disciplines – they were for grammar school pupils. As we were destined to be hewers of wood and metal filers, we had woodwork and metalwork classes at a nearby redundant school. I am still proud of my nice dovetailed jewellery box that I made. I had less success with my metalwork classes. I often started with a large sheet of metal hoping to make something grand. After measuring mistakes and cutting too much off and despite endless filing I ended up with a coat hanger. Some of the boys were much better than I was and made nice coffee tables or metal toolboxes. As for the girls, they had separate cooking and sowing classes. We also had technical drawing but I never got my pencils sharp enough for neat drawings. Our teacher was a former army officer who had fought in North Africa and had time off school because of recurring bouts of malaria. We also had fine art classes that were fun if somewhat messy. I remember doing an ink drawing that was my pride and joy. It was inspired by my school trip to the Rhineland in West Germany. Partial colour blindness hampered my efforts to follow in the footprints of Michelangelo – finding difficulty distinguishing between my pinks, purples, reds and oranges. My older sister Dorothy and younger brother Vincent are both very good at art so family honour was saved. One unusual lesson we had were dancing classes – waltz, tango, foxtrot and charleston. The fact that rock and roll was the rave seemed to pass our teacher by but I admit I did like putting my arm round Geraldine Gallagher's waist. We had regular morning assemblies that gave Mr O'Connell a chance to sing the praises of our school and his ambitions for the future. Our morning prayer of St Richard went:

Thanks to you our Lord Jesus Christ
For all the benefits which you have given us
For all the pains and insults which you have born for us
Most merciful Redeemer, Friend and Brother
May we know you more clearly
Love you more dearly
And Follow you more nearly
Day by Day

Perhaps St Richard was an apt name for our school as he choose a life of abstinence and poverty and shared his university gown with his brother if memory serves me right.

Only a few years after I joined the school the words of this prayer became world famous as lyrics for the song "Day by Day" in the Broadway musical "Godspell".

THE GIRLS FROM LIVERPOOL

At St Richards we were fortunate to have the support of the local Dominican Order that is dedicated to education among other duties. They organised an annual trip to their Spode House priory in Staffordshire and it was here that I got the chance to meet other school pupils from Kirby in Liverpool and visit local places of interest. One stands out, the coal mine at Sutton Coalfield.

We were given miners lamps and helmets and then taken several hundred feet down a mineshaft on a very shaky and noisy elevator. We then had to walk several hundred yards through fire doors to get to the coalface and passing us on the way was a small train system that brought the coal from the coalface. I was surprised how hot and dusty it was down the mine and by the cramped conditions the miners worked in. All the time there were creaking noises coming from the wooden beams used to prop up the roof of the tunnel and I decided there and then that I would never want to be a coal miner. Still, it was a great adventure and one that today's children will never be able to experience.

Situated in lovely countryside the priory had a working farm that brought back memories of my time on the farm in Ireland. Despite my love for the cattle, I was now finding the girls from Liverpool a greater attraction. At our evening social gatherings, I got to know one girl in particular called Mary Murphy. I just about understood her accent but she was a very extravert girl and a great dancer. It was not long before a group of the girls invited us to visit them up in Kirby near Liverpool. A few months later in the Autumn of 1962 my closest friend Charles Bond and a few others in our class were on our way to Liverpool.

We had never been to the north of England before and were delighted to arrive at Lime Street Station and see a real working river Mersey with all its docks. Our host girls took us by bus the few miles out to Kirby which was a large post war council estate with a big Liverpool Irish population. This was to be the first time I stayed in a house other than my own in England. I cannot remember the name of the girl whose house I stayed in but I do remember her generous parents and brother not to mention the large crucifix on my bedroom wall. One of the highlights of the trip was when the girls took us on a ferry to cross the Mersey to Birkenhead. Years later when I was a teacher the memory of my trip to Liverpool was brought back to me when my school play was "A Penny to cross the Mersey". A year later The Beatles arrived and Liverpool and the Mersey sound became a world phenomena. We kept in touch with the girls and exchanged black and white photographs for some time. Years later, I received a letter from Mary Murphy informing me that she was divorced and would I like to visit Liverpool. It was too late, my infatuation with her had worn off and she would have been far too social and extrovert for me to handle on a long-term basis.

A SEARCH FOR THE COUNTRYSIDE

Outside of school I began to settle down and also to acclimatise into life in the big city. I got a job as a delivery boy for a local shop and was able to use the special designed delivery bike with a large front metal cage to hold my deliveries. I deserved some of the tips I got after having to walk up several stories to deliver groceries to a top floor flat – there were few elevators in 1930s built flats. One day I decided to take the cheap bike that I used to visit my Granny to try and find some real countryside. I was homesick for farm life and especially the cows. I cycled north about four miles to Golders Green but there was still no sign of the countryside. I carried on a few more miles toward Barnet and then I saw my first cows. The fields were not large and were enclosed by housing. Even odder was the Express milk dispenser at the entrance. I had a nice cold carton of milk for sixpence and managed to get close enough to some of the cows to stroke their cheeks – I had not lost my touch. It was much later that I learned that this was a city protected small research farm and that I was still many miles from the open countryside.

MY SISTERS, THEIR BOYFRIENDS AND ME!

My sisters had now left school and were working and their boyfriends started to appear at our house. As a fifteen year old the idea of romance completely escaped me and the boxes of chocolates the boyfriends gave the girls were often demolished by me. I can remember one boyfriend of my sister Avril – Jimmy Salisbury – was not happy with what happened to his chocolates and he put me in an arm lock and bent me over the stair well threatening to drop me down the five floors to the basement. Jimmy's Lambretta scooter provided the main attraction for Avril and the rest of us. I did manage to get a ride on the back of it but Jimmy was neither a Mod nor a Rocker and his scooter remained undecorated. I actually preferred the Vesper scooter with all its extra lights and mod badges.

Another of Avril's boyfriends was Asiam Baig who was a first class manipulator – I wished I had learned more of his ways but I was too up front and honest. He used to regularly challenge me to chess games and always won but upon reflection I think he cheated in doing so. Once he challenged me to run round the block, a challenge I was eager to take up. I got in front of him early and ran like the clappers. On the home straight I was a sure winner until he appeared from nowhere and ran past me to win. He must have known a short cut but even my sister thought that this time he had gone too far. Asiam was on his way out. In contrast to Asiam's duplicities, another of her boyfriends was a secretive gambler. He gave her a very expensive gold ring to keep for him! Avril, a very sensitive person, was constantly worrying about the ring and not being able to cope insisted he take it back. I guess that was his way of controlling his girlfriends.

My sisters met many interesting young people who they invited up to visit. One lot of visitors stood out from the rest. Avril and her friend Joan met up with three young Canadian boys who had arrived in England by boat to visit the old mother country. One of them a blond boy called Ron had a string tie with a metal skeleton bow that I liked and then there was the tall quiet one called Grant Hexamer. My dad liked visitors and was happy to let my sisters organise a party for the Canadians and others. The rock and roll of the 60s was building up a head of steam and at one stage in the party the old floor of our flat was vibrating so much dad, now a carpenter and he should know, thought it might collapse and had requested my sisters play more ballad music and less rock. As the party hit full volume, a group of lads, one with a guitar tried to gate crash the party and Aril was about to let them in when she remembered her dad's warning about the floor.Some years later she realised that one of them was almost certainly the rock star Rod Stewart who lived in the area. The Canadians were a great hit and it was no surprise that Joan and Avril took a fancy to them so much so that they later went to Canada and married two of them. They claimed at the time that it was going to be either Canada or Australia made on the toss of a coin as both countries qualified for the government sponsored £10 fare. I never really believed this as they had kept contact with the Canadians since their visit to England. My sister got a bit of a shock to find that Grant, the man that she fancied, was already married, divorced and had sole custody of his baby daughter Terry. However first love triumphed and Grant and Avril later married and had two great children and Avril gained a wonderful step daughter in Terry.

In contrast to some of Avril's boyfriends, I had a very positive relationship with my eldest sister's boyfriend Pat Horgan. Pat was a keen footballer and played to a high level. My knowledge of soccer was very limited but despite this, Pat took me to see my first game, a first division match between Fulham and Sunderland at Craven Cottage. It was the first time I had been in a stadium of 20000+ spectators. I noticed two players stood out from the others. Johnny Haynes playing midfield for Fulham was making pinpoint passes to his teammates all over the field. I was not surprised when Pat told me that he was one of England's star players. The other one was Charlie Hurley a barrel chested giant of a man, further enhanced by the vertical stripes of his team's shirt, playing in the middle of defence. He chested down, headed and kicked any ball that came his way, no one got past him and it was no surprise that he also played for the Republic of Ireland. Pat also took me to some of his club's matches. I remember seeing him play at Hackney Marches that had about twenty football fields and was a hot bed for Tottenham Hotspur supporters. Pat, despite his known allegiance to Chelsea, stood out as a hard man centre forward who took no prisoners. Some of his fellow players had been with professional clubs and liked to play extra games for Pat's team – off the record as it were. Despite this early introduction to soccer it took me another ten years to start playing the game and then only when I had left London for Reading.

My younger brother Vincent had his own set of friends and his parents gave him a lot, if not too much, freedom to roam around. He was in the local houses/flats of his friends for many hours. I can remember that he spent a lot of time with the young daughter of Freddy Stone who was a professional boxer, even at nine or ten he was developing an eye for the girls. My job was to harden him up. Once whilst throwing darts in the lounge I managed to hit a main vein in his arm. Only when I saw the amount of blood from the hole in his arm did I think

I might have gone too far. Vincent ended up in Hospital and the doctor dealing with the case wanted to know what crazy person threw the dart.

Sometimes we had no key to get in the front door to the building, not a problem if the offices were still open or someone was in our flat on the top floor. If all else failed I would climb up five floors using the old heavy metal rain downpipe and slip in through the bathroom window. My tree climbing expertise gained in Ireland came in useful. Fortunately when my little brother, six years younger than me, started to try to do the same I had enough sense to stop him.

SCHOOL GERMAN TRIP 1961 – FIRST OF MANY

I settled in well at school and made good progress with my GCEs. It was a great surprise to me to learn that the school was organising a trip to West Germany. My sister Avril had already been on a school trip to Rome and thought I should go. I still had my money from the sale of my cow and decided, as well as paying for the trip, I would buy myself a new suit. I selected a heavy woollen one and lived to regret it. The lining was not too extensive and whenever I wore the suit I was itching all over for days on end. It was good that we had to wear our school uniform on the trip and I left my suit at home.

We took the train from Victoria to Dover and many pupils got sick on the ferry but my experience of crossing the Irish sea got me through. Another train took us to Bonn, a lovely small city on the river Rhine and the new capital of West Germany. Our small hotel was at Bad Honnef about six miles upriver from Bonn. I remember this trip not because it was my first to the continent but for an incident in the hotel. We had very clean and tidy bunk beds. One morning I thought my shoes needed a good polishing and using the finest Kiwi black polish managed to drop a few bits of polish onto my pristine white bunk bed sheet. I did not notice it at the time but I certainly got to know about it when we returned that evening. Just as we sat down for dinner, the Hauswirtin walked towards the Head teacher's table carrying what I thought was a large white flag but as she held it high above her head pointing to some black marks it quickly dawned on me that this was my bunk sheet. I did not understand her German but I got the message. Mr O'Connell, red faced with embarrassment stood up to ask whose sheet it was. As I stood up our Hausfrau expanded with glee, she had her culprit, job done. I was grounded for a day but Mr O'Connell had left his cane back in London so it was a bit of a let off for me. The next time that the head teacher called me in to see him was to tell me that he was going to expel me from his school.

EXPELLED FROM SCHOOL

Catholic schools across London organised regular day retreats for older pupils at the Brompton Oratory. Various Catholic dignitaries gave talks to the pupils and when we attended there was a nationally known dignitary present. My close friend Charles Bond was the leading and trusted member of our group, which also included Noel Baker and Geraldine Gallagher among others. Our group met boys and girls from other schools through our organised discussion sessions. As well as lunch we were served afternoon tea which included cakes. In those days I was a great fan of cakes as my Granny never made any cakes so they were a real treat for me. My mother did bake a very good apple pie with cloves from time to time. At the afternoon tea Noel Baker and I laid into the cakes and even got some from other pupils at tables near to us. Noel was a bit ham-fisted and I remember some spare cake dropping from his mouth. We had great banter between our group and other pupils. Next day back at school the Head teacher called and asked Charles to come with him to his office. Charles was away for a long time. We had no inkling of what was to follow. Charles returned very flustered and said the head teacher wanted to see Noel Baker and me. When my turn came to be interviewed, the Head teacher told me that I had let the school down and that a senior member of the clergy had reported my misbehaviour to him. He accused me of spitting cake at pupils from other schools and shouting and shoving tables around the cafeteria. He made the same charge against Noel Baker. He found us guilty as charged and we were permanently expelled. I was surprised how the person who complained knew our names. I am not convinced that he did even now; but concluded that the head teacher was so shocked about someone from outside of the school complaining about the behaviour of his pupils he felt the need to act and especially so because the complainant was the top dignitary present.

My mother was not very happy when I told her about my expulsion. She arranged an interview with Mr O'Connell and put a very good case on my behalf. He wavered a bit but still stood by his decision. Maybe he remembered the shoe polish incident in West Germany. I had just finished my GCEs and if I did well I could get a job or go to a Further Education College. When the results came out in August I passed four GCEs with good grades and just missed out on Art – no surprise there. However the school was surprised with my performance. The Head teacher asked to see my mother and told her they would let me into the new and growing sixth form as long as I behaved myself. Sadly, Noel Baker did not do well in his GCEs and there was no reprieve for him. I still feel that Noel was badly treated but I am sure he found useful employment.

SUMMER HOLIDAY AND PART-TIME JOBS

Many of my fellow school friends, including me, had part time jobs to help our families and provide money to buy any special clothing or outings to events. I heard that some older boys were working for Anthony Jackson a supermarket in Camden Town. They had many packages of cigarettes to sell around the school and it soon became obvious that these were stolen from the supermarket. The cigarettes were stored in a locked wooden case in the loft above the shop floor. The boys managed to unscrew the back of the case to get at the cigarettes. I only learnt later why the manager never discovered the missing cigarettes. I got a job there two evenings a week and all day Saturday. My main job was to keep the shop shelves full. The section I had to keep filled included tinned fruit, vegetables, tinned condensed milk and cream rice. Carnation condensed milk was very popular with people from the Caribbean. I did not like the thick creamy sweetness of the stuff. Some people used it as a substitute for fresh milk in tea. What a way to destroy the taste of a good cup of tea. My favourite tinned food was Ambrosia creamed rice and I would eat a whole tin of it for lunch – paid for of course. The supermarket had an outside stall that formed part of Camden Market. Getting a job on this stall selling directly to people at the market and in competition with the other stalls was highly prized and was normally only for full time staff. I was very surprised when I arrived for one of my Friday evening shifts the manager asked me to take over from the full timer who was relegated to shelf filling. When it came to our evening break I went downstairs only to be greeted by the very angry guy who I had replaced. He flung a large tin of Britvic peach slices that just missed my head and splattered against the iron pillar just behind my head. The reason the manager put me on the stall it transpired was that he was thieving cash from the till and the manager thought, correctly, that I was a lot more trustworthy. I did enjoy the stall work especially at Christmas and could not believe how many boxes of Christmas Crackers that I sold to all sorts of people including women of the night. Later the manager was transferred to another branch of the supermarket chain near Kilburn but now only as a department manager – a demotion. It seems that he too was thieving or fiddling the books. Maybe this was the reason why the missing cigarettes were never reported. I quite liked the manager and ended up working in his department in the Kilburn supermarket for the summer holidays. With my job earnings I bought myself a very nice Swiss Tissot wrist watch. I still have it but not in working order – waterproof problems. I also bought a jacket with two large red stripes down the sleeves, which I wore for about two years. We had no Brand makes to worry about in the 1960s. However, my striped sleeves certainly got me noticed.

I got a very different type of work during my first sixth form summer holidays at Camden Council. This was essentially a clerical job dealing with community rate charges. I had to sort out the cheques, postal orders and even cash that came in as payment, log them and total up each day. I soon got the hang of it and completed the job in about three hours. I then pretended to work whilst reading a novel for the rest of the day. My immediate boss was a rather large young very volatile women who took a bit of a fancy to me which I did not reciprocate and it was not long before she turned on me – especially when she found out that I was reading novels. I cannot remember the exact circumstances but one day she gave me an almighty wallop across the face. I was prepared to let it go but in her guilt she ran to her boss and God only knows what she told him but the outcome was simple. I got the sack and two weeks' pay in advance. Great result for me and I headed for the open-air swimming pool on Hampstead Heath.

The next summer I got a job a Crawford's Biscuits in Willesden finding and sorting out accounting mistakes in order to help the chief auditor balance the books. The job put me off dealing with accounts for life – luckily when I got married my wife took over our family accounts. The job had one perk besides free luncheon vouchers. Each week we could purchase for a small sum a big bag of mixed rejected biscuits- mostly ones that had broken but were otherwise ok. Despite gorging on the biscuits I was lucky that I never did develop a lasting taste for them but I am still partial to a milk chocolates digestive biscuit until I think of all the fat, sugar and salt they contain.

I can remember one incident that occurred during my time at Crawford Biscuits. The factory was near a main electric overhead railway. It was a warm sunny August day and I regretted that I did not have a job outdoors. Suddenly a large flash of light, followed by a loud bang, lit up our office. We dropped our pens and ran outside to see a railway worker sitting on the line, bare chested and with bits of a thick wooden ladder spread all around him. It transpired that he was carrying the ladder on his shoulders when the tip touched or got too near to an overhead electric cable and caused a short circuit. His chest had suffered burns but he was still conscious. Sadly he likely died later from delayed shock.

Despite my longing for an outdoor job I ended up with another summer office job, this time at Legal and General at Swiss Cottage across the road from where I lived. My main job was filing customer correspondence and claims. Some of the insurance claims were interesting. One I remember involved a man claiming for fire damage to his kitchen. Seemingly he had placed his shirt over his gas cooker hob to dry and duly forgot about it until he smelt smoke and went back to his smoke filled kitchen and a shirt in ashes not to mention the blackened kitchen walls and ceiling. One of the regular office workers seemed to spend a lot of time on the phone, even late into the evening, so much so that I thought he was the busiest person in the office. Later I discovered that he was ringing Lords Cricket Ground to find the latest test and county cricket scores, no internet or mobile phones in the 1960s..

Whilst at Legal and General, I learnt that I had passed my Maths and Physics GCE A' levels with top grades. Somehow the office manager found out and asked me to visit head office for an interview for a permanent job contract as a trainee Actuary. I had no idea what an Actuary job entailed but a paid day's leave to headquarters in the City was attractive. The interview took place in a palatial office and I found difficulty answering questions whilst sitting in a deep leather armchair holding a cup of coffee. I was very surprised how keen they were to offer me the traineeship. I found out at the interview that an actuary has a key job of working out and setting premium rates. If he or she gets the rates wrong, the firm could lose a lot of money. Attractive as the offer was, I still wanted to go to university. In 1965 only about 12% of my age group went to university compared to over 45% in 2015. In addition, there were no fees to pay and I would get a free maintenance grant. In order to be an actuary today one is expected to have a PhD in a mathematical subject – how times have changed.

During one of my summer vacations at university I did manage find a job that was a bit more exciting than the usual clerical office job – Walls Sausage factory in north west London. The job was in the product development department and a science background was an advantage.

My first day was a day to remember. I arrived at 7.30 am to the screams of pigs in an adjacent building and to the screams of women on the sausage production line, which I had to pass through to get to the product development laboratories. Let me deal with the women first. The main sausage assembly hall contained scores of women on benches stretching for hundreds of feet. At one end, the sausage meat was put into piles according to the type of sausage to be made. Further along the line was the sexy bit where the sausage meat squirted out of pipes to be funnelled by the women into long tubes of sausage skin covering and then divided up into sausage length packages. Finally, individual sets of sausages were wrapped into the familiar sausage packages of six or eight sausages. The few men present in the large hall moved the big boxes of sausages to the next room for distribution. I had to walk through this area several times a day to get to the canteen and other parts of the factory. The first few women to see me (or any man) entering would start to scream and wave a sausage at you. By the time, one got to the end the screams were as loud as in a football stadium but full of sexual references to male body parts. You might think that this was great fun for the man, but it could be quite terrifying at times so much so that I resorted to going around the outside of the building even in the rain.

It took me a little longer to experience the full screams of the pigs. After the second or so morning of my arrival, I asked a colleague where all the pig squealing was coming from – the entry pens to the slaughterhouse was his reply. It took me another few days to get enough courage to visit the slaughter area. Early morning the day's quota of pigs for slaughter was unloaded from several Lorries into pens outside the slaughterhouse. Unfortunately, the pigs could smell the spilt blood of the other pigs ahead and so added to the crescendo of gut wrenching squealing – pigs are not stupid and I am sure they sensed their end was near. As a pig went through the final pen it was electrically stunned and a chain clamped on to a hind leg. It was then hoisted up to the first floor of the slaughterhouse and the slaughter man in a leather apron and rubber boots slit its throat, the blood flowed into a collection tray – probably used to make blood pudding. The carcass then went through a flame furnace and steam room to burn off hair and dirt. The conveyer belt then moved to the next stage where the entrails were removed and later the carcass was sliced in half and so on through different stages. In the later stages, individual men with sharp carving knives cut up different sections of the carcass for hams, shoulder, and other cuts. They were very handy with their knives and I would not like to get into an argument with any of them. It is surprising – if sad – how one can get use to this daily slaughter but no way would I like to have to work in that slaughter house on a permanent basis.

One of the product tests that we did was to see how packages of sausages would fare when weights were put on top of the packets. The idea behind this test was to make sure that the sausage casings were firm enough to take up to say a kilogram of loading before the sausage meat came out the ends. No housewife – it was the 1960s – would be happy when she got home and took her packet of sausages out of her shopping bag to find sausage meat all over the bottom of the bag.

We also tested how sausages would last intact at temperatures over a range of 30 C. The fun bit was testing them for frying because you got to eat some as well. The lesson I learnt was that the sausages must be put into very hot oil and completely submerged; in my experience most cooks do not do this. What made me wary of buying the cheapest sausages was the amount of fat they contained. Chunks of pig bits with only about ten percent lean meat and the rest fat were thrown into big grinders with many other additives.

THE OVERCOAT

My dad gave me two memorable presents and unlike the kids of today I can remember the giver many years later. The football came as a present from Santa, but I knew who Santa was and he was on a Christmas visit to Ireland in 1956. The football "kick started", as I stated earlier, my Gaelic football career. The second memorable present that dad gave me was when I was about eighteen and it was a beautiful mohair three quarter length overcoat. I had always admired my dad's traditional heavy Crombie Cavalry Twill overcoat that he wore for years. It was a great surprise when he gave me a very modern mohair overcoat that became the envy of my fellow A' Level students when I was studying at the North Western FE College in Kentish Town. Three students in particular vied for the coat and they were all Greek Cypriots. The coat not only looked good but also was lovely and smooth to the touch. They tried everything to get the coat off me – money, coat swap, sex with a fellow Cypriot girl student – not much to look at but a great body (and they should know). Tempted though I was, no way could I give my dad's present away. I did tell him about the offers I had and surprisingly he was not against me driving a hard bargain – ever the businessperson.

Many years later I was at an international rugby match in Dublin with my old friend Andy Sloman. We had a good drinking session after the match and decided to visit one more pub around midnight for a final nightcap. With pints in hand we stood to enjoy the folk music when we both noticed a man in his early thirties coming into the pub wearing a heavy Crombie Cavalry Twill overcoat. It did not take long before we got talking to him and discovered that the coat belonged to his father and he allowed us to try it on for size. He was wearing it in memory of his father and at that moment, I remembered my father's Crombie coat as a teenager and was surprised how big and heavy it was. My dad's coat was around for years and I regret now not keeping track of it. The company that made it, and still makes Combie coats, was established in 1805. They made coats for Russian and Confederate armies and later Ronald Regan and Mick Jagger among others.

French Trip 1962

Michael Heaney was a close friend of mine at school. He was born on Achill Island off the Mayo coast and the family emigrated to England in the mid 1950s. Michael came up with the idea that he and I should go camping in France. We bought a basic tent in a local ex-army store and applied for Irish passports. In August 1962, aged sixteen I set off with Michael for France. Our plan was to hitch to the south of France armed with Michael's 'Teach Yourself French' book. At Victoria rail station, we went through passport control. No queuing for us as we had our own Irish passport officer who wished us well on our adventure. It was late evening by the time we got to Calais and too late to hitchhike. We walked a few miles along the coast trying to find a suitable camping spot as it grew darker, eventually putting our tent up on a cliff with a nice sea view. Unfortunately, we had great difficulty trying to get the tent pegs into the ground and later discovered in the morning that we had set up our primitive camp on top of a Second World War German gun battery. We got little sleep on the hard ground and the local cockerels made sure that we were not able to have a lie in.

We walked miles the next day before we got our first lift. The driver of a small Citroen stopped and we managed with great difficulty to get into the back seats with our large rucksacks. The driver spoke French and we spoke English. I did glean that he wanted to know where we were from so I said Hibernia and that really confused him. Clearly his Latin was not as good as his French. Michael did a little better using his dictionary. We did not get too far as our driver was a local farmer. We walked for the rest of the day, failing to get a lift. It might have helped if we had an attractive girl with us. In the evening we decided to set up camp in a cornfield that had been recently harvested. Using the straw as a ground sheet and as a blanket, we decided that there was no need to put the tent up on a warm and beautifully sunny evening. We were wrong. I woke up during the night to be greeted by a clear starry sky and covered in heavy cold dew. I had not yet taken my O'Level Physics and did not realise that a clear night sky in August led to rapid ground heat loss and condensation. We carried on towards Rouen for several days getting the occasional short lift from the locals. Our dream of getting to the Mediterranean was rapidly disappearing. We eventually got lucky when an English couple in a Hillman Imp gave us a lift all the way to Rouen. We soon got very unlucky when Michael could not find his wallet. We reasoned, correctly, that it had fallen out of his back trouser pocket onto the car's rear seat. We found our first and only campsite a good walk from the centre of Rouen and set up our tent before we headed back into town to the Gendarmerie station in the hope that the English couple discovered the wallet and handed it in. At this time in the early 1960s, France was on full military alert because of their Algerian crisis. When we arrived at the station we were greeted by fully armed Gendarmerie who did not take kindly to two young sunburnt youths speaking in a foreign language.

After a time we got them to contact the local English counsel but we were not confident that we would ever see Michael's wallet again.

The English Councillor came to the station and invited us back to his flat. It was not long before we realised that he was gay and finding the wallet was low in his priorities. Still we enjoyed the wine and managed to escape unmolested. We gave up all hope of ever getting the wallet back and from then on we would have to rely on the little money that I had and luckily Michael still had his passport. We wondered in and around Rouen for several days. Occasionally I would lose Michael as he wondered off on his own. Michael was a bit of a dreamer and I was glad when we decided to head back for the port of Dieppe. It took several days to get there, surviving only on a diet of French bread, cheese and some vegetables from the fields. We slept in the fields by night and lifts were difficult to come by. With all the road walking I got badly sunburnt, my nose blistered and I ended up with a deep scar split along the ridge. We both lost weight and at night I would dream about being back home in my comfortable bed only to wake up and find that I was lying on very hard ground and aching all over. We managed to keep enough money for our ferry fair and when we arrived back at Folkestone we bought a Hovis loaf and some butter- we were in heaven. We had no problem hitch hiking to London and my parents were shocked when they saw my emaciated appearance. It took weeks to regain my normal weight but it was great to be back in my own bed. Some weeks later I had a surprise phone call from Michael informing me that his wallet had been handed in at Croydon Police station. The English couple did not trust the French police and knew that at least we would get the wallet back – better late than never. I did not go camping again until I met my Norwegian wife who knew what real camping was all about.

CHAPTER 5

IRELAND REVISITED 1965

A lot had happened in the five years since I left Ireland and I was looking forward to going back to see how the farm that we sold had changed and to hope my neighbours remembered me. It was even stranger going home with no home to stay in. My closest friend Charles Bond would be my travel partner on his first visit to Ireland. The plan was to travel round the south and west of Ireland staying in Youth Hostels and to finish up in the east, north of Dublin where I used to live. Luckily for us it was very easy to hitch hike in Ireland – unlike France in 1962.

On the ferry from Holyhead Charles and I had a Guinness because everybody else seemed to be drinking the black stuff. Amazingly we did not like it but finished off our bottles anyway. At Dun Laoghaire we visited the house where I was born, 1 Lower George Street. It was an end of terrace Georgian style three-storey house with the ground floor converted into a shop. This was a thriving vegetable shop during the war when my father was in charge. It was now a carpet shop. We then got the train into Dublin where we got our photographs taken by a tout on O'Connell Bridge. We paid his fee, gave our London address, but never saw the promised photographs.. He must have correctly taken us for two young fools. Later we climbed up Nelson's Column and got a great view of Dublin city, the bay and the Dublin Mountains. Less than a year later the IRA blew up the column, which most Irish people saw as a symbol of the British Empire. There is a similar column of the Duke of Wellington – still standing surprisingly – in the nearby town of Trim. The fact that he was born in the area might have saved him although he never overstated his Irish origins. There is an apocryphal story that when a fellow MP at Westminster referred to him as an Irishman, the Duke responded to the effect that "being born in a stable does not make you a horse". Where upon another MP shouted "does that make you a jackass then?"

We managed to get tickets for a hurling match at Croke Park, which was the theatre of dreams for me as a kid; but I cannot remember anything about the game. We were inspired by our trip to Trinity College to see the Book of Kells – an illuminated Latin manuscript of the four gospels ca 800 AD. Later on our tour we visited the town of Kells and the stone house scriptorium where the book, or part of it, was scribed.

We then headed south to Waterford, a Viking settlement and the birthplace of John Barry, the founder of the US navy and America's first Commodore commissioned officer appointed by President George Washington in 1797. Next stop Cork and its National University. We made a point of visiting Ireland's national universities as we wanted a foretaste of university campus life before we started at London University a few weeks after our return.

It was not until we got to Mitchelstown caves in Tipperary that we sampled our second Guinness. Whilst waiting for the caves to open we went into a nearby pub and ordered two pints of Guinness. In 1965 Guinness was still sold in bottles and draught Guinness only became popular in the late 1960s. I still remember a poster in London stating that there were six million bottles of Guinness sold each day. This time we failed to complete our Guinness and went down the road to sit on a lovely stone bridge to wait for the caves to open. About half an hour later a farmer on a horse and cart came over the bridge. He stopped and looked at us in amazement. He then said "Are Ye the two fellows after leaving yer Guinness glasses half full in the pub?" He certainly had never seen anything like it in his life before. Years later I was to make up for this insult to the Irish people by drinking copious amounts of Guinness with my sons and nephews at international rugby matches.

The tourist highlight of our trip was to Cape Clear Island off the coast of Cork. We got a lift with a middle aged Irishman who decided to visit a pub on the way to Skibbereen. Several pints and hours later we eventually arrived as the boat was about to depart. The boat only went to the island every other day and was delayed by difficulties in loading a cow on board. The small population of the island was Gaelic speaking and we stayed at the local youth hostel. The island was popular with foreign bird watchers and the island pub was the focal point for all entertainment. After a walk around the island we arrived at the pub for evening entertainment. It was very quiet with a few Gaelic speakers, although one local seemed to know a lot about boat engines and was happy to regale us with his knowledge, helped by the constant flow of Guinness. After an hour or so the pub began to fill up and the musicians arrived. I noted on the wall a list of names that had gained the Guinness Bath Badge. To achieve this dubious honour you had to submerge your body in a bath full of Guinness and then sign your achievement certificate using your own blood. I only hope the person seeking this honour had a proper bath before being submerged, because I am sure the bath Guinness would have gone to waste. Midnight came and went and the party was just getting going. Unlike the mainland, there were no police on the island to worry about. Some revellers were heading for Spain in the morning and decided there was no point in going to bed before taking the morning boat off the island. After being up most of the night Charles and I were glad to get back to the hostel and to bed.

Some of the hostels were in scenic locations but difficult to get to. I remember staying in a mountain shooting lodge that once belonged to one of the many English landowners in Ireland. The place was very damp and it was not surprising that Charles ended up with a mild bout of fever.

I have little memory of what other places we visited until we got to Kells where I made it a priority to visit the farm that we sold. The new owner and his wife of six years had improved the dairy cowherd and milking facilities. It was clear that the farm was going to prosper. Recently in 2015, I visited the area and was informed by Mrs Ward (87) and the oldest surviving person in Cookstown, that the son, who now owned the farm had 300 cows and he had bought and rented more land around the area – a long way from our 20 milking, or semi-milking cows.

It was fortunate that I met two of the local characters on the road – Tom Gahern and Tony Brady. Tony Brady was our cowman and he still had a few teeth left. Tom was Sheila Rennick's uncle and a confirmed bachelor, as was Tony. I could never understand why these men, handsome men in their days, never married. As kids in Ireland we never heard about gay men or women with the one exception of our allegedly gay teacher at the Christian Brother's School. In Tony's case he ended up looking after his mother in a council cottage. Once again and many visits later Mrs Ward provided us with the finest tea and homemade brown bread. We visited my old national school in Cortown and then walked into Kells where we stood in the courtyard of the Christian Brothers' School. I asked Charles to listen carefully. It was not long before he heard male voices shouting and the crack of cane or leather straps echoing around the courtyard. I could see the frightened look in Charles's eyes. "Welcome to school life in Ireland: the land of saints, scholars and child beaters", I said to him. Charles was already on his way out before I could say anything else.

From Kells we got a lift to Drogheda where the name Oliver Cromwell even today is not forgotten. In parallel with his infamous declaration to the native Irish – to hell or to Connaught – he singled out Drogheda for special treatment after the town failed to surrender to his invading army and performed one of the largest massacres of defending soldiers and civilians of his time. It is said in mitigation that some of the leading soldiers within the walls were English Royalists. Not long after a famous resident of the area, the catholic Archbishop of Armagh and Primate of Ireland, Oliver Plunkett (later raised to sainthood in 1975) was convicted for treason at Westminster. Deemed to be innocent by many of his peers, he was found guilty and hanged, drawn and quartered at Tyburn in London. His head is preserved in a shrine in St Peter's in Drogheda. Our visit to this church brought back memories of my maternal Uncle Tom who suffered from schizophrenia. During his worst periods, Oliver Plunkett featured strongly in his hallucinations, a bit terrifying to a ten year old boy. This visit helped give me some consolation and understanding of Tom's suffering.

Our final visit was to Ardee the hometown of my Granny who sold the farm and was now living in England. We visited her brother Frank's Pub on Main Street. One of Granny's sisters, Bessie, lived with Frank and both never married. Later we visited two more of granny's siblings, Joe and Aggie, at the family farm at Richardstown 3 miles outside Ardee. Again, Joe and Aggie never married. Granny had another brother Jim, who owned a pub in the town about 500 yards from Frank's pub. Jim was married and had 13 children to make up for his childless siblings. I have a reunion photo of these now grown up children from 2014 – they are all still alive, from the youngest around 60 to the oldest, Father Jackie, a retired priest about 86 years old. They are a very talented family, among them three nuns, two teachers, a priest and engineer. I am a similar age to Sister Angela McKeever, a nun working with the poor in Santiago Chile for nearly forty years. I was the first ever relative to visit Angela when in 2005 I ran the Santiago Marathon to raise money for her local charitable work. As I write (Feb 2016) I have arranged for my sister Dorothy to visit Angela on the last day of their South American cruise in Santiago on Feb 17th. Angela will come home to Ireland for good in 2017, ending a lifetime of charity work on behalf of the poor of Santiago.

My mother told me that her McKeever granny had paired off her children so that they would have to support each other in the pub and farm business. I am not sure if the unmarried siblings approved of her scheme, but they were well provided for. This arrangement was very much resented by Aggie who remained bitter throughout her life at being denied the opportunity to better herself in the wider world.

Charles and I were a bit suntanned after our hitchhike around Ireland and Charles, being half-Italian, was a lot darker skinned than me. At Frank's pub we got plenty of orange juice and biscuits with Frank leaning close to me to ask "who is this Blackman ye have with you"? I do not think Charles was too impressed but we were in rural Ireland. We went upstairs to see his sister Bessie who poured out her deepest sympathies and pities for us in this cruel world. This was a bit of a surprise to us as Bessie had never left her hometown, never mind Ireland. We found Bessie's tearful concern a bit disconcerting, as it appeared that she herself would never have to face too many problems. Her deep pity for others did not stop her living beyond ninety years!

Our next stop was the farm of Joe and Aggie. This was the birthplace of my maternal granny Theresa and during my stay with her she always made sure to visit her homestead at least twice a year. I loved the two hour car journey with the half way pub stop in our Morris 8. Joe and Aggie put on a great afternoon tea of homemade brown bread, apple tart and jams. Well actually their niece Angela (soon to be nun) did most of the work. They regularly used the children of their brother Jim in the town as resident house servants. They worked them hard feeding the racing greyhounds, chickens and cows and lavished great praise on their work efforts. Speaking to Angela years later – which played a similar role to mine with my granny in Kells- she never resented the hard work and actually enjoyed the years she spent with her aunt and uncle. However more valuable to Joe and Aggie than physical work was spiritual work. Angela was good at school and when she decided to become a nun, Joe and Aggie were delighted. Now they would have someone to do the hard work of praying for them before they shuffled off this mortal coil.

Joe got his little used car out of the barn to take us to the main Dublin road where we had a better chance of getting a lift. We had run out of money and near Dublin we were walking past a parish presbytery and took our chance to call in and regale a young priest with our hard luck story. We impressed him enough to get a few pounds to buy some food on the ferry back to England. Thank you Father.

CHAPTER 6

MY DEBATING ODYSSEY – FROM SCHOOL HALLS TO THE CAFE ROYAL TO LONDON UNIVERSITY

Sometimes in life the unexpected happens and I never dreamed that I would enter the world of school and university debating. In our small sixth form at St Richard's School, I studied for three A'Levels in Pure and Applied Mathematics and History. I had private free lessons in Latin and started Physics O'Level at the local Further Education College. The high point of my two years in the sixth form was reaching the final of the London Metropolitan Schools Debating Tournament held at the Cafe Royal, Piccadilly, London. How a team of two students from a secondary modern school could defeat some of London's top Grammar and Public schools to get to the final was at least a small miracle.

At St Richards we were fortunate to have support from the local Dominican Priory and the Rev Simon Blake was our school chaplain. He was also chaplain to the actors union and he knew and helped some famous actors living in London. We also had some young aspiring teachers who started their teaching careers at the school on their way to greater things. One particular teacher was Mary Afron Jones – nee Ellison. Mary was my History teacher and she was studying for a PhD in Modern American Trade Unionism at University College

London. She went on later to be Professor of History at Kiel University.

The London Evening Standard, in conjunction with the London University Debating Society, had recently set up a debating competition for sixth formers attending schools in the greater London area. Our school was one of many invited to participate. My history teacher Mary Jones thought that she could find a team to enter. After a trial debate my great friend – later my best man, Charles Bond and I were selected to represent the school.

The first round of the competition in our part of London took place at The Jewish Free School in Camden with eight teams. The motion was "Patriotism is the last refuge of the Scoundrel" – a quotation from Samuel Johnson. We were selected to propose the motion. At the time, I was very much an Irish patriot and did not see myself as a scoundrel; but in the debate I was able to link country with empire. I am certainly no imperialist and I can think of many imperialist scoundrels. Problem solved. Charles and I were fired up and well prepared by my history teacher and others and just did enough to win.

Next debate up was "Popular taste is the best guide to good music" – horrors on this one as Charles and I knew nothing about music and besides I was tone deaf. Surely this was the end of our budding debating careers. Well, we might not have known much about music but others did. Our school chaplain arranged for us to have a talk with Danny Wolgar, the Prior of the local Dominican Priory. Danny was a very knowledgeable man and opened up the classical world of music to us. I can still remember Danny explaining the role Hungarian folk music played in the musical compositions of the composer Bella Bartok. Some of his works were adaptations of folk tunes from Transylvania that were played on fiddle or shepherd's flute. Making the link between the folk music of the common people and highbrow orchestral music was a key argument for this debate. Danny furthered our classical music education by taking us to a performance of Beethoven's Ninth Symphony at the Royal Albert Hall. The final choral movement made a lasting impression on me. I was not completely devoid of a classical music appreciation. My mother occasionally played Beethoven's Fifth and Pastoral Symphonies that I came to appreciate. In passing, I was also impressed by the long hours that the Prior worked, up at five am and in bed after midnight. He did reveal his secret of surviving such a long day – a half-hour power nap early afternoon.

My history teacher came up with another trump card for this debate. She contacted the BBC research team to find out the most popular requested songs. We were all surprised with the result. This being around 1963-64, the swinging 60s were just getting going so no Beatles at the top yet. The most popular song requested was "When You Come to the End of a Lollipop". This seriously questioned the notion that popular taste was a guide to good music. Blackfriars Hall was the venue for this debate and we got through to the next round thanks to good homework and being able to predict the opposition's arguments.

There were two semi-finals on alternate evenings at Lambeth Town Hall and we were allocated to the second evening. This time the motion was "The Establishment is a Barrier to Progress" and we were selected to propose the motion. This was just what we wanted. In the 1960s only about 10% of 18 year olds went to university compared with nearly 50% in 2015. Most students going were from private or grammar schools. Things were changing with the beginning of comprehensive schooling and maintenance grants for some poorer students. There were no university fees unlike today. In 1965 when I gained admission to London University, I was one of the first groups of students to benefit from the wind of change that was sweeping through British society. A key source of information about the Establishment was the recently published book "Anatomy of Britain" by Anthony Sampson (1926-2004). Sampson was educated at Westminster School and Oxford and spent his early years as a young journalist in South Africa. He was well qualified to take a close look on how power was distributed and exercised in the UK of the 1960s. He wrote to 200 of the great, the good, the obscure and the most powerful; all but three agreed to be interviewed by him. He discovered some interesting facts: there were still 600 butlers employed, the church was Britain's third biggest landowner, the select few ruled the upper echelons of society. The judiciary, law, medicine and the civil service were in the main the preserve of those educated in the private sector. Many of the establishment figures belonged to private clubs. These clubs often paid more attention not on selecting members; but who to exclude.

Even in 2015, the judiciary and top posts in the civil service are largely occupied from the 7% that are privately educated. Some 47% of the current Conservative government were privately educated and a sizeable minority of all party MPs went to Oxbridge. Upon reflection, I believe that Sampson's book was the inspiration for selecting the motion for the semi-finals.

Charles and I attended the first semi-final and we heard all the arguments of both sides and realised that we were well prepared for our debate. I decided to wear a black tie for the event and made the point to a full chamber that I was wearing it in mourning for the Establishment. This went down well and we were clear winners, knocking out two well know public schools in the process. As the Establishment is still not dead and has in fact been augmented by new money and our celebrity culture, maybe I should be still weaning my black tie.

The motion for The London Metropolitan Schools' Debating Tournament final was "Of all her Colonies, England takes the greatest pride in the United States" and took place at the Cafe Royal. The judges for the debate would include the American Ambassador and the Secretary of State for Education, Edward Boyle. The big difference for the final was that we would not know whether we would oppose or propose the motion until the morning of the debate. We were not very inspired by this motion and I would have preferred to oppose the motion.

Unfortunately, we were selected to propose the motion on the day.

Once again, we got good support in doing our research. Mary Jones arranged for Charles and me to attend a lecture by a visiting American Professor of History, one Henry Steele Commager (1902-1998). His books "The Growth of the American Republic" along with "The American Mind" (pub 1951) were standard reading for two generations of Americans. Commager was a believer in American exceptionalism – that the country fashioned by the Founding Fathers was a uniquely perfect polity, living realisation of what the European Age of Enlightenment dreamt of, but could not achieve on their own scared continent. (Obituary, Independent Newspaper 1998). A good reason here as to why England should take pride in America perhaps. For this debate we needed also a literary input and our School Champlain Simon Blake put us in touch with Olwin Wymark, an American playwright and wife of the British actor Patrick Wymark. We met her at her house in Hampstead over tea and she gave us a quick review of American literature. She thought the poetry of Robert Frost and his take on the American dream would be useful to us. A lot of his work is based on nature and life in New England in the early 19C. In Frost's poetry, there is a constant idea or dream that there are many paths that one can take to fulfil one's life. People have choice and are free to dream and to accomplish their dreams and this for many could improve their economic and spiritual prosperity. We have all to decide what path to take and once gone down that path you keep on going, hopefully with no regrets. His poem **"The Road Not Taken"** opens with the lines:

Two roads diverge in a yellow wood
And sorry I could not travel both
And be one traveller, long I stood
To where it bent in the undergrowth
Then took the other, just as fair
And perhaps having the better claim,

Because it was grassy and wanted wear,
Though as for that passing there
Had worn them really about the same.....

The American dream compares with the limited horizons of the European who must know their place and serve their betters as well as being restricted by social barriers that cannot be crossed. Our thinking here was the Frost's poems should not only apply to Americans but to everyone else in the Old World.

The Cafe Royal is a rather grand place. By the 1890s it was the place to see and be seen. Its patrons have included Oscar Wilde, D H Lawrence, Churchill, Brigitte Bardot, Muhammad Ali and many more. Before the debate we had a five course meal with various dignitaries present. I got confused in selecting my cutlery for each course and would have preferred to debate on an empty stomach. This debate would be the first time we did not face the audience. We were seated House of Commons style with the opposition facing the proposition. In fact with the bright lights focused on the debaters it was impossible to see the audience. I prefer to make eye contact with audience members as well as fellow debaters. Charles and I were not prepared for this format. Charles always spoke first and my job was to finish off the job. When Charles was speaking, I heard a strange knocking noise and soon realised it was made by one of his legs vibrating on the floor – that is how nervous he was. Our performance was a little wooden and we lost. The Education Minster in his summing up stated that I would make a good political scientist as a career. Later I looked up what the work of a political scientist might entail and concluded they might make good scholars but not necessarily good debaters.

Charles and I had come a long way, especially as we were the only non-grammar or private school students in the competition. Our school received a Gavel and Sound Block made from wood from one of London's old coffee houses frequented by Samuel Johnson. It was only later that I appreciated the significance of this award.

Coffee houses were popular in the towns of the Ottoman Empire but it was not until 1652 that London had its first coffee house cum stall at St Michael's Alley, off Cornhill in the City of London. By 1700, there were hundreds of coffee houses in the city despite Charles II's attempt to stop them in 1675. It concerned the king that for a one-penny entrance fee anyone could discuss politics freely in the coffee house. At Lunt's coffeehouse in Clerkenwell Green, patrons could sip coffee, have a haircut and enjoy a fiery debate on slavery. Jonathan's coffee shop near The Stock Exchange – now a private member's club, traded the first stock and share dealings. Conversation and debate were the lifeblood of the coffee house. Pepys records a coffee house debate on the futility of distinguishing between a waking and a dreaming state. Isaac Newton once dissected a dolphin on a table in the Grecian coffee house, now part of the Royal Society. Dr Samuel Johnson spent a large portion of his life in coffee houses in the Fleet Street area -"...so a man is sooner ask'd about his coffee house than his lodgings". He also said, "When a man is tired of London, he is tired of life, for there is in London all that life can afford".

Sadly today's coffee houses may have much better coffee but the coffee drinkers are too plugged into their iPhones and iPads to engage in conversation with each other. A few years ago in Reykjavik in Iceland my wife and I observed two male friends come into a very comfortable coffee bar, each on their own iPhone, ordering by hand signals whilst still conversing, staying for 15 minutes, paying by hand signals and then leaving, still on their iPhones. They never said a word to each other, and this in one of the least populated countries in Europe, famous for its Icelandic Sagas.

The power establishments in the US hold the Gavel and Sound Board in great esteem. The Senate uses an ivory gavel without a handle and the House of Representatives the traditional hammer shaped wooden one. Members in Congress or the Judiciary dare not speak once the gavel hits the soundboard. I now understand why the presentation of the gavel to schools participating in the final was a very appropriate prize and it has taken me a long time to understand and appreciate it.

TAKING THE FLOOR- UNIVERSITY DEBATING

My interest in debating was rekindled when I went to Queen Mary College, London University in 1965. As luck would have it, Charles Bond ended up at the same college so we were able to enter as a team to represent the college in the inter-collegiate university debating annual tournament. There were at least twenty colleges and medical schools participating and we got as far as the semi final held at Goldsmiths College in Lewisham. Goldsmiths specialised in the Arts and Education so had a majority of female students. I cannot remember much of the debate but I do remember drinking with many female students in the bar afterwards. I have no doubt that they were impressed by our debating skills although fortified with drink it may have distorted my opinion of myself. Charles certainly got on well with the students, so much so that he passed out on the upper deck of the bus taking us home just before Westminster Bridge. The conductor ordered us off the bus and I was able to get some students to help me carry Charles to the nearby Westminster Hospital. The night nurse arranged for Charles to have a stomach pump and then decided to admit him to one of the wards. I made my own way home – just about. According to Charles, he woke up in the morning thinking he was in his own bed but could not understand why the ceiling was so high. He then had a panic attack and though he was dead or near to it. The nurses were quickly present to reassure him that he would survive especially with a strong coffee. When he went to get dressed there was no sign of his expensive new jacket, somehow it came off in the struggle to get him to the hospital. On the positive side we had made friends with two Goldsmiths students who would later be part of our London University Debating Society Committee.

The main university debates took place at the Student Union in Malet Street or in Senate House near the British Museum. These debates were open to all students from the various colleges and for the more popular debates the hall was full and doors closed. At London and at Oxford and Cambridge we could attract many national and international figures to participate in our debates.

For one of the first debates I attended the motion was "Wogs begin at Calais". I am sure that this would not be acceptable today and it would probably be changed to a statement of the obvious "Foreigners begin at Calais". In early December it was traditional to hold a motion titled "This House has no Confidence in Her Majesty's Government" at Senate House. For this debate we would have a cabinet and shadow cabinet minister present. Students got a chance to speak from the floor after the main platform speakers had their say. Charles and I took our opportunity to speak and be known to the committee and soon we were invited to the pre-debate sherry reception. Sherry was the drink of choice in the 60s and certainly helped to calm the speakers' nerves. I can remember one cabinet minister, Quentin Hogg, later Lord Chancellor, who arrived by bike and had no problem helping himself to the sherry – a real professional. I assume that he kept the same balancing skill on his bike on the way home remembering that he also attended an after debate dinner at a nearby restaurant. Tough chaps are these cabinet ministers. I can only assume that the female cabinet ministers who came later learnt from the likes of Quentin Hogg, or maybe not.

For the London University Debates our format was to have four invited speakers for the proposition and four against and facing each other across the despatch box in House of Commons style. I, as President wore the robes of office representing the chancellor and colours of the university and sat on the high chair overlooking the speakers and the audience with the minute taking secretary to my left. The Chancellor of London University for many years was Queen Elizabeth the Queen

Mother. I had a traffic light system to control the duration of speeches and speakers always had to give way to a point of order. The fun started when I opened the debate to the floor and the students let rip.

Our first debate had the motion "There is too much litter in literature and sin in the cinema" and one of our key guest speaker was John Trevelyan, Secretary to the British Board of Film Censors (1958-1971) and whose name always appeared on screen at the start of all films in the cinema. I was quite nervous as this was my first debate as President but it went well in front of almost a full house. Trevelyan had the skills and diplomacy to pass films that were revolutionary in terms of explicit drug use, swearing, frontal nudity and relatively graphic sex scenes. Yes, it was a lively debate from what I can remember of it.

Our most successful debate was "Modern Man has no need of God". We managed with some difficulty to assemble a strong line up of speakers. The main speaker against the motion was Lord Longford, then Leader of the Lords in Harold Wilson's labour government. He nearly failed to turn up for the debate and I had to start without him. He was delayed by proceedings in the House of Lords. He managed to get a taxi, still in his Lords regalia, and arrived only a few minutes late – he did get a standing ovation when he entered the Hall. Longford had a reputation as a reforming peer of the realm and was famous or infamous for his work with prisoners and sex offenders. As a committed Christian and a convert to Catholicism, he believed that sinners were forgiven if they truly repented. His prison visits to the child murderer Myra Hindley and his investigations into the sex trade caught the public imagination for better or for worse. His family were the Pakenhams, landed gentry from County Westmeath, Ireland who received lands in the Irish midlands as part of the English colonisation of Ireland. They managed to survive and keep their estate during the Easter rising and the creation of the Republic of Ireland. Although educated at Eton and awarded a double first from Oxford, Longford always considered himself Irish. Some years ago, I saw him ambling along towards Twickenham for an England versus Ireland rugby match and took the opportunity to remind him of our debate and seek some sponsorship for The Thomas Coram Foundation and my participation in the Boston marathon. A few days later I received a cheque – Coutts Bank – from him and wishing me luck.

Supporting Lord Longford for the opposition was The Reverend John Robinson, Bishop of Woolwich who also had achieved an element of public notoriety. His book "Honest to God" was a best seller- a million copies sold. In it he suggested that God was not up or out there but was very much earth bound. He questioned the idea of miracles and the virgin birth. He could also be termed a relative moralist rather than an absolute one. He defended the publication of Lady Chatterley's Lover. Certainly having Longford and Robinson debating together was a real treat for the students.

Professor G O Jones, physicist and novelist from my own Queen Mary College agreed to propose the motion. He made his name in Low Temperature Physics and later as the Curator of the Museum of Wales. A debate like this one also needed a philosopher and we got Professor Ted Honderich (1933-) from University College London. Born in Canada, son of a Mennonite German father and of a Scottish Calvinist mother and force-fed a religious diet throughout his youth. By his late teens he could see nothing in religion that could be possibly true – just the man to propose our motion. In the early 1960s he joined Bertrand Russell on CND marches. He was and is a strong believer in consequentialism – one is judged by the consequences of their actions and not by one's own personal morality. It was no surprise that he is not a fan of Tony Blair. His philosophy covers: Right and Wrong, Determinism and Freedom, Mind and Brain and much else. In 2002 his book dealing with political philosophy and the use of violence in which he asserted the moral right to resist ethnic cleansing with violence was banned in Germany and made him a figure of hate in some quarters.

To add to our eclectic collection of speakers we had the President of the British Humanist Association. This Association, formed in 1896, campaigns for a secular state, challenges religious privilege and promotes equal treatment for all regardless of religion or belief. They want non-religious people to be confident in ethical matters and to have a life fulfilled based on reason and humanity.

We were also hosts to the winning North American Universities debating team from McGill University, Montreal. They were unhappy about being listed as support speakers, but such was the strength of the line up that I had already made an exception in getting them a place on the front bench.

We had a packed hall for this debate and I cannot remember much of what was a lively exchange. I do remember Professor Jones, a committed atheist, saying that he was honoured to be in the presence of so many earthly Lords.

My sister Dorothy and her husband Pat as well as my Uncle Philip were also present at the debate and dinner afterwards. We had one interesting happening at the restaurant. I got a phone call from the Bishop telling me that he had taken the wrong overcoat. It transpired the he had Lord Longford's and he had his, so they arranged to meet each other to exchange coats at a well known London club and no doubt continued to explore the finer points on the existence and nature of God.

One person who liked coming to our debates was Viscount Patrick William Barrington (1908-1990), 11th Viscount of Ardglass, County Down, Ireland. 11th Baron Barrington of Newcastle, Limerick. 5th Baron Shute of Becket, Berkshire. On his death, his titles became extinct, but whenever I called upon him to speak from the floor of the debating chamber I used his titles to impress the students. Educated at Eton and Magdalen College, Oxford, Viscount Barrington could be guaranteed to add a bit of "Class" to our often-grubby student existence. He could call upon his humorous verse that often appeared in Punch Magazine to enliven any debate. His best know work was "The Diplomatic Platypus". I often got the feeling that he was a bit lonely and sought solace in the company of the lively students. It was nice of him to reciprocate our hospitality by inviting Charles and me for tea in the House of Lords.

Whilst on the subject of their Lordships, I debated with one The Earl of Arran at Leicester University in 1966. He succeeded his brother to become the 8th Earl of Arran. I remember asking him which Arran Island he was master of and he replied that he was linked to the Irish Aran Islands and the Scottish Isle of Arran. In fact, the Earl of Arran is a title in both the Peerages of Scotland and Ireland. The title is still active as his son, the 9th Earl, is an elected hereditary peer. His popularity as a debater was enhanced by his regular column in The London Evening Standard where he was billed as "the Earl you love to hate". His nickname was Boofy Arran but he did some useful work in the Lords where he thrice introduced a Sexual Offences Bill as a passionate advocate of homosexual rights and also campaigned for the protection of badgers. When asked why his homosexual bill was passed and not his badger protection bill. He replied," that there were not enough Lords who were badgers"!

I had intended that my legacy debate would be one on Ireland. Matters were beginning to hot up in Northern Ireland. Republicans – Catholic and non- Catholic – were discriminated against in jobs and housing allocation. There was widespread gerrymandering to keep unionists in power in areas where they were the minority. Northern Ireland's second city Derry (Londonderry) was controlled by unionists despite being in the minority. The selection of Colerain as a site for a new university and not Derry was widely condemned. The civil rights movement in America inspired republican protest marches. There was a larger than life character that stood out from the rest – The Reverend Doctor Ian Paisley – the title he insisted that people refer to him by. He was a big man with a big ego and an even bigger booming voice. He had two clear sound bites "No Popery Here" and" No Surrender".

I had no problem in getting speakers for the republican cause. Charles and I met a Mr MacAteer of The United Ireland Association in a pub in Covent Garden. He was a bit of a control freak and wanted to make sure his Association had a lead role in the debate and under the influence of Guinness we were a little too influenced by him. His competitor for the lead republican role in our debate was a national figure, Gerry Fitt (1926-2005).

Fitt had recently been elected as the Republican Labour member for West Belfast and was Northern Ireland's only nationalist MP at Westminster – amazing since nationalists made up about 40% of the population of the province. We met him at a meeting at Camden Town Hall and he impressed me with his passion and his ability to talk. That should have been a warning sign because later on as we got closer to the deadline for fixing the motion for our debate he got quite slippery and was capable of going back on what we thought we had agreed. This trait was later to undo him in his political career when he lost his seat to Gerry Adams in 1983, partly because he did not support political status for the hunger strikers. Still, Thatcher thanked him by making him a life peer a few months later. Later on, he even voted against the disbandment of The Royal Ulster Constabulary who had beaten him up in a very bloody demonstration in 1968. He also did not want Dublin to be involved in any power sharing agreement in Northern Ireland. Was he perhaps in the end a true "turncoat"?

Like Fitt, Ian Paisley was charm itself but it was impossible to get him to agree on anything. After several expensive phone calls to Northern Ireland, I could not get him to agree a motion that would in any way question the constitutional status of Northern Ireland. The only motion that he would agree to would be one about the financial support Northern Ireland got from the UK government. He knew very well that the nationalists would not want to debate such an anaemic topic. We were also in contact with the leader of the Orange Order in Britain as a possible speaker. While he seemed to be a little more amenable than Paisley to a more political motion, it was clear that he was in cohorts with Paisley behind the scenes. So no joy here either.

We had already printed Green and Orange Posters to advertise the debate throughout all the colleges and medical schools of the university. However, after hours of debate about The Debate we had to give up and cancel. I was not surprised that it took another thirty years to get any sort of agreement to power sharing in Northern Ireland. Tony Blair may have made many enemies in power but his success in Northern Ireland was the hallmark of his premiership.

We did have more success with our end of term "No Confidence in Her Majesty's Government" debate at the end of term in Sennet House. The main speaker for the proposition was John Boyd Carpenter (1908-1998) who held four ministerial posts under three conservative prime ministers. Charles and I happened to be at Westminster tube station when we spotted him and got him to agree to come to our debate, subject to his diary commitments. As a former president of the Oxford Union, we knew that he would be a good speaker and we were not disappointed. Opposing the motion was Reg Prentice (1923-2001), Minister of Public Buildings and Works. Not the most exciting of HaroldWilson's ministers but serving minsters are not easy to get to come to student debates. In 1976 Prentice was deselected by militants in his Newham East London constituency – a portent of things to come for the Labour Party. He switched to the Conservative Party and served as a minster in the early Thatcher government. He ended his political life as a conservative in the House of Lords. The debate was not very exciting but we did have some heated contributions from the floor of the chamber.

The time was rapidly approaching when I would have to get down to serious study and the Christmas vacation was devoted to catching up with a lot of missed lectures and laboratory work. Today I would have been given a sabbatical year for holding the Presidency of the Debating Union.

One of the more chastening experience of my tenure as President of London University Debating Society was my trip to Glasgow University to debate a motion on education at their renowned Student Union. The invitation was a bit of an honour as the Presidents of the Oxford, Cambridge, Durham, Trinity Dublin Debating Unions besides me were invited. My ever-loyal Vice President Charles Bond joined me on the trip. We arrived at Glasgow main station mid-morning and both of us agreed on the quality of the shapely legs of the Glasgow girls as they came off the commuter trains on their way to work in the city. Two members of the students union came to meet us and after an early lunch invited us to enjoy the best of Scottish whisky.

I was designated to the Liberal Party and had to learn very quickly what their policy was on education – this came as a big surprise. I did not realise that the debate was organised on a House of Commons format and would start at 2pm and go on until early morning finishing at about 5.30 am the next day with a break for a Cabaret at midnight. There would be a full served Scottish supper and breakfast. This debate was the highlight of the academic year, and most of the Scottish MPs and other dignitaries would be present. The whole occasion was a bit too much for me. Added to this was the fact that the Scottish student speakers were high calibre and knew their stuff and the format of the debate. Some of the top Scottish politicians and professionals were former Presidents or members of the Student Debating Society. I recently visited the Student Union (2015) and the layout of the hall was exactly as I remembered it in 1966. I now had time to see the list of past Presidents on the honours board: Donald Dewar, Charles Kennedy, John Smith, Sir Menzies Campbell, Lord Irvine and many other notables. The pain of my experience there also came back to me – if only I knew then what I know now!

I was expecting to speak by late afternoon but they told me that I would not be speaking until after the Cabaret – 2am in the morning. I was not happy and by early evening whiskies had gone to my head and this is a drink that sets me off into an aggressive mode if I am frustrated. The only time I ever had an argument in anger with my father was fuelled by whisky. I stormed off and went back to my student residence hall. Some hours later, they persuaded me to come back to the hall but my mood was still negative. It was considered an honour to speak in the final session of the debate but I was beyond caring. The complications of amendments and extra points of order that were raised over the hours of debate did not inspire me. Add to that the constant drone of the strong accents of the Scottish speakers over the hours depleted further any drive and emotion for the topic of Education that I had in the first place. I preferred our own straightforward motions at London and besides I was not an aspiring Scottish MP. My speech was fairly detailed but lethargic. I remember fiddling with a box of matches, something I never did before. I survived until breakfast, which was a grand affair with waiters in kilts delivering all sorts of delicacies including the famed Haggis. Charles and I then fell into bed exhausted. My Glasgow experience was a very chastening one and I was very glad to get back to London.

CHAPTER 7

MEETING THE LOVE OF MY LIFE

A few weeks before I met my wife to be in July 1967 I had met a very good-looking girl at my summer vacation workplace. Feeling a bit flush with my job earnings, I invited her for a meal at a restaurant in Golders Green. I have no idea why I selected an expensive fish restaurant but my guest ate very little of anything that we ordered. I noticed that she had very cold hands – fish cold you might say – and was quite the silent type. I decided that one date with this beautiful ice queen was enough for me. I prefer warm hearted and warm handed women who are also good talkers. I do not like long silences or using silence as a weapon of control in a relationship. The next girl I met was the exact opposite to the ice queen.

My old school friend Michael Heaney and I arranged a game of tennis and afterwards with no particular plans in mind we walked past the Europa Club in Finchley Road. We were not dressed for clubbing – I was wearing a lamb's wool pullover with a hole in one of the sleeves – but as it was early evening we decided to make a quick visit. We saw two very blond girls – from the back – and Michael said he would ask the taller of the two to dance and I was more than happy to ask the shorter girl. My girl seemed to have some shiny metal pieces on her teeth. Earlier on TV I had seen a programme about Finland and noticed one person had similar metal on her teeth. I asked her if she was from Finland. She was from

Norway, close enough I thought. It transpired that she was wearing braces to straighten her front teeth and this was the first time I had seen them. They were so rare in 1967 that she had to attend University College Dental School to have them regularly adjusted. It turned out that her name was Turid Alice and of course I had difficulty pronouncing Turid- silent d- and she said just call me Alice, which I have done now for nearly fifty years. I noted her lovely blue eyes and warm hands and that she was even talking more than me. I decided that the Cosmos, a coffee bar and restaurant across the road would be a better place to talk. This coffee bar was popular with Jewish refugees from Germany and I often played chess with some of them.

Well, when Alice said there were seven political parties in Norway and named them all with the policies they campaigned on I was astounded. We also discovered a commonality in outlook coming from two small countries. It was not for us the glory of empire, but rather the struggle of small countries for freedom. Norway had been under the rule of Denmark and later Sweden. It was only in 1905 that the country became an independent constitutional monarchy but unlike Ireland the separation from Sweden, although involving great tensions, was peacefully achieved – a velvet divorce. Alice opened up my mind to how the Norwegian poets, playwrights and musicians of the 19C., like Bjornson, Ibsen and Grieg who had awakened and forged national identity and nationalism. This parallels Yates and the Gaelic awaking in Ireland. She was aware of the Norwegian founding of Dublin and other Irish coastal towns. The Irish were also aware of their Viking city origins as exemplified much later on 1988 when I ran "The Viking Millennium" marathon in Dublin, that was organised to celebrate a thousand years since the city was founded by the Norwegian Vikings.

I was very surprised to find out that Alice was only seventeen years old. She had been to England the previous year for a short stay as an au pair and had completed a year at her local Gymnasium (grammar school) in Hamar, a county town about

120 km north of Oslo. This time she intended to have a year out to improve her English and to learn another language and then return to finish off her schooling with the intention of taking linguistics at university.

Meeting Alice was almost love at first sight, drawn by our similarities physically and culturally. I found our differences of language and national landscape also attractive and it was clear that meeting her would open up new horizons for me, not to mention the Northern Lights that would illuminate our future.

After some time – that seemed to be just an instant – I walked my Alice home to Baker Street a little over a mile to the small hotel where she worked. I gave her a good night kiss mostly on her metal braces. I walked back to Swiss Cottage on cloud nine with my head spinning and trying to comprehend all the information that Alice had told me. In terms of talking, I had met my match. I wondered how she could do it all in fluent grammatically correct English.

Late September 1967 I started my final year at Queen Mary and the expectations were that we would have to study far harder than we did in the first two years. The college professors designed the courses and tailored them to their research interest. QMC had the first university research nuclear reactor in the UK so Nuclear Physics was a necessary course. The college had the first aeronautical research department with its own wind tunnel (1909) so aerodynamics was a strong specialism. The college had strong research interests in Low Temperature Physics and Astronomy. My main interest was the new love of my life but somehow I managed to keep studying even though I lost interest in some of the lecturers who were not very inspiring. They may have been strong in their Physics speciality but lacked the skill and personality to communicate effectively to their students. I believe that the lecturers today are far more student focused and take account of student feedback. One can also plug in on the internet to free quality lectures from universities around the world.

For my final year, I was able to get a grant to live away from home. Students from outside London were able to get priority for places in the university halls of residence and QMC had a new student resident campus at South Woodford a few miles east of the college. I had no chance of getting a place but did secure a rented room including half-board in a typical suburban semi in South Woodford. Mrs Pratley, my landlady, was a divorcee whose grown up children had left home. Sometimes I visited the nearby hall of residence and realised how well the students were looked after. The big advantage they had over me was the intellectual stimulation from fellow students and links with the college. I was a bit lonely in my digs but Mrs Pratley fed me well. Sometimes on a Sunday when she went to her local church I would go into the front room and play some records. I discovered that the flip side of a child's record had an Irish rebel ballad recounting the battle between the United Irishman and the British Army during the Irish Rebellion of 1798 – The Rising of the Moon, with opening lyrics:

And come tell me Sean O'Farrell tell me why you hurry so – Husha buachaill hush and listen and his cheeks were all a glow – I bare orders from the captain get you ready quick and soon – For the pikes must be together by the rising of the moon....

The title later formed the final line of the last entry of the diary of the hunger striker Bobby Sands "... *the day will dawn when all the people of Ireland will have the desire for freedom to show. It is then we'll see the rising of the moon.*"

I introduced Alice to my parents in a pub at Swiss Cottage and all went well fortified by a few pints. At that time the drinking culture between Norway and England was very different. Norwegians used their homes more for entertaining and drink in those bar-restaurants that served alcohol was prohibitively expensive. In England and especially in big cities, peoples' homes were much smaller and the pub was the focus for social meeting. Alice and I got closer in love and commitment to each other as autumn progressed. I took her to a formal Ball at Senate House in the presence of Elizabeth the Queen Mother and to an all night do at my own college. We both fell asleep at 4am watching the musical "Annie get your Gun" but we woke up in time for breakfast.

THE PROPOSAL

Our relationship had developed to the point that I decided that I wanted Alice to be my future wife and hoped she also felt equally in love with me. On the 11th October on a lovely autumnal evening we strolled through Russell Square when a great rush of emotion came over me and I could resist no more, stopped, looked into Alice's eyes, and asked her to be my wife. To my joy and relief, she said "Yes". An engaged girl needs an engagement ring and that costs money and we all know diamonds are a girl's best friend or were, until Alice informed me that Norwegians do not do diamond engagement rings. Instead, the engaged couple wear similar gold rings that also becomes their marriage bond symbols. This was a less expensive option but a trip to Hatton Garden to look for suitable gold rings soon changed Alice's mind when she saw all the sparkling diamond engagement rings. Besides, as the gold rings were a Norwegian custom it would be more appropriate to purchase them later in Alice's hometown. I still had some of my student grant left and dwindling summer earnings and decided to buy Alice a single solitaire diamond ring. As I then needed to live on some of Alice's earnings, one could say that Alice helped to pay for her own engagement ring, but then thankfully, love is blind.

Our engagement changed Alice's plans and we decided it was better that she went back to Norway at Christmas to restart her studies and I would concentrate on finishing my degree.

She had already invited me for Christmas and it would be my first one away from my family.

MY FIRST CHRISTMAS IN NORWAY 1967

In December 1967 we set off from Kings Cross to Newcastle to catch a boat for the two day trip to Oslo. It would be twenty-five years until the arrival of the low cost airline and still a few years before the start of the large car ferry. We travelled third class, meals included, in bunk bed accommodation in the bow of the ship. The first thing I noticed was the strange names on the rucksacks of my fellow mainly student passengers: Kristiansen, Jensen, Olsen, Hagen. The strange names increased my excitement at the prospect of what was to come. We went up on deck to watch the passing harbour lights and ships as we sailed out of the Tyne to the open sea. I remember Alice telling me that Norway had the third biggest merchant navy in the world and how travel by sea was the only way to get to the western and northern parts of Norway to places that were hundreds of miles up the fjord indented west coast of the country. I was glad I was in the care of a young woman who was a knowledgeable seafarer. Until that is our small ship began to hit the rough open North Sea. Our ship had no modern stabilisers and Alice began to turn a little green in the face. Then she was gone. I remained on deck for a while and quite enjoyed the rolling of the ship but then went to check on Alice who was tucked up in her bunk bed. It was clear that our Norwegian seafarer would only be emerging again in the morning when we entered the sheltered waters off the coast of Kristiansand.

INTERLUDE – THE DUVET.

I had a top bunk bed in the male dormitory and could not understand why I had so many sheets and no blankets. In the darkened cabin I managed to pull what I thought was a thick white sheet half over me but with the ship rolling and not feeling too good I gave up any further effort to sort out my bedding and fell asleep. In the morning I could still not figure out why I had no Blankets. Alice came to my rescue. Norwegians do not use blankets; they use a duvet, called a "dyne" in Norwegian. What I thought was a thick white sheet was the duvet. I came to realise what a wonderful invention the duvet was when I rapped myself up in it on the next night at sea and later during my stay in Norway. No more blankets falling off the bed and the need for a quilt to cover the blankets, which could also slip onto the floor. I also learnt that the Norwegians used summer, autumn and winter duvets that contained different quantities of eiderdown to cope with the range of seasonal change in temperature. In fact, I was so impressed with the duvet that on my next trip to Norway, Alice got me one – double bed size- to take back to England. I had a big problem at Newcastle where I had to pay a hefty import duty. The Customs impounded my duvet because I did not have enough money to pay the duty. Eventually some months later, after I paid the duty plus a parcel post charge, I had my beloved duvet in London. It would take many years before the British came round to seeing the advantages of moving out of the Victorian era and using the duvet. Today blankets are history all over Europe and beyond. On looking back, I could have made a fortune importing duvets to Britain but 1967 was too early, people must be ready and persuaded to see the need for change. The duvet that I imported finally went to a heavenly slumber land in 2015 after a lifetime of nocturnal service.

As our ship approached the harbour lights of Kristiansand I could see the snow clad streets lit up by Christmas lights and could not believe that this would be my first White Christmas. We were able to disembark for a couple of hours and walked up the main street on beautiful clean white powder snow to look at the lit up shop fronts. The temperature was the coldest I ever experienced but I did not notice it in this magical world of fairy lights and dazzle. In one butcher's shop there was a whole pig decorated in tinsel with an apple stuffed in its mouth. I quickly learnt that pig in the form of pork ribs and sausages were the main Christmas fare.

On the second day morning at sea we sailed around the south coast of Norway and up the Oslo fjord into the heart of the city. No sea sickness to worry about now in calm waters, time to enjoy looking at the small ports and landscape and finally we were in sight of the towers of the new Town Hall, and the start of a lifelong romance with Alice and her country.

TANTE(AUNT) MARTHA

My first impressions of Oslo were viewed through romantically tinted glasses. It is a relatively small capital city but on occasion is one of the coldest cities in the world in mid-winter but in summer one of the most beautiful, set at the head of a fjord and backed by pine clad hills. In Oslo one is always close to nature on land and sea. Alice had already made sure that I had the right clothing so cold weather was not a problem. In fact, I often felt colder in London with damp and almost daily varying weather – three seasons in one day as they say.

We were to spend a couple of days with Alice's aunt- Tanta Martha- who lived in a flat in a well established part of the city, not too far from the Palace and close to a tram station. Although occupied by the Germans during The Second World War the city had escaped bomb damage and the central streets were typical of continental 19C design and construction. I was very lucky to meet Tanta Martha early in my visit because she was quite an extrovert and had spent some years in America and had worked on a Norwegian cruise liner. It was not long before she showed me her magnificent wall mounted wooden carved frame headed by the figure of Neptune and containing more than one hundred silver or silver plated spoons from cities across the world. I asked her if she had been to Dublin and of course she had and pointed to a spoon with a handle headed by a shamrock. Tanta Martha had married Otto in her 30s, in stark contrast to our early planned wedding, and had two young children called Annette and Ketil – more strange names for me to learn. We were given Annette's bedroom and she took the upper bunk of a double bunk bed in her brother's room. She used this as a launch pad to launch herself fearlessly down on us as we played with them.

The main event of our stay was the arrival and assembly of a kitchen table from America. Tanta Martha had an eye for quality and a bargain. We were to sit at this table many times in the years ahead. Also about fifteen years later a great friend of ours Maria, who Annette was an au pair for in her summer holidays in England, stayed with Martha and got the table story. Sadly, Martha died a few years ago at the age of 75 years having moved to a new flat in Oslo with the kitchen table still in service. Martha, being open minded and worldly, was a great support to us in the early years of our marriage and continued to be so until she died and we greatly miss her.

HAMAR THE TOWN I CAME TO LOVE SO WELL

The final leg of Alice's homeward journey was the 120km train journey north-east to Hamer. This was to be my first view of the Norwegian landscape and I had plenty of time to view as the track was a slow single line one with some tunnels, bridges and spectacular lakeside cliffs to traverse.

It was dark when we arrived in Hamar and as we walked along the snow clad platform we were greeted by Alice's older sister Ragnhild who was similar to Alice in height and figure but not as blond and a little nervous of meeting this foreigner who was going to spend some time in her home. I learnt later that she thought I was good looking and had lovely curly hair like her late father. Like Kristiansand, the town was covered in a pure white blanket of snow, and lit up for Christmas. I saw some more decorated pigs in the shop windows as we walked the kilometre to Alice's block of flats.

Alice is one of four children. Two younger brothers called Odd Egil and Einar Magne and her sister Ragnhild Beate. Many Norwegians use two first names that is also sometimes the case in Ireland.

Sadly, Alice's father, Ragnar, drowned in the local lake Mjosa aged only 35 years. The mother, Gudbjorg, was left alone to support four children aged 2, 4, 9 and 10 years at the time of the accident. Ragnar was a machine mechanic in the local Nestle factory but it was the local paper that stepped in to support a collection for the bereaved family. They also gave Gudbjorg a job that involved collecting the paper's subscriptions, a job she could fit around her family commitments. She also got some money from the sale of her husband's boat. It is difficult to image what Gudbjorg must have endured losing her husband in such dreadful circumstances and still have to bring up such a young family on her own. She managed to accumulate enough savings to buy a share in a newish two bed flat with a lovely view of lakeMjosa. By 1967, Gudblorg had gone back to her pre-marriage job as a chef at the Hotel Astoria as her family were older and more able to cope with her shift hours.

In England in the 1960s it would be unthinkable to have a foreigner coming to stay for Christmas, even more so if they had only a two bedroom flat. The flat had a very large lounge and individually allocated storage facilities in the cellar and loft. Only Ragnhild could speak good English so generally I was reliant on Alice as my translator.

As a twenty one year old I appreciated my food and was delighted with the family's custom of dining together and allowing one to serve oneself from full dishes of food. This meant second and even third helpings. (My mother, admired for her efficiency if not generosity, dished out the food before the meal on individual dinner plates and then kept the servings warm in the oven. You collected your ration when you came in to the kitchen and that was that – but we did not starve.) I particularly remember the large pot of meatballs in a wonderful rich sauce, I had three helpings but I was not the only one so was not too embarrassed by my greed.

The biggest difference between Christmas in Norway and England and Ireland is that their Christmas Eve is our Christmas Day. Christmas Eve morning is still a normal working day but in the early afternoon there is the tradition of visiting the graveyard to light candles for the departed. When Alice and I visited the grave of her father and her grandfather we placed flowers and lit candles next to the headstone. It was very moving to see the whole graveyard lit by candles with their flickering light reflected in the snow. It is also customary to attend church for nativity hymns and then home for celebrations.

Most Norwegians have a big Christmas tree placed in their large lounges so that one can dance around it. Presents are placed under the tree on Christmas Eve morning and the lights are turned on for the first time – not two or three weeks before as often is the case in England. The family link hands – Maypole style – and dance around the tree singing Christmas traditional songs and afterwards open their presents.

The Christmas dinner was a big surprise to me – no turkey but pork. One had pork ribs, sausages, ham, cabbage with caraway seeds, tyttebar(wild cranberry) sauce and other delicacies unknown to me. I was a little disappointed that there was no turkey but soon realised that this meal took a lot more preparation, was traditional and had more variety. After all the turkey is an American import and a long way from English Christmas fare of olden times. There was no Christmas pudding for dessert. I did bring one from England but the family found it very rich and strange. Our Norwegian dessert contained preserved multe (cloudberries) and cream whipped into a very tasty flan. It is traditional to pick multe in August on high open damp ground. They are very rich in vitamin C and it is said that the Norwegian polar explorer Amundsen had a supply of multe when on his trip to the South Pole in order to prevent scurvy. The English sailor's solution to scurvy was to have a supply of

Limes aboard ship. There was one more surprise, no wine but instead we drank lager with a small glass of Aquavit. These drinks go well with the juicy fat of the pork ribs, especially after the second top ups and toasting. My dear wife has continued over the years to have a Norwegian Christmas meal that we have on Boxing Day (St Stephen's Day in Ireland). Sometimes we have as many as twenty extended family sat down and use our Norwegian real silver cutlery for this special occasion. After some initial resistance, our extended family would be now very disappointed if they did not have their Norwegian Christmas fayre.(We had 19 people for Christmas 2015)

On Christmas Day Alice and I visited some of her relatives and enjoyed more food and cakes. At this time in Norway tea drinking had not caught on although a few people drank lemon tea. When visiting people it was usual to offer boiled coffee, served with cream and homemade cakes. The coffee could be very strong especially if it had been in the kettle for some time.

FIRST TIME ON SKIS

To ski in Norway is like riding a bike in England. In 1967 cross-country skiing was the norm and alpine downhill was to gain in popularity several years later. It is written into the Norwegian psyche to escape to the mountains for Easter skiing. While most people would be glad to welcome a walk in the woods in spring, the Norwegian heads for the mountains for one last trip on skis. This is not as daft as appears because Norwegian winters can be much colder than in the Alps, often below -20C and a wind induced extra chill factor is not the best conditions for pleasure skiing. Easter temperatures are higher and the sun much stronger up in the mountains and with the reflection of sunlight off the snow as well, it is very easy to get a nice suntan or Paskebrun as the Norwegians say.

Alice found me a pair of her mum's old cross-country wooden skis and it was not long before we were skiing along the lake and up to a hill called Hedmark Toppen. Of course I fell several times but was determined to succeed. Alice had balance gained as a child on skis so could spend time to lift up her now covered in snow snowman lover. Compared to modern cross-country laminated skis and lightweight boots, my heavy long wooden skis and big strong leather ski boots seemed to weigh a ton. After some early lessons from Alice I skied on my own a couple of kilometres to a ruined monastery where I nearly got buried in the deep snow – no mobile phones to the rescue then – managed to get back and shock the neighbours by my snow Yeti impression. After a hot bath my spirits were restored and I decided to take an easier tour next time to my favourite pub – The Stallgarden where I stacked my skis outside the main door and entered the pub to the amazement of all therein – they had had never seen anyone ski to the pub before. When they found out that I was Irish and was trying to learn their favourite mode of transport they were forgiving but probably wondered who this crazy foreigner was. On one occasion I surprised everyone by buying a round of drinks – it was my first and last time for many years. Norwegians buy their own drinks unlike using the English round system because the price of a beer is far more expensive than almost any other country in the world. Even today wine and spirits can only be bought in the state owned Vinomopolet.

My stay in Hamar was not all love and fun and I had brought some Physics textbooks and studied for a few hours most days. Alice's mum may not have been impressed with my drinking habit but she was impressed with my notes that were in compact writing on both sides of my foolscap paper. What impressed her most was the way I used all the space. She was brought up on a farm in the bible belt of Jaren, south of Stavanger in western Norway where land often had to be regularly cleared of rocks and stones to have enough space for growing grass and oats but the rich black soil was a left over from the last ice age.

Before returning to England there was one more important job to do, buy our engagement/wedding rings. Alice got admiring looks from her friends for her diamond ring but they would not believe that she was engaged until she wore the traditional Norwegian gold band. This time I needed Alice's financial support for our two rings that we bought in the local goldsmiths. It is also traditional to have the inside engraved with your beloved's name and date of the engagement. Mine reads **"Your Alice 11-10-1967"**. I could now leave for England knowing that Alice would always have my name close to her heart and solid symbols of my love for her in my absence.

I did return in May for a week and this trip served only to demonstrate that we were really in love.

CHAPTER 8

1968: THE YEAR OF REVOLUTION, THE GRAPES OF WRATH AND THE ROAD TO GRETNA GREEN

I finished my degree course at the end of May and would normally have returned home but my parents along with my younger brother Vincent, then 13 years old, had moved from Swiss Cottage in Hampstead. My mother was fed up with caretaking and hoovering offices for our landlord Match and Co, even though they gave us a good sized rent free flat in a great location. Her decision was probably more to do with letting my father off the hook from having to pay any rent. They rented a small flat with a second bedroom just big enough for Vincent south of Finchley Central that meant there was no room for me. At 22 years, it was time that I did make my own way in the world. My sisters had already left home in their late teens and by the standards of the day that was late and people got married much younger than today.

Alice was due to arrive from Norway so I rented a double room nearby but that needed money. I applied for the first and only time for social security as a homeless person and managed to get a few pounds to tide me over until I got a job. I had seen an advert for fruit pickers in Norfolk that also provided basic accommodation. This was a chance to get out of the city to the countryside and near to the sea. Upon Alice's arrival we stored her luggage in the rented room and headed for Norfolk.

The fruit picking had not started when we arrived and this turned out to be to our advantage. The farm manager, a Mr Seed, allowed us to live in his detached house on the lovely Norfolk Broads. He and his new young girlfriend had to go to Eastern Europe to finalise the recruitment of Polish and Czechoslovakian student workers. We had some work to do which was to place straw under the ripening strawberries to keep them clean, especially when it rained. When Mr Seed returned it became clear that he had other plans for us. He gave us our own caravan and the job of running the campsite bar and catering facility. He assumed that as I was Irish I knew all about bar work, in fact, I had never pulled a pint in my life but we went along with his plan. During the daytime when the pickers were at work, we would often join them to make some extra money.

Alice did a good job in preparing sandwiches and other snacks as well as serving in the bar. Company Reps used to visit the farm and gave out free beer mats, whiskey water jugs and much else, so I had a good collection before the main body of student pickers arrived. We served lager and beer from kegs under pressure as well as spirits and the infamous Blue Nun German white wine. Add to this mix the ever-popular Babysham, Snow Ball and sherry.

We had some local customers from other farms and the men liked their pint of mild. Mild beer was a dark porter like session beer with low alcohol strength of 3.5%. I remember one humid evening when one of my local customers, with wife present, told me that his second pint of mild tasted strange and asked me to have a taste. Not alone did it taste terrible but it smelt like cat's piss. I could not believe he had drunk a pint of the stuff. Luckily his wife was on Babysham. By way of apology, I offered him and his wife free drinks for the rest of the evening – and do not tell your mates. I had learnt my first lesson in bar work – flush out with water the beer pipes every day, this is very important with weak beers that can go off quickly if contaminated.

I noticed that the students had arrived when all my beer mats and water jugs disappeared. The faster I replaced the beer mats on the tables the faster they disappeared. As most of the student pickers came on special visas from the eastern bloc countries they valued anything different and colourful from the west as souvenirs.

The main fruits to be picked included: strawberries, raspberries, loganberries and blackcurrants. Depending on the weather the fruit ripened at different times, so some days there was plenty of fruit to pick and other times less which meant that the pickers could not always earn the same money each day. With the less ripe fruit it took a lot longer to pick a basketful and so you earned less which often led to disgruntlement from the pickers. On a few occasions we had to deal with striking pickers. At the time I was reading the **"Grapes of Wrath"** by John Steinbeck about the plight and abuse of fruit pickers in California in the 1930s and so I had some sympathy with the plight of our pickers. On the 20th August we had far greater problems to deal with than striking pickers.

At around midday I was cleaning the bar lounge – not forgetting the beer pipes – when a news flash came up on the TV, Russian troops along with other Warsaw pact troops, including Polish troops, had invaded Czechoslovakia. Russian tanks were on the streets of Prague. It did not take long for the news of the invasion to spread to the pickers and within the hour all fruit picking had stopped and we had scores of pickers in the bar watching the TV. Tension began to spread between the Polish and the Czechoslovak students when it was realised that there were Polish troops involved in the invasion. Action was required to stop a possible riot. My experience at London University Debating Society and my participation in anti-Vietnam demonstrations came to the fore. A quick meeting with the farm owner, the farm manager, Mr Seed, and the pickers was arranged. The outcome resulted in Mr Seed hiring several coaches to take the pickers to London. We were taking them to the Russian Embassy to protest. The Poles choose to go together as a group as did the Czechs. Riot avoided at least for now.

They returned late that evening and headed for the bar arm in arm and singing. They now had a common cause on which to unite – hatred of the Russians. The drink flowed, my beer mats disappeared but now it was our turn to get some presents. One Polish student insisted in giving me a full glass of homemade vodka and others gave Alice some small dolls and miniature bottles of plum liquor and the party continued late into the night.

Next morning as I cleaned out the bar I found a glass with a black smudge at the bottom behind one of the sherry barrels. I soon realised it was the glass of Polish vodka that was given to me and had been too busy to drink any of it. It must have been over 90% alcohol and thankfully had mostly evaporated overnight.

As the fruit picking season drew to a close we managed to visit the seaside and Charles Bond came up to spend a few days to share our caravan and enjoy the traditional August downpours.

Degree Result

Towards the end of August I rang Queen Mary College for my degree result. I got a 2.2 Physics BSc (Hon) as expected. This was classed as a good degree and was the main classification with very few students getting first class degrees. About 11% of the year population went to university in 1965. Today with nearly 50% of the age group going to university or "Uni", 75% get first or upper second-class degrees. How standards have improved, makes me feel a real failure!

THE HIGH ROAD TO GRETNA GREEN OR THE LOW ROAD

Alice and I were very keen to get married but we knew Alice's Mum objected since Alice had still not finished her schooling. As love is blind, we looked at the possibility of getting married at Gretna Green in Scotland where people over 16 years old could get married without parental permission. We thought that her mother would accept a fait accompli if we were married when we arrived in Norway later in the summer. We saw a local solicitor in Norwich and that was a waste of time as Scotland has its own law jurisdiction. In any event, we decided to head for Gretna Green on our way to Norway.

HOT WATER BOTTLE AND BED SPRINGS.

We hitched hiked north to the Lake District and stayed in a B&B in Carlisle. We were shown to our double room by the very friendly daughter of the landlady who was about eighteen and as we soon discovered was a bit odd. I found out how friendly she was when we entered the bedroom. She grabbed me by the testicles and gave them a big squeeze that gave me the shock of my life. Later we discovered that she suffered from Down's syndrome. That night our double bed also sprung a surprise on us. When we got in it caved in towards the middle with springs popping in all directions. Alice and I were physically forced together more than anticipated but as we were young lovers it did not matter. After more ball grabbing attention from the daughter the next morning, the landlady suggested we join them in the evening for a night out at their country club. During the day we visited the Lake District that reminded Alice of parts of Norway – was she getting homesick I wondered.

The club had strange sexual undertones that were reinforced by some of the acts during the stage shows. One act involved a semi naked man blowing up a hot water bottle to at least half his own size, and that was not the only item he blew up. I also noted that our ample landlady and her partner were very colourfully dressed. We were glad to get back to our lodgings and next morning we headed for Gretna Green.

GRETNA GREEN AND THE BLACKSMITH

Then and now Gretna Green is one of the world's most popular wedding destinations, hosting over 5,000 weddings each year and one in every six Scottish weddings. It is thought that Gretna's famous runaway marriages began in 1754 when Lord Hardwick's Marriage Act came into force in England and Wales. Under the Act if a parent of a minor under the age of 21 wishing to marry objected then they could legally veto the union. The Act did not apply to Scotland where at that time boys at 16 and girls at 14 could marry with or without parental consent but since 1929 both have to be at least 16 years old. The opening of a toll road in the 1770s into Scotland and passing near Greta made it the first reachable village in Scotland and the elopements from England arrived in great numbers thereafter. The local blacksmith and his anvil soon became the lasting symbols of Gretna Green weddings. If a declaration of marriage vows was made before two witnesses almost anybody had the authority to conduct the marriage ceremony. The blacksmiths in Gretna were known as "anvil priests", culminating, with one Richard Rennison performing over 5,000 ceremonies. The ceremonies today are always performed over the iconic anvil.

It seemed a simple task for Alice and I to get married over the anvil but there was a problem. In 1856 Scottish law was changed to require 21 days residence. This residential requirement was lifted in 1977, but still applied to us in 1968. It was a good way of making money for the locals, although it could be argued that it gave a cooling off period for the passionate elopement arrivals. It was not possible for Alice and me to stay three weeks in Gretna, as I had to be back in England two weeks later to start my job as a teacher. I am sure that this would have been a relief to Alice's mother if she had known about our plans. As consolation, we bought a small anvil as a souvenir, which still resides on our lounge sideboard as a symbol of our everlasting love for each other. We said farewell to Gretna and hitched to Newcastle on our way to Norway.

This time we decided to take the 24-hour boat trip to Bergen, the gateway to the Norwegian Fjords and then hitchhike across the mountains to Hamar in eastern Norway. The west of Norway is best visited in June to view the apple and cherry blossoms lining the fjords, but August, with the first colours of autumn in the mountains is a good time as well. We stayed a couple of days in Bergen, famous as an old Hanseatic town, birthplace of Edvard Grieg the country's greatest composer, old wooden houses and quayside wharf with its popular fish market. It also has a reputation for its rainfall but we were fortunate to head out along the fjord in fine weather.

Our journey across Norway is memorable for two of our hitchhikes. We got a lift with a young Norwegian who drove along the fjord's winding roadside, through several tunnels and up hairpin bends into the mountains, at breakneck speed. It did not take long to realise that he had had a few drinks before he picked us up. After several miles, he revealed that he was going up to a remote hydroelectric power station where he was going to have a few drinks with friends. Today in Norway almost nobody drinks and drives, not even the night before. Norway has an almost zero blood alcohol level and if caught over the limit you can end up in prison. In the old days, they joked that a drink driving offence was the best chance of meeting a politician or other public personality in prison. Years later, I can remember staying with Alice's sister for some Easter skiing and one morning as I loaded up the car with ski equipment to drive about one kilometre across the public road down the track to the ski centre, we got a phone call from the ski centre informing us that the police were stationed half way down the track breathalysing every car driver coming down. I had a few drinks the previous night and even 12 hours later this would have been enough to put me over the Norwegian limit. So imprisonment was avoided as well as a hefty fine.

Our driver dropped us off in a lovely scenic part of the mountains and headed off at speed down a dirt road to the power station in the distance. Alas, we were in the middle of nowhere. It was getting late in the evening and we still had about 80 miles to go to the ski centre of Geilo where we intended to book into the youth hostel. Very few cars were coming up the mountain but being in love and ever optimistic we were oblivious to what could be a cold night stranded in the mountains. As it grew darker our hopes were lifted when a Mercedes car approached and passed us, oh dear! Then the car stopped further down the road. We ran with our rucksacks and piled in. It transpired that the driver took pity on us as he realised our chances of getting a lift were minimal as darkness descended. Alice and I remember talking to him about why he would not buy a British Jaguar car – similar to the Mercedes. He confirmed what we already knew – Britain was the sick man of Europe racked by union strikes and poor workmanship. I suppose we were lucky that he did not have a Jaguar, as we might never have made it to Geilo. I am pleased that now Britain is no longer the industrial basket case it nearly was and benefited from a bit of Japanese efficiency in management and in manufacturing techniques.

We stayed overnight in a youth hostel and after several more hitchhikes, plus a ferry crossing, we arrived in Hamer late the next evening. On reflection, hitchhiking is now outdated but I think young people today miss out on the element of adventure and the trip into the unknown – but at least they will not be at risk from drunken drivers or worse.

It may seem strange that soon after we arrived in Norway Alice and I went to a local farm to pick fruit, having just come from a fruit picking camp in England. It did make sense financially. The fruit season in Norway is later than England and can lead to quality fruit because of the longer ripening period. Hourly wages in Norway then and now are much higher; rental accommodation cheaper but food, alcohol and eating out is a lot more expensive. Some basic food like milk and some dairy products are cheaper because of government subsidies. So as long as we lived frugally we could save some money from the fruit picking. I enjoyed my first experience of the long summer evenings and swimming in the beautiful lake Mjosa but we soon had to think about our future.

Alice's mum wanted Alice to continue at school in Norway and that was not unreasonable. One had to be over 21 to be able to marry free of parental consent so we would have a long time to wait. However, Alice getting pregnant changed everything. When we were in Norway in August 1968 Alice had bouts of morning sickness and tests revealed that she was expecting. I returned to London alone with the intention that Alice would join me in late September.

I found a two room downstairs flat with shared toilet and bathroom in Squires Lane, Finchley Central. The landlady was Jewish and I got on well with my Jewish lecturers and with those that had given me Saturday jobs. She was pleased with the fact that I had a secure job but she still wanted me to look after the front garden. I had previously cut hedges and weeded several gardens belonging to Jewish people in Finchley and Golders Green. The good news was the Jewish house owners knew less about horticulture than I did, so when I tidied up the flowerbeds I removed not only the weeds but also some flower plants as well hoping that they were weeds. My hedge cutting was my strong point. During the two years we occupied the rooms our landlady was pleased with my gardening efforts and I was able to talk her into putting in an air extractor into our damp back room and to keep the rent the same in a period of high inflation.

THE TELEGRAM

On her way to join me Alice stopped off in Oslo to spend a few days with her aunt Martha. One morning she woke up with a skin rash that her aunt Martha correctly thought was German measles. This type of measles can cause blindness in a developing foetus and Alice returned home to Hamar to see her local doctor. I received a telegram from her giving me the bad news. After some reflection I sent a telegram requesting her to avoid an abortion if at all possible. Fortunately the doctor judged that at her stage of pregnancy there was a low chance of damage to the foetus and Alice was able to join me a week or so later.

CHAPTER 9

OUR MARRIAGE AND THE START OF MY WORKING CAREER

This most eventful year would happily conclude with our marriage at St Philip the Apostle RC Church in Finchley Central on 2nd November 1968. Alice agreed to marriage in a RC church as she was not a practising Lutheran and she was happy that any children from our marriage would be brought up Catholics. We were at one for our children to be brought up within a Christian moral and spiritual framework and for them to choose their own way of life as adults. We were not great believers in the absolute authority of religion over life but equally we did not want to inculcate our children with Atheism at an early age. I believed then and now, that it is important for children to have a sense of wonderment and curiosity about the world around them. God as the great heavenly father and maker of the world is a concept that can help them to expand their imagination. We all know what great imaginations children have and the last thing as parents we would want to do is to stunt it.

In preparation for our marriage, we had a few sessions with our local parish priest Father Thomas on the importance of marriage and the need to give a lifelong commitment to each other. We decided that we could not afford a big wedding and that only my parents, brother and my best man Charles Bond would be present. My sister Avril was in Canada and I did feel a bit guilty about not inviting my sister Dorothy in Kent. It would also have been appropriate to invite Alice's mother from Norway but as she had objected to our early marriage, this was not appropriate. It was difficult for me to even think of having a large wedding when we were living in two rented rooms, a pregnant girlfriend and just a few months into a new job. However we did redress the balance when Alice's mother later attended the christening of her first grandson Ragnar, named after her deceased husband, in the church that we got married in and Dorothy and Pat were Godparents for our second son Fingal.

To save money Charles and I hired morning suits for the occasion and Alice managed to acquire a lovely wedding dress. We had our official wedding photographs taken by an elderly women photographer in her studio near to the church. The equipment she used seemed to date from the early 1900s and we wondered if she had disappeared, Houdini like, when she put in a big glass photographic plate into a human size wooden box and then went out of sight under a large black sheet. In the developed – eventually – photographs we appeared a bit like porcelain figures in pasty black and white.

We planned for a small wedding but it got even smaller when my father did not turn up, preferring to have a Saturday morning lie in. I wondered if he was embarrassed by our small scale wedding plans compared to the magnificent wedding that my sister Dorothy had four years previously. However, this could not be the case as there were only a few people at his wedding in Ireland. The real reason I believe was that he thought that Charles and I had taken over some of the proceedings at the reception for my sister's wedding. In retrospect we were a bit loud and did mess up or lose some of the reception photographs.

My mother was as always well presented and made sure my younger brother was as well. The priest was astonished to see Charles and me in full morning dress and we may have lacked numbers but not style. After the wedding we went back to our two-room abode for some food and drink and guess who turned up? My father. After a few drinks he was in full swing and later we all went for dinner at the Tally Ho pub in North Finchley. I got a little drunk and remember running round the block to sober up – I hope not in morning suit.

MY FIRST JOB SEPTEMBER 1968

I never liked the idea of working in a factory or office and the 9 to 5 routine. I was still interested in continuing education and the pursuit of knowledge so a teaching post seemed to be an option. It may not pay well but it was secure and I would not be stuck in one place with just a few work colleagues. Later in my teaching career I asked new potential teachers "What makes for a good teacher?" Their answers focused on empathy with the pupils and ability to work with colleagues. The answer that I wanted – honed by experience – was to attend regularly, have loads of personality and have a love and understanding of your subject. A teacher cannot achieve anything if they are away a lot and no matter how learned they are, they cannot convey knowledge and learning to the pupil if they do not have the personality and charisma to engage them.

Ideally I would have liked to carry on with study and research and be a university lecturer, but this would take more time and having to live on low pay which combined with my new family circumstances was not an option.

I did not impress my new colleagues by arriving three days after the start of the school autumn term – boats only sailed twice a week from Oslo and my intended sailing was fully booked. I had to take classes on my first day with no formal teacher training and no induction period, which would be unthinkable today. I had to learn very quickly from my mistakes and hope I could keep my pupils on board with my enthusiasm and force of personality, which in the main I managed to do.

This was my first time in a Grammar School and I soon realised that the facilities and quality of the teachers were far superior to anything I experienced in London as a pupil. For a start the teachers wore academic gowns and pupils could study subjects that included: Philosophy, Greek, Ancient History, Further Mathematics and much else. Some pupils stayed on for a third year in the sixth form to prepare for open entrance exams to Oxbridge. I taught Physics to one such pupil who a few years later I visited at Trinity College, Cambridge where he was an admissions tutor and Professor of Applied Mechanics.

Science teachers did not have to wear a gown in the laboratory situation. On one occasion I wish I had worn one. I had just bought a nice new jacket at Selfridges that I took off and hung on a water pipe on the demonstration front desk. I was demonstrating to the pupils how bromine diffuses much quicker through a vacuum than through air. The experiment involved the use of a vacuum pump and two long glass tubes with a bromine glass capsule in each. The idea was to crack each bromine capsule container in a rubber tube sealed with a rubber bung at one end and connected to the bottom of the long glass tube at the other end and then watch how the rusty coloured vapour spread at different rates through the tubes. It took less than a second to spread through the vacuum tube and several minutes through the tube containing the air. However, when I squeezed the bromine capsule for the vacuum tube the bung came off and the capsule shot out and across the bench smashing into the water tap and burning a large hole in my new jacket. The pupils had a great laugh and then began to panic when they smelt the bromine. I had to evacuate the lab for an hour or so but pupil safety was not in danger as the bromine vapour took a lot longer to diffuse and disperse through the air in the laboratory. Back then we were not overburdened with government health and safety regulations. We were mindful of basic safety requirements and we did learn fast on the job. Some pupils showed unexpected creativity. I remember the son of the well-known comedian Spike Milligan bringing a contraption into the laboratory. He positioned it on the end of a bench and asked me to pull a lever where upon a naked figure shot out jack in the box like and urinated water all over the floor. Like father like son, you might say.

I started my teaching career on the cusp of a revolution in science teaching. Lord Nuffield, who made his fortune in the car industry, bequeathed a large sum of money to create The Nuffield Foundation to promote new ideas and teaching equipment in science teaching. The main idea was to teach science using an experimental approach and to get the pupils to discover for themselves the laws and patterns of physical, chemical and biological systems. New equipment and work sheets were designed to help the pupils to work the way a scientist would. The role of the teacher was to facilitate this approach and to guide them in drawing the right conclusions from their experiments. What one did not do was to tell them the laws in advance and get them just to verify them. This was hard but exciting work for teacher and pupil alike. The Physics curriculum was revamped to include the latest advances in Electronics, Astronomy, Thermodynamics and Nuclear and Atomic Physics. The discovery and experimental method was to be my main approach to teaching throughout my teaching career. I was a strong supporter of using similar methods in other subjects. The way we examined our pupils also underwent radical change. The invention of the photocopier meant we could set multiple choice, long and short answer question papers and project work. The Physics GCE O'Level multiple-choice paper was the first in the UK to be marked using the Optical Mark Reader and appeared as an item on the BBC programme Tomorrow's World.

Even in a Grammar school pupil discipline could be a problem. I taught an integrated science course to younger pupils that involved human biology and reproduction and as a young teacher I was a little too helpful in trying to answer some of the pupil questions when it came to female reproduction. I got over familiar and they got a bit too personal with me. I had to get nasty to regain class discipline and my relationship with this class never got back to the way I wanted it to be. No doubt, familiarity bred contempt in this case. On another occasion, when out of school, my wife and I went regularly to a teashop in North Finchley. One of my pupils decided to call names and insult us, thinking of course that he would not be caught. I was faster than he thought and when I caught up with him, I found out who he was and told him I would be seeing him in the morning. I knew he would have a restless night wondering what was going to happen to him. The next day I sent a pupil to collect him and bring him to my laboratory. As he walked into my lab he duly collapsed on the floor and ended up with blood all over his shirt. I felt sorry for him and was sure that he would not annoy teachers outside of school again. I was never a vindictive teacher and saw it as my duty to help young people to learn the finer arts of human behaviour. However not all teachers were the forgiving type. The staff at the school were a conservative middle-aged group in the main and there were only a few teachers under 25 years. I made friends with the new maths teacher called John Blodwell from Manchester and we are still very good friends today. John remembers my first day in the staffroom as a young confident eager person who initiated interactions with staff.

BALL SPIN

In time John was happy to follow my opening lead into, at times, controversial issues with his own take on the topic at hand. He remembers my "ball spin" argument with a well-established member of staff, Joe Linnean who was a season ticket holder with Tottenham Hotspur and was known to be the staffroom expert on all football matters.

I had watched on TV several matches from the 1970 World Cup in Mexico and noticed that South American players seemed to be able to bend the ball, which European players did not do and found that after a lot of practice at my local park I could bend the ball left or right. To bend it right I kicked the ball with the outside of my boot slightly off centre to put clockwise spin on it. To bend the ball left I used the inside of my boot to put anticlockwise spin on it. This was in accordance with the laws of dynamics and the Bernoulli principal. Joe told me it was not possible to bend a football through the air and he had never seen a player do it at his club. He may have not seen English players doing it because of the muddy pitches and heavy leather football they used. I got a football from the PE department and proceeded to demonstrate to Joe in the staffroom that it was possible. I did not bend the ball much because I needed to kick the ball quite hard and for the ball to travel at least 10 yards to see it bending. John as the main applied maths teacher stepped in to support my case. Joe was not too pleased to see his football expertise being challenged by two young staff in the presence of his colleagues and stormed out of the staffroom.

It was nice to hear that John thought I got on well with the pupils and inspired them with my enthusiasm for Physics. I started a part-time MSc course in Nuclear Physics at London University, to prove that I could master the subject at a higher level. John followed my lead and in taking a higher degree in Maths and eventually got his PhD. I often engaged my students in science topics beyond the syllabus. One particular student liked my lectures on elementary particle Physics so much he ended up studying the subject at Imperial College. Whilst at school he told his medical doctor father about John and me and we got invited to his house for dinner. We ended up having a keen debate about drug use at a time when pop stars were influencing young people by their drug usage and references to it in their music. John and I were at that time a bit naive and upon reflection; I think the good doctor was a lot wiser and knowledgeable than we were.

MANCHESTER TRIP

John was and is a northerner who takes great pride in Britain's industrial heritage and is not over enamoured with London and its city financiers and their lack of investment in engineering and manufacturing. Born near Ashton under Lyne close to Manchester his home was surrounded by industrial enterprises that ranged from mining and milling to computers and textiles. This world of industry was completely unknown to me and John intended to show this by now soft southerner, what put the Great into Britain. I had visited Liverpool for a few days, but girls were my interest on that occasion and they were my interest when I went on school retreats to Staffordshire, although I did go all the way to the coal-face of a working mine in Cannock Chase.

We went up north at half term in late October and took the bus from the main rail station the few miles to John's Victorian semi-detached house. On the way, we passed factories, mills and a coalmine, very different from the industrial suburbs of London. When I entered my allocated bedroom I was surprised to be greeted by a glowing coal fire at one end of the room. Nearly every room in the four-bed house had its own coal fire and they made a change from the stinking paraffin oil heaters common in the south. At the back of his garden John pointed out the ruins of an old mill from the 18C. The next couple of days we walked and bussed around the city including visiting the famous Manchester Ship Canal and the stadium at Maine Road, home of John's beloved Manchester City FC.

We did some walking up on the moors nearby, climbing over the dry stonewalls and avoiding the challenges from some of the more aggressive rams as we passed close to sheep flocks. John pointed to Oldham in the next valley and to the city of Sheffield in the far distance. I am always surprised how many northern industrial cities are so close to wonderful countryside. But then the cities were built after the discovery of coal, iron and other minerals in the area.

John was keen on horse racing and had specialist knowledge of most racecourses in England that involved flat races under a mile. He read the horse form and knowing the contours and bends on a particular course would bet on the horse that would cope best. He did not have large stakes but normally came out with a small profit. We attended one of the last ever summer evening meetings at Alexandra Palace in London. I put my money on the jockey rather than the horse, but the jockey in question was the great Lester Picket.

I stayed at Finchley Grammar School for three years and could have stayed there for life but for me it was time to move on. I was attracted to the new comprehensive school movement and saw a job as Head of Physics at Holland Park Comprehensive School in west London. This was a purpose built school with a well know Chair of Governors, one Caroline Benn. She was the wife of the Labour politician and recent Peer of the Realm Tony Benn who later became a government Secretary of State. Caroline was an American who was an advocate of universal comprehensive education and wrote about its advantages as well as heading up a campaign. I applied for the post and got a typed letter inviting me to interview –computerisation was still a few years away. A week later I was surprised to get a phone call from Mrs Benn asking why I had not turned up for interview. I had my letter to hand and told her the interview was in two days time. My letter had the wrong date and there was nothing they could do because they had appointed someone else. Still my application did catch her eye and I often wonder what direction my teaching career would have taken if the school secretary had not made that typing error.

A few weeks later, I was interviewed for Head of Physics at Burnham Grammar School west of Slough and was offered the post.

FIRST CHILD A BOY, OUR SECOND CHILD, A BOY

Our first child Ragnar Sean was born on the morning of 10th April 1969 at The Victoria Maternity Hospital in Barnet and weighed in at six pounds two ounces. It was not an easy birth. Alice had been in the maternity ward for 24 hours before the birth and needed regular doses of oxygen using a mask. I was one of the first fathers that was allowed to be present at a birth. The maternity nurse was very chatty, even flirty with me, to Alice's annoyance. After some serious pushing on Alice's part Ragnar arrived into the world without a squeak. The maternity nurse lifted him up by the feet and gave him a few gentle back slaps but still no crying and Ragnar started going blue. I got worried and was glad when the Doctor was called. A very relaxed Indian female doctor strolled in slowly with her hands deep inside her white coat pockets. I was not impressed with her lack of sense of urgency. Seeing my distress and the nurse's now frantic efforts to clear mucus from Ragnar's mouth, she finally got the message that we had an emergency on our hands. An oxygen supply was wheeled in and a mask put over Ragnar's face and thankfully he reacted immediately and he made his first weak sounds. He got a quick cuddle from his mother and was then put in an incubator where he remained for two days.

Most Norwegian babies were breast fed in contrast to England where bottle-feeding was de rigour. My mother bottle fed all of her children including me and thought it strange that Alice wanted to breast feed. For me it was a no brainer. Before I left Ireland – as mentioned earlier – my Granny gave me an orphan white calf and I was determined to hand feed my calf to grow as quickly as other calves left to suckle with their mothers. I gave my calf extra helpings of linseed oil, cereals and put her to graze on the best grass fields. No matter how hard I tried, my white calf did not grow as quick and strong as the calves suckled by their mothers. Lesson learnt. It was very irresponsible of western food companies such as Nestle to exploit poorer nations, who discouraged breast feeding by selling them dried baby powder milk substitutes to boost their profits. Some claimed they were helping to kill babies by depriving them of immunities provided in the milk of breast-fed babies.

In 1969 maternity wards were still organised on Victorian lines with all babies kept in a separate room and there could be as many as 20 mothers in a separate ward. Baby feeding was organised at four hour intervals and mothers normally stayed in the maternity wards for a week. Today a mother is in and out in a day or two and their babies are in a cot beside their bed. Ragnar was weak and Alice found it impossible to breast-feed him, especially as he was hungry most of the time. She expressed so that he could be bottle-fed. After a few days she could recognise his crying next door from that of the other babies. One day he was gently crying in between the four hour feed sessions and she sneaked out to try and breast-feed him. As he was not too hungry he was more relaxed and took to her teat and started to suck and never stopped for the next year or so.

We had no problem deciding what to call our first-born son. He was to be Ragnar after Alice's father Ragnar who was drowned in a boating accident in Harmer at the age of 35 years. We also wanted to give him a second name reflecting his father's Irish roots so we choose Sean that in English is John. In keeping with this tradition our other two children are called Fingal Erik and Astrid Colleen.

RAGNAR'S CHRISTENING

It was a pleasure to have Alice's family over in the summer for Ragnar's christening at St Philip the Apostle where we had been married less than a year earlier. Alice's mum Gudbjorg was a very proud first time grandmother. I still have vivid memories of Alice's brother Odd Egil in his red velvet trousers and his ability as a fifteen year old to down four pints of Guinness. I still wonder what Gudbjorg thought of meeting my parents in the local pub and seeing us all drinking with gay abandon. My father had a hard time convincing her of the benefits of the British pub life – at least she knew that the drink was a lot cheaper than in Norway. She did appreciate our trip to London Zoo and looking at the shops in the West End and of course Buckingham Palace. I am still amazed how we put up Gudbjorg and her two sons along with Alice's twenty year old sister Ragnhild in our two roomed flat for several days.

Fingal arrived into this world in the early morning of 20th October 1971 at Victoria Maternity Hospital, Barnet. The birth was quick, relatively easy and he weighed in at 8lb 7oz. I managed to call an ambulance from a public phone box late evening and was surprised to find that when I phoned the hospital early next morning that Alice had already given birth to a baby boy. I would like to have been with Alice but I had to look after Ragnar and a close a friend of mine, John Blodwell who was staying with us for a few days. I still had the presence of mind to cook John a full English breakfast and Ragnar got his sausage and baked beans. We chose the name Fingal as it was the Gaelic name for the blond haired Vikings and Erik after Alice's uncle. Sometimes I think Fingal feels a bit left out as his birth does not get the attention oft the more dramatic and problematic births of his sibling.

Fingal was christened in Mary Immaculate and St Gregory The Great RC Church in Barnet and my sister Dorothy acted as Godmother and her husband Pat his Godfather. Dorothy was very impressed with the lovely white shawl that allowed his blue suit to be seen through the holes.

CHAPTER 10

MOVE FROM LONDON: BURNHAM GRAMMAR SCHOOL 1971-73: NEW HOUSE

The chance to get a council house with Eton and Rural District Council influenced my decision to take the Head of Physics job at Burnham Grammar School. Windsor Castle is within the jurisdiction of this council and even though there were several spare rooms within Her Majesty's Windsor Castle I do not think we would be considered suitable residents so it would be a place well outside the castle walls for us. Alice searched the local papers within a twenty miles radius of my new school and discovered that a large private housing development was under development in Reading, Berkshire. In those days you only needed to put down a small deposit but you could not raise a mortgage more than three times your annual salary. My new salary put this at a maximum of £6800 and this would allow for the purchase of a terrace or end of terrace three-bed house on the Reading development. The council could not find me a vacant property for a few months so I had to commute from Barnet to Burnham. To get to school for 8.35am, I got up at 6.30am, then had a 20 minute walk up Barnet Hill to get the Northern Line (end of line station), then a 40 minute tube ride to Euston where I surfaced and had a 10 minute walk to Euston Square tube station to catch the Metropolitan line to

Paddington. I then boarded the 8.05 express train to Swansea which stopped at Slough. At Slough, after a wait of 5 minutes, I caught a local train to Burnham. After a brisk twenty minute walk I arrived at school to the ring of the school bell for assembly. The journey home took longer as I had to take a local train to Paddington and if there were no hold ups would be home at 7pm, in time to see my boys before their bedtime. I ended up doing this journey for nearly a full academic year. Occasionally I stayed overnight when I had Parents' Evenings, Prize Giving and after school management meetings, but mostly I made my way home arriving just before midnight – if lucky. It was not easy on Alice as we had no phone so at times she had no way of knowing when I might be home.

Six weeks after starting my new job a phase release of another batch of new houses on the Reading development was due. I arranged to stay with a school colleague overnight at Reading so I could be at the site office at 9am on Saturday morning when the 100 or so new sites were allocated. There were only five terrace houses that we could bid for, the rest were way above our budget. After school on the way to Reading, I suggested to my colleague that as we had a bit of time before dinner we call at the building development for a quick look around. When we got to the site office I noticed a row of about 10 cars parked outside. The office was just about to close but I managed to ask the site manager what the car queue outside was about and he told they were waiting for the office to open the next morning. I quickly checked with those in the queue and discovered that there was just one end of terrace house left of the five we could afford. The manager wrote me a note to confirm my place in the queue and the plot I wanted. I told my colleague that I had to stay to keep my place in the queue and that was the end of my planned evening meal and pub visit. He did come back later with some sandwiches and others in the queue let me stay in their cars during what was a cold October night. I did not see the site plots or the existing estate, which was called Caversham Park Village. The next morning there was a long queue of cars stretching into the distance and a photograph of the queue subsequently appeared in the Reading Chronicle that I still have as a memento. I did not return to Reading until our house was ready. We had no car so Alice, our two boys and I travelled by public transport from Barnet to Reading. We took a bus from the station to the site office, collected the house keys and then walked for the first time the half mile through the estate to our new house. The removal van was waiting for us with our meagre belongings and we proudly opened the door to our new home and stepped over the threshold into a new phase of our family life.

THE BULLY TEACHER.

My two years at Burnham Grammar school were enjoyable enough except for one particular senior teacher. He had served in the army and still acted as if he was in it but without the personal discipline of the army officer. It appeared that one of his main jobs was to get the staff out of the staffroom quickly after the morning tea break so that he could continue to smoke his pipe. He had a mountain of unmarked pupil exercise books in his office. Occasionally I had problems with my lengthy journey to school and would arrive a few minutes late and he would be waiting for me to show his displeasure. The fact that he was already late for his own lesson never did occur to him. He was the staffroom bully and most of the staff were afraid of him but not me. The science department was pioneering new examinations where some of our exam papers could be several pages. We had to use photocopiers that were still nowhere near the quality of modern ones. Once he complained that printing on a page on one of my exam papers was too feint and then handed back all my bundle of exam papers telling me to photocopy the whole lot again. This was the last straw for me and I rammed the lot into his rather large belly as he collapsed back over a pile of his unmarked exercise books. I shouted at him that he was nothing but a bully and he was not going to bully me. I slammed his office door shut and walked away. The staff heard the commotion next door and then saw the bullyboy run from his office straight to the head's office. It was the first time they witnessed a member of staff taking him on and silently they were delighted. Half an hour later I was invited to the head's office where the bully was sitting red faced, puffing on his pipe but sure that he had his victim. The head told me that the bully said that I had assaulted him in the course of doing his job. Well I let loose. I told him he had dropped my exam papers deliberately on the floor and as he turned round fell over a large pile of unmarked pupil exercise books. He was always late for his lessons, bullied the staff etc etc. If he carried on displaying antagonism towards me, I would have no other course than to seek the advice of my teachers' union. Secretly the Head was delighted because he knew every word I said was true, even the Head was intimidated by him. The outcome was that he managed to get a sort of apology from me and I shook hands with the bully who never came near me again. My reputation with the staff soared.

THE GIRL ON THE TRAIN

Burnham Grammar School was the first school where I taught girls as well as boys. Towards the end of my teaching career I taught in two nationally renowned private all girls schools. Over the years I have come to learn that on average girls are far neater and more conscientious in the presentation of their work. Boys tend to be a little more slap dash and leave matters to the last minute. Their practical skills are better and they can be reprimanded without taking offence. Boys on average do not hold grudges against their teacher – they forget like goldfish. Girls have much longer memories after a reprimand and are far more sensitive. They want to be accepted by the boys in the class and boys can take advantage of this by borrowing equipment and even some of their work off them. Above all girls can develop a crush on their teachers more often than boys with their female teachers can. I am pleased to say no boy ever developed a crush on me but girls have.

After a few months at Burnaham I noticed a teenage girl sitting with her eyes trained on me on the seat in front of me on the train on the way home to Reading – a journey of about 20 miles. She was quite attractive and not in school uniform. On several occasions I saw the same girl again always seated in front of me where ever I sat on the train. One day I recognised her at school, this time in school uniform. Later I would see her waiting outside some of my classes and I began to get a little concerned more because of the time she was wasting having a crush on a teacher ten years older than she was and one near penniless as well. Eventually I had a word with the senior teacher in charge of girl's discipline who interviewed her. I never saw her on the train again but when I saw her round the school, she gave me a real evil look. Love and hate are close relatives.

FIRST ELECTRONIC DIGITAL CLOCK

As a science teacher I have always wanted to link the science curriculum to the world of industry. The lessons from our Industrial and Research Establishment visits for students were incorporated into the curriculum. Nuclear and Coal Fired Power Stations, The Nuclear Research Facility at Harwell with its Particle Physics Accelerator, The National Physical Laboratory, University Science Departments including attending lectures and Electronic Companies were all on my list for student visits in support of the Physics curriculum.

I established an industry link with Essex University. They arranged a visit to Racal Electronics in Slough for my Physics students. The men – no women – in suits met us in the front office. They passed the sherry around and talked about how good the expensive frequency measuring instruments they made looked. I soon realised they knew little about what was inside the instrument case and certainly not the Physics underpinning the workings of the meters. We did get to meet the design engineers and I discovered that one of them was not very happy with the management and felt that he was being patronised by them. He even asked what it was like to be a Physics teacher. We got on well and he "found" four state of the art Nixie tubes to give me and back at school, using some modern integrated circuit chips and a suitable power supply, we constructed an electron digital Nixie Tube 24 hour clock. Back in 1972 you only had mechanical driven clocks. A few years later Nixie tubes were used as digital read out in petrol pumps so we were well ahead of the time with our clock. A big thank you to our design engineer who I hope was not caught for giving us the Nixie tubes. In 2016 I Googled Nixie tubes and discovered you can buy Nixie clocks ranging from £100 DIY to fully assembled and cased ones for £1000 and this forty years on from when I made mine!

THE END OF MY GRAMMAR SCHOOL ODYSSEY

On the sixth form leaving date near the end of my last term at Burnham I went out for a drink with some sixth formers and staff. In the afternoon we had a leavers' assembly and staff sat on the stage in their gowns behind the Head teacher who gave a farewell speech. The pupils were quite boisterous – fortified by their pub experience and unknown to the Head. He told them to stop behaving 'Like drunken Irishmen on a Saturday night'. Well the hall exploded with cheers and laughter and all eyes were on me. The Head was at a total loss as to why they were even more unruly until he realised that this Irishman was sat behind him. He managed to collect himself and said that he did not mean to include me among the Irishmen in question. Little did he realise I had been in the pub with the sixth formers and by now I was far more like a God to them than a drunken Irishman was. Later in the staffroom he apologised to me, which I had not expected or asked for; but the incident certainly helped in getting me a good job reference. Much of the shire counties in the early 1970s were white middle class and the Irish were the butt of jokes and discrimination for higher-level jobs. This was further compounded by the growing troubles – war – in the north of Ireland that was spreading to England.

LIFE EXPERIENCES BEYOND THE CLASSROOM
MY FIRST SKI TRIP

The school organised an annual ski trip to Austria and the German teacher Stas Lenton asked me at short notice if I would take his place. Most of the pupils were 15 year olds but a few sixth formers came as well. Stas had been on the trip the previous year as had one of the sixth form girls who was coming again this year. I soon came to realise that the sixth former had a strong crush on Stas and that was why she was coming again. Maybe Stas had worked on his escape plan which I unwittingly was now part of.

The women teacher in charge of the trip was a very mercurial Welsh Latin teacher who liked to spend time at London Welsh rugby matches especially in the bar after matches.

My wife was generous in letting me go on the trip even though as a Norwegian she never had the opportunity to Alpine ski. She did make one request that I bring a back a pair of Lederhosen for our eldest son. We had already met a German friend of Stas whose name was Hans and it was agreed that he would still drive up from Munich to visit me even though Stas was not coming.

I joined the learner group of pupils for ski lessons near the ski centre and although I got my beginners certificate at the end of the week I did not go up the mountain. This was partly because an experienced American pupil broke his ankle and I had to keep an eye on him in the local hospital and later at our hotel while we tried to contact his mother to come out to take him home. Telecommunications in 1972 relied on the use of international operators using semi-mechanical switchboards and it could take hours to get through to England. Language problems meant that when a call did get through one of the teachers had to be present to take the call and that was normally me especially as one of our teachers had severe hearing problems.

Hans arrived from Munich early one afternoon and surprised me by suggesting that we take an evening trip back to Munich. He also suggested that we bring the two sixth formers that hung out with me. The Problem was that they were on a group passport and did not have individual passports with them if they had any at all. No problem. He saw that my Irish passport was green, the same colour as his German passport. When we got to the border he showed the border guards his passport while I held up my closed green covered passport. The guards would note his German registered BMW and would conclude all four of us were German. It worked a treat.

We arrived in Munich and went straight to the Hofbrauhaus Bier Keller where Hitler in the 1920s gave a speech to nearly 2000 people outlining the principles of his new party – The National Socialist German Workers Party later shortened to Nazi. There were scores of drinkers and buxom frauens and frauleins serving large beers in steins. I quickly discovered as the steins were opaque it was difficult to assess how much beer they contained even though they appeared to be full as the froth spilled out over the top. I estimated they were about two thirds full when the froth settled but the beer was strong and most of the punters did not notice – or care. In between the split lever floors of the beer hall there was a band playing German umpa music at a frantic pace. After a couple of steins- including two for Hans – we went to one of Munich's top restaurants. Uniformed waiters in white aprons carried silver plated trays containing chunks of beef or pork on their shoulders to the tables. We went for the beef. Some of the waiters were Gastarbeiter from Turkey and Hans had nothing good to say about them. At that time they could work for years in Germany and never be granted citizenship and certainly not German nationality. Only in recent years has the law changed to allow for several million guest workers who had lived and worked in the country for decades to take up German citizenship.

We got back to our hotel at about 1am in plenty of time to go to the local nightclub where we found our Welsh ski leader almost blind drunk. She clearly fancied Hans but was not happy about the girl sixth former being there – no problem with the male sixth former. She was decidedly cool towards me for the rest of the trip but it meant I escaped her amorous clutches. Unfortunately when we got back to school, in collusion with her fellow classics teacher – the senior woman in the school management team – she reported me to the Head teacher. She said that I had taken the sixth formers out drinking late at night in one of the ski resort bars. She did not know I had also taken them to Munich and did not tell the Head that she had herself been out late on several nights without informing her fellow teachers on the trip. When the Head teacher interviewed me I told him that we went out looking for her and found her blind drunk in one of the bars and that this was not the first time. I also told him that she was very unpredictable in behaviour and he said do you mean 'mercurial'? "Exactly spot on" I replied. He already knew about the reputation of this woman outside of the school. Later I saw her in the staffroom very red-faced and ruffled. She never spoke to me again.

THE TRAGIC DEATHS OF COLLEAGUES AND STUDENTS

During my years as a teacher one meets large numbers of pupils and colleagues and the chance of experiencing accidents and death of work colleagues and pupils is high. At my first school, a fifteen-year-old boy was electrocuted in bed. He had the flu and was confined to bed. Perhaps he was a bit bored and started to play around with a side lamp. He managed to short circuit the electric current through his chest and electrocuted himself. Salty sweating hands make electrical conduction a lot easier and he must have had both hands on the brass bulb fittings whilst the lamp was on. Lying down in bed gave him no chance of falling or pulling away from the lamp. Some years later I attended the funeral of a school governor – an identical twin – who was an electrician but still he got electrocuted at his work place – he forgot to turn off the electric supply fell onto the lives wires he was trying to disconnect.

At Burnham my fellow Physics teacher John Langdon, who took over from me was killed on his way to work on the first day of the new autumn term. He had recently passed his driving test and was driving along a duel carriageway into Slough when his nearside front wheel hit the central reservation kerb and the car flipped over and he was decapitated. He was married to a lovely Portuguese woman and they had two young children. I stayed at their house overnight on several occasions to save me the long journey back to London. I cannot imagine how his wife felt when she got the news of the death of her husband. RIP.

When I was a deputy Head at Cheshunt school in Hertfordshire, two pupils rushed into my office just after school to tell me that a car on the nearby dual carriageway had hit their friend and could I come immediately. We ran the two hundred yards or so for me to see a fifteen-year-old girl lying in the middle of the road with blood coming from her ears and nose. The car that hit her was parked further up the road. She was killed instantly. The three girls were waiting for the traffic lights to change when one of them in deep conversation with her friends stepped backwards onto the road and got hit by the passing car at speed. This was not the first time we lost a pupil at this dangerous dual carriageway that was meant to be a bypass for Cheshunt but cut three secondary schools off from the town centre. It took several more fatalities and many years later before they built an overhead bridge. This tragic accident was just before Christmas and having to tell the parents that they had lost their lovely daughter is painful beyond reason. Her funeral service took place a few days before Christmas day at the local St Mary's Church next to the school. I still have vivid memories of her family carrying her white flower bedecked coffin towards the main alter. It was difficult to celebrate Christmas that year without thinking about the loss and suffering that the girl's family were going through.

Later in this book I describe how an identical twin pupil from the City of London Girls' School was killed on a school trip to South Africa.

The probability of a work colleague been killed by an act of terrorism abroad must be very small. The probability of two work colleagues been killed by terrorism on two different continents must be infinitesimal. Nevertheless, it happened.

Chris Rolf was a young science teacher in my science department at Cox Green School in Maidenhead. He was very interested in alternative energy and for a time lived in a specially constructed van that used alternative energy sources. He was a very mild and gentle teacher and did have some discipline problems. He applied and got a job working on energy projects in Africa. Eventually he moved with his young family to Uganda and a few years later I read in the newspaper that a young British family had been killed in a hotel lobby by a bomb thrown into the lobby. That such a caring, internationally minded and environmental activist was killed in that manner is unimaginable.

When I was a deputy head at Ashylns School, Berkhamsted we had a young dynamic teacher of History who wanted to work abroad. He had an international outlook and wanted to serve more disadvantaged youngsters in Asia. Some years later I was reading the Times newspaper when I saw his photograph. He was killed by a terrorist bomb planted in a bar in Bali.

Another colleague of mine, a very gentle man, was murdered by his son's best army friend who was high on drugs at the time. There were other tragedies that I will not recall here. But there go I by the grace of God and good luck.

PRIVATE TUTORING

Throughout my early teaching career I have given private tuition lessons in order to provide badly needed extra income. When I started tutoring I went to the homes of my tutees because I had no separate space at home or worried about their willingness to come to our flat in a large council estate. Most of them were the children of well-heeled middle class families. Whilst it was nice to go to big houses in Hampstead or large country houses, I often had to use public transport so for an hour's tuition I could be away for up to three hours. It was far more profitable for the students to come to me and this was the case when we became house owners.

When we lived in Reading, I tutored a student called Simon who had boarded at Taunton School in Devon but had failed to get good enough grades to get on an army officer-training programme. His father was a British army colonel serving in NATO and certainly was not pleased with his son's academic efforts. I agreed to tutor Simon in Physics and Mathematics over a six-month period so that he could retake these subjects in the January examinations. The good news for me was that Simon was very good at sports and was an outstanding sailor. He also had his own car. In my time tutoring Simon I learnt more from him than he did from me. He took me sailing and taught me the basics of handling a small sailing boat- we even competed in a few races. We battled it out on the local squash courts and I introduced him to Real Ale. Simon worked as an orderly at the Berkshire Hospital and was able to take me to their social club for some real cheap beer and introduce me to his girlfriend who was a nurse at the hospital. We also visited the local army social club for even more cheap beer. Because we got on so well socially he woke up to doing some serious academic study and I was able to stimulate his interest in Physics by demonstrating how this subject was fundamental to understanding the science behind sailing, squash and the car. Simon passed his exams and gained admission to the army staff college. His father was so pleased that he invited Alice and me to dinner with no expenses spared, especially on the quality of the wine and on the silver service.

Normally I am reluctant to tutor the son or daughter of close friends but I did make one exception. Cathy, the daughter of a close drinking friend of mine, was struggling with her Higher Maths paper. She was a keen student but maths was not a strong point. Unfortunately, her mother was a chartered account and wanted her to get a grade A. Any shortcomings in her daughter's abilities were the fault of poor teachers. She was also a strong conservative party supporter and The Daily Mail was her paper of choice. I was reluctant to take this student mainly because of her mother's righteous attitude and her willingness to play the blame game. I also thought it odd that as a chartered accountant she did not help her daughter with her maths – but later it became clear that she did not have a clue about the new mathematics syllabus that included vector analysis, statistics and algebraic methods.

I agreed to take on the job under one condition, that I test Cathy's current understanding of maths and then decide which level of paper to take. I tested her deliberately in the presence of her mother and decided that she should take the intermediate level and not take the higher-level paper. Her mother would like to have objected but realised how little of modern Maths she knew and how much had changed from her days at school. Her daughter was relieved. Cathy would stand a much better chance of getting a grade B that was necessary for university entry. The course of lessons went well and Cathy got her grade B. Needless to say I got no special thank you from the mother, after all she had paid for the lessons and that was that. In fact I had not charged my usual rate because I did it as a favour for my drinking friend.

By way of contrast I had a model student from Harrow Public School who needed some intensive revision for his GCE A' Levels who paid well and appreciated my service. A sixth form girl from St Alban's Girls' School was a pleasure to teach and told me all about her experience of playing Lacrosse for England Schools. Some years later I was to get the chance to have a little go at playing Lacrosse at St Paul's Girls' School and found out that it is almost as difficult as playing Hurling.

MY TERRITORIAL ARMY EXPERIENCE

Substituting for Stas on the ski trip provided me with some unwanted excitement but he had another idea to provide me with another adventure. Stas was very good on drilling German grammar into his pupils but he was even better at military drill. Before starting as a teacher he served as a full time sergeant in the signal division of the British army in Cyprus and elsewhere. His father, a Lithuanian, was a captain in the German army and fought on the Russian front. Stas inherited his father's visceral hatred of Russia. With his clean Slavic features he was selected as a poster soldier for army recruitment. With the cold war in full swing senior officers got concerned about the high profile of someone of Lithuanian extraction working in the sensitive area of signal communication and moved Stas to an infantry battalion. Stas was delighted as he took this as a sign that the army was taking the Russian threat seriously. As a teacher Stas joined the Territorial Army that was now moving away from its dad's Army image and its members were expected to go on short tours abroad to work with the professional army. Stas told me what a great time he had on manoeuvres in Germany and his visits to the Hamburg red light district. The school was obliged to give him paid leave and with additional pay from the TA, made joining the TA an attractive proposition for an impoverished teacher. After a lot of persuasion from Stas I joined the local Reading TA which was part of the Wessex regiment. Going down for a weekend exercise and shooting practice on Salisbury Plain was fun but tiring. One weekend we went on a military manoeuvre to Thetford forest in Norfolk, leaving Reading on Friday evening on a specially commissioned military train dressed in full military infantry combat gear. The train moved slowly through the night to arrive in Thetford at 5am. We then had a full 10-mile march through forest paths to our military camp. Luckily the weather was nice but I got bored with the hanging around and not knowing what the overall plans were – we were just cannon fodder after all. I did learn that we were due to embark on a dawn attack on a group of buildings defended by another TA unit and that we had to sleep whenever we got a chance. It was late March and there was quite a frost on the ground. I remember dozing off while waiting for the dawn attack. I woke to find a large white object lying near my feet. It turned out to be a sheep who also wanted a share of the heat underneath the tree.

At about 4.30 am we began our march. I agreed to carry a heavy Bren gun whilst someone else carried my rifle. Soon we were in place to launch our attack and waiting for the flares to rise to light up the buildings and to signal the attack. I decided to have a last check on the safety latch of the Bren gun. In the dark I could not see the latch and decided to give the trigger a little squeeze to check for resistance. The gun went off, the flares went up, an officer shouted down the line – who was that man?, the response went back up the line – "O'Reilly" Sir. Too late, all soldiers moved forward firing on everything and anything. My embarrassment was total. After the exercise, we had a good cooked breakfast and then the commanding officer interviewed me. I told him exactly what happened and as he had a good breakfast he was not too hard on me, especially as the manoeuvre was deemed a success – a surprise to me. We made the long train journey home to Reading to arrive early Sunday evening. Next day at school I was exhausted and Stas had a great time telling staff about my experience with the Bren gun.

What surprised me was the number of Irish people in the TA. For centuries the Irish have been a major force in the army especially around the Empire. On the military coaches on the way home from Salisbury some of the lads would sing IRA songs and the officers would pretend to take offence but enjoyed the craic. Some of them had bullets and other bits of army equipment as souvenirs in their homes.

The troubles in Northern Ireland in the early 70s were catching world attention. Stas decided that he would play a joke on me. One Saturday morning he arranged for two military Lorries on their way to Salisbury Plain to come via my house. They arrived in the close next to my house and set up two machine gun emplacements. The soldiers had blacked out faces, one of them knocked on the door, and when my wife opened the door the soldier said they had come to arrest me for IRA activities. My wife, not sure what was going on called up to me that there was a army man who wanted to arrest me or words to that effect. As luck would have it I had already looked out of an upstairs window and seen Stas, face unblackened, behind one of the machine guns. We had a bit of a laugh and Alice gave them some tea and biscuits. God knows what the neighbours thought not to mention the risk Stas took playing games with Her Majesty's army. Not long after I resigned from the TA but Stas carried on in the TA for many years – the love of his life.

MY GRANNY'S FUNERAL: MRS T FITZSIMONS 1890-1972

I had kept in close contact with my Granny since we moved to England. She was quite happy staying with her youngest son Philip and his wife Agnus at their house off Green Lane in Haringey, London. For most of the twelve years before her death, she was able to go shopping and purchased her beloved Gold flake cigarettes in the nearby shops. She did not need me anymore to walk the mile or so to O'Connell's country shop in

Ireland. My Granny was a large woman so it was not surprising that she got breathless with age and eventually ended up in the Middlesex Hospital in north London. X-rays showed a dark shadow on one of her lungs, which might be cancer. When Alice and I visited her in hospital she complained about the pain in her legs due to very poor circulation. There was the possibility that she might have a leg amputated. Soon afterwards she suffered a major stroke which mercifully ended her life.

Granny's body was taken to Ireland to be buried in the Fitzsimons family grave in Kells. When I asked my Head teacher for permission to go to her funeral, he refused my request because she was not a close enough relative – had to be a sibling or parent. I pointed out that I had lived for eight years with my Granny and that she was like a mother to me. Eventually he relented. It is my experience that some English do not cope or deal well with death or funerals. They appear to be events that are strictly private and emotional displays kept to the absolute minimum. Those who do display their emotions openly – mostly foreigners and Irish – are viewed with a degree of distain.

The Irish do know how to do funerals well. No employer would dare refuse a request to go to a funeral, even if you do not know the deceased. One of my best friends in Ireland has attended hundreds of funerals over his working life of fifty years. It is a surprisingly short time interval from deathbed to grave – three to four days. On the first two days the body is prepared and takes pride of place in the parlour and neighbours come to the house to pay their respect. Some volunteer for the overnight vigil – the corpse is never left alone and soft drinks and sandwiches are served. On the third or fourth evening the corpse is taken to the church and after a blessing lays there until a funeral mass and burial next morning. Back at the house there is drink and food a plenty as all regale the life of the deceased – the Wake. Unfortunately, we could not give my Granny a proper wake as it took several days to arrange to fly the body to Ireland. My mother and I along with her brother

John were driven to Holyhead to take the ferry to Ireland by my Uncle Philip. My mother's two other brothers found their own way there.

There was a great turn out in Kells for the funeral mass. At the end of the mass there was a collection which shocked me in the manner it was done. A table was placed in front of the alter and the congregation invited to come up and place their offerings on the table in full public view. It was very noticeable if someone did not go up and if someone put down coins instead of notes. Some of those priests and Bishops have a lot to answer for and it is not just child abuse.

We all walked the half mile behind the hearse to the graveyard where Granny was finally laid to rest with her husband Patrick and one of her sons who died aged only four years old. Afterwards we had a great celebration of her life at the Headfort Arms Hotel. The next day we met up in Granny's home town of Ardee to continue celebrations in her brother Jim's pub in Main Street. When I got back to school all I got from my colleagues was their displeasure for having to cover for my lessons.

CHAPTER 11

A NEW START – THE AGE OF COMPREHENSIVE EDUCATION

In 1973 the move towards comprehensive education in England was gaining momentum but there was no legislation in place to make it compulsory for all Local Education Authorities to go comprehensive. Most labour controlled authorities embraced the spirit of comprehensive education enthusiastically but conservative controlled ones were more hit and miss. Even today Kent County Council has the 11plus in place for all pupils. Some other counties retain pockets where Grammar schools are still in place. For example, Colchester has two grammar schools for boys and girls and selects from a wide area is that way beyond the confines of the town and so in effect are super grammar schools. The two ex grammar schools in the town of Maidenhead, Berkshire where my new school Cox Green was located still creamed off some of the brightest pupils through sibling connections but catchment area was the main criterion for pupil selection. There was one main problem with basing pupil admissions on catchment areas. If they area included large council and industrial estates it was difficult to have an intake that was a true cross section of the general population. Cox Green's pupil intake was skewed towards the more disadvantaged but we did have a lot of nearby new private estates. In my experience when people talk of good schools they mean schools in well heeled suburbs with a high proportion of middle class parents. However with the advent of value added assessment, the achievements of all schools can be more favourable compared; but ambitious parents will still want to get their children into schools in more socially favourable areas Some even move house to achieve this and estate agents actively promote house sales in favoured post code locations.

The real good news about my new job was that I was in at the start on the building of eight new science laboratories. The bad news was that I still had staff that were from the old secondary modern era. However, that would change because the school roll was increasing and we would be able to appoint new staff. During the seven years that I was at Cox Green we recruited a Cambridge Chemistry graduate, a teacher who was educated at Eton, a Biology teacher with a first class degree and another teacher who was the daughter of the Principal of The Berkshire College of Agriculture among others. The number of pupils taking GCE A 'Level increased and consequently more went to university.

My technicians were willing but did not know much about science – more like secretaries. One of my woman technicians believed all science equipment should be kept in the boxes that they came in. She had to learn quickly that I was a strong believer in practical class experiments and this meant all equipment had to be in trays, on trolleys and in sets of up to sixteen items. I was lucky to have a grant to purchase class sets of the latest equipment to teach the new Nuffield supported science curriculum. I did have a few luxuries – a LASER and one of the first desktop commodore PETT computers. The Maths department were a bit envious when we started teaching computer programming, but my main reason for the computer was for statistical analysis in thermodynamics and to control and measure physical quantities like temperature and pressure over time in experiments. The LASER I used for transmitting sound by light beam, optics and holography. Our experiments on Open Days impressed the prospective parents and pupils and increased our recruitment figures. The LASER and Computer cost many thousands of pounds but today they can be bought for a small fraction of the price. Nevertheless, it was nice to be in on the start of the LASER and microcomputer age.

CORPORAL PUNISHMENT – THE FINAL SLAP.

During my time at school the use of corporal punishment was institutionalised and went unquestioned by pupils and parents alike. Now a teacher is suspended if he or she as much as touches a pupil in anger. In my early teaching days, when angered by extreme pupil misbehaviour, I was sometimes tempted to give a pupil a clip round the ear but never laid a hand on a girl pupil. An incident occurred at Cox Green that finally convinced me never to lay a hand on a pupil again even if they climbed up the walls and jumped out the windows of my laboratory.

The Head teacher was angry about the of pupils using their own loud music boxes in school and at a staff meeting 'harangued' the staff for not doing something about it – not good leadership! Soon after this meeting, I was just about to leave school and take my wife to Heathrow airport so that she could fly to Norway to see her terminally ill mother. On my way out of the science block, I went to the toilet only to find a pupil, one Gary Paske, blasting away on his expensive music box. I immediately challenged him and his response was "what has it to do with you?" I grabbed the music box from him but he did not let go of it and then I clipped him across his rather fleshy cheek with my right hand and threatened to drag him to the Head teacher's office. Tears came to his eyes and I relented. Instead, I pushed the music box into his stomach and told him to get the hell home and count himself lucky. I forgot all about the incident until the next morning when during a fire drill the Head teacher wanted to see me in his office immediately. This was very odd as a fire drill should be the top priority. When he interviewed me with a witness present, he told me Mr and

Mrs Paske (who were in the office next door to his study) wanted to take legal action against me for assaulting their son. I discovered later that Gary was an only child and his parents worked in the City of London so Gary was very spoilt. Self-preservation made me deny assault as a first option. I told him that I had tried to take the music box off him – following advice from the staff meeting by the Head teacher, he did not like that. As Gary was aggressive towards me, I had to fend him off with my right hand, which in the struggle to get him to release the music box may have caused the box to rub against his cheek. Game on – Head teacher flustered. Now on the front foot I then informed him that as I was threatened with legal action, I would need to contact the teachers' union for legal advice and support. He decided to go next door to talk to the parents to work on a compromise. It was agreed that I apologise to the parents for the incident but no legal action would be taken. There and then, I decided that I would never lay a hand on a pupil again and felt much better for making that decision. The age of corporal punishment whether as victim or perpetrator was finally over for me and a few years later this was nationally reinforced in law.

THE SEQUEL

Gary left school a year later and got a job as an office junior in the City. One day he came to school on his flash motorbike and fancy riding gear. I heard a knock on my office door and upon opening the door, I was surprised to see Gary. He told me he had come to apologise for reporting me for the music box incident. In fact, I was one of his favourite teachers and the incident had really taught him a lesson to take more responsibility for his own actions and not to blame others. No problem Gary, there is really no need to apologise but nice all the same and glad to see that you are doing well. Keep up the good work – forever the teacher in me. This incident was a life changer for pupil and teacher alike. It is also a warning to those who think education is only about teaching the basics. Note, I have used the pupil's real name but I am sure that Gary will not sue me!

OUR FIRST CAR AND PROBLEMS THEREAFTER – TALES OF WOE.

It was not easy to get from Reading to my school at Maidenhead and initially I had to get a bus to Reading station and then a train to Maidenhead station followed by a long walk of nearly two miles to my school.

I played tennis with a neighbour who gave me a lift on occasion to school but had to rely on public transport to get home. After I got to know the staff at school better, I discovered that a maths teacher Harry Kianni lived in Reading and a geography teacher Maria Prattico and I got a regular lift to school with Harry. Harry was a member of the Baha'i religion and regaled us with his beliefs on anything and everything. He had the unnerving habit of wanting to look at you when talking to you and that was not too good an idea when driving and one was sitting in the back seat of the car.

Alice got a job at the Gillette factory in Slough that involved shifts of 3 nights, followed by 3 mornings, then 3 evenings and then 3 days off and it was not long before she was promoted to inspector. The company supplied a free bus service. The problem was that we had two young children to care for. On occasion I arrived home just in time for Alice to catch the company bus but the effort was worth it as the money was good. The company had a high turnover in salesmen's cars and Alice put her name down in a lottery open only to employees to get first buying preference and it was not long before her name came up and we bought a year old Ford Cortina 1300cc with 40,000 miles on the clock. Today 40,000 miles is not a problem but in 1972 it was considered high mileage and it was not long before we needed a new short engine and later a gear box and disc + drum brakes. We now had a car but no driving licences. Maria had acquired a red minivan and she gave us some driving lessons. We both failed our driving tests but got through the second time. I failed my first driving test trying to reverse round a corner in the minivan mainly because the van had no side windows and I ended up scraping the offside wheels along the curb. Later we took the underpowered Cortina to Norway and the engine over heated going up the hairpin bends to Geilo. Solution, take out the thermostat to improve water circulation and hope the engine gasket did not blow. Our second car was also a Ford 2000cc second hand Sierra with high mileage bought at a car auction and again we hoped for the best. This one lasted two years before an engine blow out on the way to Maidstone for my sister's silver wedding anniversary. Luckily, we were only a few miles away from home so I was able to go and get our second hand Vauxhall Cavalier, also bought cheaply at a car auction. A few months later the gearbox blew in the Cavalier on the way home from my school in Berkhamstead and that car was a right off. We then bought another lower mileage Vauxhall Cavalier from a car auction that did last a few years before an electrical fire late at night on the way home from a party. The fire brigade came and just about stopped the whole wire system from a meltdown. Some of the all white firefighters, and they were all men, had nothing better to do than make racist comments about the Irish. I was too stressed out to take them on, but thankfully institutionalised racism in the police and fire services is now being addressed – I hope. Later this car was stolen from our driveway by local travellers and found outside the nearby traveller site. They realised they could not keep it inside the site because it was security marked. The contents of the car had been removed and I hope they enjoyed using my squash kit and playing my Irish folk tapes!

The car that gave us the most trouble was the Austin Princess that we purchased at British Car Auctions. It was a luxury model and a great looker but sadly not a great goer. I noticed too late after I bought it that there was a spare bottle of automatic gear box oil in the boot and it was not long after that the Borg-Warner automatic gear box went. I got it rebuilt by a former RAF mechanic at great cost. Later it needed a new engine – despite an engine size of 2.2 litres it needed an extra oil cooler to tow our caravan but even then the engine went. We got a short engine in a garage in Hertford that my wife Alice managed to carry on her bicycle the mile or so to our house for a technical teacher friend of ours to replace. It was only in 2006 that we bought our first new car – a Honda CRV 4WD. It was at a reduced price because a new model was due out six months later. We did not know this and certainly, the sales representative did not tell us. Unfortunately this car struggled in towing our modern style caravan and the gear box went just outside the 3 year parts guarantee period. At the time of writing we have had the alternator replaced at great expense and loss of our time. Therefore, overall, like most other people we have had interesting and expensive times over the years with our motorised transport.

MORE WORK FOR ALICE

After Gillettes, Alice did night shifts at Mars Chocolate factory near west London. She did five nights in a row from 9pm to 7am. The money was good but it was hard on both of us. Later still she got an evening job at Huntley and Palmer biscuit factory in Reading and this involved me getting home in time from work to take charge of the boys. Alice was now taking her A'Levels over two years at an annex of Bracknel FE College in Reading and this involved two days a week of lessons. By now Ragnar was at the local Primary school and Fingal was in a local convent nursery near her place of study. In the summer of 1975 she completed her three A' Levels with grades ABB and got a place at Reading University. She also got a government grant that helped ease our financial problems.

Selfie Ireland 1965

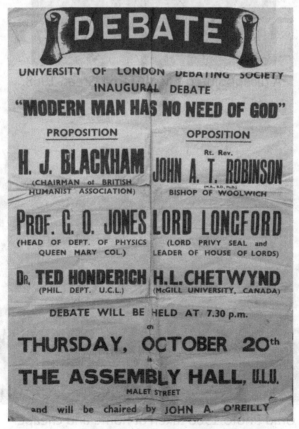

Debating Line Up 1967

A disappointed Alice, Gretna Green 1968

Grad Photo 1968 taken at home and cheaper
than in The Royal Albert Hall, London

Wedding Alice and me with Fsther Thomas
Finchley London 2nd Nov 1968

Brother Vincent and me Wedding 1968

Alice Ragnar Fingal and me circa 1975

Me with beard Fingal as baby Mum and Dorothy 1972

Alice and me Hamar Norway circa 1974

Alice, taken and developed by me circa 1975

Eating Crayfish Oslo circa 1976

With Dad Camping Suffolk circa 1980

In Denim Jacket Norway 1975

Best man at Charles Bond's Wedding Chesham 1975

Alice has the boys in velvet 1975

Salmon caught of Norwegian coast 1976

With Minister for Industry in my School
Lab - Maidenhead circa 1976

CHAPTER 12

THIS SPORTING LIFE: A LIFETIME OF ADVENTURES BEGINS – THE TEAM PLAYER.

Prior to 1971 the last time I played a team sport was just before I left Ireland in late 1960. Most people end team sports by the time they are twenty-five. I started at that age. Throughout my late teens and early twenties I kept up my fitness level going for runs. My running adventures are covered elsewhere (**Ref Marathon Adventure across Europe and Beyond**) but suffice to state here that I was always fit enough to play in the occasional staff football or cricket matches against the pupils.

The first amateur football club that I joined was Emmer Green in Reading mainly because my next-door neighbour Pete played for this club. Pete was not much of a footballer but he was a far better player away from home with other men's wives. He had no moral compass and once when we held a party for neighbours and friends he tried to take advantage of my wife in the upstairs loo while we partied downstairs. A married Norwegian girl across the road was also the subject of his advances. He could not resist telling me about his conquests – I assume he did not tell his long-suffering wife. He was an occasional taxi driver and took every opportunity to invite himself into the houses of lone women that he took home from parties or nightclubs. Once he told me that he was distracted by a women's Alsatian dog licking his backside while he had sex with her on the sitting room couch. It takes all sorts!

Normally I played for the reserve team and occasionally for the first team. I found it hard to transfer and change my Gaelic football skill set to soccer. My kick was much stronger out of hand then off the ground and in retrospect Rugby would have suited me more. But I liked playing in the midfield position and could cover as much as six miles in a game. As our sons got older I would take them to matches and they would muck around with other kids. Some of the places we played had no showers so my sons and I looked forward to getting home for a joint bath afterwards – sometimes we had to shower first to remove the caked mud that we were covered in. In 1972 I also joined the Caversham Park Village club which played on a Sunday morning. Surprisingly this was quite a high level of football because some class players from Saturday leagues also liked to play Sunday as well. In 1973 the Emmer Green Reserve team won the league and reached the cup semi-final. Some of the first team players wanted now to play in the reserves and a few of them were allowed to do so because other teams were doing the same thing.

Our semi-final match played on a hard dried out pitch in March was a bit of a disaster for me. On the Friday night before the match we went to a party at a flat rented by my fellow bachelor science teacher Geoff in a country house near Bray outside Maidenhead. Geoff shared the flat with two British Airways staff who had access to duty free drink. It had a large sitting room and several bedrooms. We brought our boys to the party who later slept in an upstairs bedroom a bit away from the party music. Just before the party started Geoff and I went out for a pre-party drink and sat on bar stools next to the great George Best who was drinking with his friend and biographer Michael Parkinson, a well know TV presenter. I could see looking into George's eyes that he was well ahead of me in alcoholic units consumed. Unfortunately by 3 am as the party was in full swing to Rod Stuart we had to leave and I was now ahead of George in alcoholic units consumed. Alice hit a guest car backing out of the car park and I went back in to tell Geoff but no one seemed to care. They were well on the way to oblivion. Alice rang Geoff late next day and he told her no one had reported a damaged car but someone had driven their sports car into a nearby field.

When we got home, I was too inebriated to bother getting out of the car and woke up only when some of my team mates came to collect me the next day. We took a one-goal lead at the end of the first half and I was sincerely hoping that we would hold on to it to win and avoid extra time. Late in the second half the opposition scored an equaliser and we went into extra time. I was feeling dreadful and even more dreadful when they scored late in extra time to win the match. Our manager thought that I was not my usual self in terms of leadership, drive and energy. Of course he was right but I kept quiet about my late night partying. I felt bad and knew I had let my side down especially as the team viewed me as their midfield dynamo.

MY RED CARD

I the late 1970s it was common for some players to drink a few points before a match and even more so after a match. I never drank before a match and rarely afterwards because I preferred to get home with my boys. I can remember playing in a match in Prospect Park, Reading and smelling alcohol on the breath on several opposition players. We scored a couple of early goals and the swearing and aggressive tackles put in by our opponents got to the point where the referee threatened to abandon the game. Just before half time one of their midfield players who was reeking of alcohol nearly maimed me in a tackle and unfortunately I reacted and we ended up fighting. The referee sent both of us off. Lesson learnt, never retaliate, and leave it to the referee.

We moved to west of Reading and I joined a club called Gladstone – no connection to the 19C British PM. The club played in a different league to Emmer Green. I remember one game in particular when we took a premiership team called Berkshire Sports to extra time in a county cup match. I played centre back and managed to contain their forwards to the surprise of everyone. My performance was good enough for Berkshire Sports to accept my application to join them. This team was comprised mainly of Berkshire County Council employees and had use of a magnificent sports complex near Reading. I played for the club until I left Reading in 1980.

MY BRIEF ROMANCE WITH RUGBY AS A PLAYER
RATHER THAN SPECTATOR

My next door neighbour in Caversham Park was Welsh and no surprise played rugby for Abbey Rugby Club in Reading. He was a medical rep who bought a similar house next door to us for 30% more than we paid for ours. He missed the six-month price rise that we benefited from but a few years later, he sold it and still got a handsome profit. One memorable weekend he took me to the old Cardiff Arms Park to see Ireland hammered by the all-conquering Welsh rugby team of the 1970s, with a brilliant performance by their full back J P R Williams. A few years later in 1984 I got my revenge on Williams when I beat him in the London marathon by 20 minutes. Before the match my Welsh neighbour took me to visit his family who lived at the head of one of the many Welsh mining valleys. Mining was still active as evident by the turning wheels of the mineshaft lifts and large slag heaps. A decade later most of the valleys fell silent after the battle between the miner's unions and the Thatcher government.

After the match we went to the hotel where both teams stayed and had a few drinks with the players before they went in for their formal dinner. Today this is not possible. In the 2015

World Cup we saw Ireland play France and later Argentina in the new Cardiff Millennium stadium and got nowhere near the players. In the age of professional rugby one would have to pay big money for a hospitality box to get near one of the players and that may well be players who were not playing due to injury.

I was never too sure of the rules of rugby and they keep changing over the years. My very first rugby game was a trial for my Queen Mary College rugby team at the college's sports ground in east London. I managed to get some dirt in one of my eyes and had difficulty seeing for the rest of the game. Needless to state I was not selected. A few days later my eye was streaming water and I could not see the lecture board. My GP gave me some eye drops after a very quick look into my eye. Some days later my eye was worse and I could see an inflamed red streak across my eyeball. Back to my GP and this time he did examine the eye properly and gave me an urgent appointment with an ophthalmologist at a hospital in Baker Street. When I was examined in the hospital the ophthalmologist accused me of neglecting my eye condition by not coming earlier and wondered if I wanted to lose the sight of my eye! I left the hospital with a large bandage around my head that certainly got me noticed on the tube line home. My flirtation with rugby was over for some years to come.

The social life in rugby clubs is far superior to pubing it with the local soccer club and changing in country huts with a cup of tea at half time if one was lucky. Most rugby clubs have a club bar, kitchen facilities and decent changing rooms with showers and even a large hot bathtub. Abbey RFC had very good facilities and a decent rugby pitch. It was not long before my Welsh neighbour asked me to stand in for The Casual 15. The main qualification for the front three was to have a large beer belly to give you a low centre of gravity in the scrum. I preferred to be in the backs and preferable at full back where speed and kicking skills were required – assuming you got the ball if it ever came out of the scrum. I played a couple of local games before playing an away match at Chichester. We had to leave Reading by hired coach at 11am for a two hour plus journey and then change and warm up for a 3pm kick off, During the game I handled and kick the ball about six times and twice nearly got maimed by a forward determined to take me out. I did enjoy the hot shower needed to get the dried cake mud off my legs. We then had the usual sausage, beans, eggs and chips. The first shared jug of beer was followed by several more and we staggered well inebriated out at 7pm for our waiting coach arriving home at 9pm. I had missed a soccer club match to go on this trip and realised that soccer gave me more exercise, less booze and my boys could come and kick a ball around with the other kids. That was the end of my rugby career except for one staff-sixth form match several years later. In that game several staff and pupils got knocks and I had to cover for staff who did not turn up at school next day because of injury. Today staff v student rugby matches are banned for health and safety reasons.

I have always been keen to support the Irish National Rugby team. Jimmy Farrell owned the neighbouring farm to ours in Kells. Jimmy played for Ireland and then went on tour with the British and Irish Lions to Argentina in 1927 and to Australia/ New Zealand in 1930. He was also a founder member of Kells Golf Club. He married a socialite from Wales and lived the high life to such an extent they went bankrupt and had to sell their farm in 1958. I can remember attending an open auction at their big house where lovely antique furniture and paintings were sold off very cheaply. We sold our farm in 1960 and came out of it with money in our pockets but we never did party like the Farrells. One of Jimmy's sons became quite a famous artist in France and when he died age 60 years old, his ashes were interned in the family grave in Cortown. Another son an emeritus Australian Professor wrote a biography of his brother in 2006. Recently I tracked down one of Jimmy's surviving daughters who now lives in Virginia, County Cavan. In her day she was a rather glamorous air hostess and over tea and cakes she showed me some wonderful photographs of her father in his rugby days. One photo stood out of Jimmy in his Lions rugby blazer and slacks relaxing on ship deck on his way to Australia. Well Jimmy Farrell may have lived the life of Reilly, but one of Ireland's greatest players was Tony O'Reilly. I can remember the time the great – and later the very rich O'Reilly was recalled late in his career to play for Ireland against England. Over weight and unfit he lasted about twenty minutes in the match against England at Twickenham. A few years later I saw my first rugby international at Twickenham when Tom Kiernan, the Irish full back secured a 3-3 draw with a penalty in the dying minutes of the match. Later in the 1990s I saw Ireland hammered at Twickenham, but in 2006 along with my daughter Astrid we saw Shane Horgan get a last minute try to beat England at Twickenham. The next year more joy as I saw the boys in green thump the Red Roses 43-13 in the historic and famous match at Croak Park, the home of Gaelic Games, in Dublin in 2007.

GETTING TICKETS FOR RUGBY INTERNATIONALS.

In the late 1960s and early 1970s, one could turn up on match day and get the cheaper standing only tickets. By the 1980s one had to know or be a member of a local rugby club to have a hope of getting tickets or rely on the ticket tout. Ireland v England matches were very popular and always oversubscribed. In the 1980s I was able to get five standing tickets for the Ireland game at Twickenham from my Head of Careers John Atkinson who worked for me at Riversmead School. I have to admit to a bit of corruption here. John was for many years President of The Hertford Ruby Club and was recently awarded a CBE for services to rugby. John had a light timetable load because of his Careers work with individual pupils and the need to keep in contact with local employers. He also was social and bar secretary at the rugby club. He asked me to timetable all his lessons so that he could have Thursday and Friday off to be at the club. I was able to do this for him without affecting too much on other staff's timetables. My reward was to receive some of the club's allocation of international rugby tickets.

I used the tickets to allow my brother-in-law Pat and his Maidstone friends to come to the match. We would meet up in Kilburn in time for three or four pints of Guinness and travel by overhead rail to Twickenham and then have a few more pints before walking to the ground. After the match we returned to Kilburn for a serious drinking session at Biddy Mulligan, then over to The National for more beer and to listen to the band. Then down to China Town for a Chinese nosh up. I would then go to King's Cross the get the first morning train to Hertford. But the Maidstone lads, were made of a stronger constitution, would then head for spiritual nourishment at the 6am Mass at Westminster Cathedral and then on to the The Style Bridge pub near Maidstone for a lunchtime session before 'finally' going home.

Our rugby days out were often very memorable and not always for the rugby. I can remember a close friend of Pat's, Bill MacMullen losing his dentures in a toilet at 3am in a restaurant in Chinatown. I tried to partly dismantle the toilet to retrieve the dentures but to no avail. Bill did not turn up at work for several days – he was a bank manager in Maidstone, until Keith, our driver and Dentist made him a new set. Bill was also involved in another memorable incident. One occasion, a Dublin man from Gravesend, joined out party. From the start there was a bit of friction between him and Bill. Things really kicked off between them late in Biddy Mulligans when Bill almost knocked him out with a left hook on the dance floor. The fellow customers were astonished to see two men in their fifties in full battle. Anyway we helped to add to the reputation of the fighting Irish in Kilburn. For a time Pat had his own access to tickets from a fellow commuter who travelled up to London daily with him. Once his son, a policeman, joined the Maidstone lads, and as customary had a warm up session at a pub in south London owned by one of Kevin Whelan's contacts. The policeman showed them the way in the drinking stakes, but they did try to warn him that it was going to be a long day. After the match they finally got to Biddy Mulligan's in Kilburn and by now our policeman was out of it. They decided to let him sleep it off in the car. One of the group came back later and found that he was gone. They assumed that he must have made his own way home by train. Later on they found that he had been arrested for being drunk on the street and spent the night in the local police cell. He was unable to convince the arresting officer that he was a policeman himself. When Pat met his father at the station on Monday morning he was cold shouldered and that was the end of his rugby ticket supply.

I was very pleased when one year my father agreed to join us for an Ireland game at Twickenham, but in view of what happened I am not sure if he was after he was robbed. As usual we made our way from The Three Kings pub to the ground to arrive only just before the match started. As we ran up the stairs into the stadium we were joined by two men telling us to hurry up – strange I thought. In the rush we later discovered that they had managed to relieve Bill MacMullin and my dad of their wallets. In those days it was not so easy to use bank cards to empty your account and Bill being a bank manager was able to stop any card transactions. I am not sure if my dad knew too many of the rules of rugby but he did not let the robbery spoil his day out or his beer consumption.

In the late 1980s I started to support London Irish and more so when they became professional and joined the new premier league. The music and the Craic at their ground at Sunbury where they celebrated their 100th year as a club in 1998 was the envy of many other clubs. I remember being at Sunbury on a wet and windy Saturday afternoon with my friend Andy Sloman when Irish beat Rotherham to gain promotion to the premier league. We gained access to a hospitality suite pretending to be representatives of Ashlyns Electronics. Our Hostess was impressed with someone from the Electronics World mainly because of her declared ignorance of anything to do with science and electronics.

It was very emotional to be at Twickenham a few years later to see Irish beat Northampton to win the Powergen Cup, their first major trophy since the founding of the club. I was in Norway when Irish lost 10-9 to Leicester in the Guinness Premiership final in 2009 at Twickenham, but my daughter Astrid was there to witness this historic event. I was present again at Twickenham in 2008 with Astrid, Andy Sloman, son Fingal and Adrian Horgan when Irish lost 15-21 to the French club Toulouse in the European Cup semi-final. They had as a club come a long way in less than a decade of professional rugby.

On several occasions a group of us enjoyed the St Patrick's Day match at Reading where they share the stadium with Reading FC. Sometimes it was worth paying extra for hospitality that included dinner, own band and a meet the players session. On one occasion, it proved a very long day for Pat and Adrian Horgan who missed their last train home from Reading. Even though I lived in Reading seven years I never got the chance to sleep over night at Reading Rail Station. As of 2016 London Irish are struggling and one hopes that their current New Zealand manager will get them back on course. Sadly, in the age of professionalism the club has to recruit some top quality players from abroad to stay competitive. The club has fewer Irish born players now but the management keeps and promotes its Irish heritage.

GOLF – THE LONG PAR 5

I have always contended that you should only play golf when you get older and that is how it has worked out for me. That is not to say that golf is not a great and rewarding game and like most games you should learn to play them when you are young and flexible so that you can acquire the basic skills. One accepts that it is much harder to learn sports that require balance and timing when you are older. Try learning to ride a bike or to ski for the first time when you are in your sixties. Ideally I would have liked to have had golf lessons in my early teens with the intention of taking it up in later life. The problem with Golf is that it takes up a lot of your time and costs a lot of money. A round of Golf can take up to five hours and with socialising at the 19th in the clubhouse can take up most of the day and that is why we have jokes about Golf widows. I also like cricket but have similar issues with the time that it takes to play.

As a sport, golf stands out as the one that can cause extreme frustration. I have seen players smash their clubs and walk off the course. I have seen normally gentle people male and female use expletives and vent their frustrations in ways that they never do in normal life. It is possible to get a wonderful birdie on one hole followed by a triple bogey or worse on the next hole. The same level of maximum joy and frustration applies even to the top professional Golfers. Upon reflection it is not surprising that Golfing can cause big mood swings – it is the Physics man. The task of hitting a 4 cm ball on the ground at great speed with a meter and a half long club by definition is not going to be easy – not to mention the added difficulty of a poor lie or finding oneself in a deep sand bucker.

My main inspiration for taking up Golf in my late fifties was down to my mother's encouragement. She came from a family in Ireland where some of her uncles were keen Golfers. Her uncles, Frank and Gussie McKeever, were members of the Ardee Golf Club in County Louth and Frank was Club Captain of the 1920s. I had the honour of playing the course around 2006 and was impressed with their new two-storey clubhouse. I was disappointed to see that the honours board did not go back far enough to include Frank's name. As with most courses Ardee was initially a nine hole course and each hole was a former farm field. This meant that every hole was shielded from the other holes. Later it was expanded to 18 Holes and some fairways had to cross- over each other because of lack of space and the need not to have too long a course. I remember getting a few pars and having an excellent real steak burger after wards in the clubhouse. My mother's hometown Kells had a similar set up to Ardee; but now has two 18 hole courses taking in some the land belonging to the former Lord Headfort estate as well as a superb clubhouse. My mother never played Kells but I did take her to see the new club facilities in 2003.

Once she moved to England, she got time to participate in two passions in her life, Golf and Bridge. She first joined the municipal Trent Park Golf Club in north London, a fine parkland course. My father and I played there a few times with her. Later on she joined the well established Mill Hill Golf Club. It was here that she got Bing Crosby's signature. Bing often played at Mill Hill when in London. He was getting on in years when he met my mother and was playing with just a few clubs when my mother spotted him on a nearby fairway. She was not shy in making herself know to him. Sadly a few weeks later Bing Crosby died in Spain. Later on it was on a long par 5 hole that my mother noticed that she was a bit breathless and asked a playing friend if she was finding the going tough – she was not. This was the first indication that my mother had a heart problem. She had rheumatic fever as a young woman and claimed this may have "weakened" her heart. Three of her brothers died of heart attacks but they were quite heavy smokers and liked a pint or six. John, a younger brother, had quite severe asthma for most of his life but lived until he was 79 years old and her youngest brother Philip had rheumatic fever as a teenager but is still going strong at 79 years. Then what explains her fit eldest son Sean – me – having a double heart bypass at 66 years old? Someone has to draw the genetic short straw I suppose.Once my mother had a pacemaker fitted she was able to continue playing golf for several more years.

In my mid fifties I finally got round to joining a golf club but only as a five day member. I still like to keep my weekends free for a family Sunday lunch and a good run or walk. I play off a

21 handicap and I would like to get down to 18 but I am not too concerned if I do not. When in form I can raise my game especially when playing other clubs in our summer league. A high point of my golfing "career" was in a foursome scratch competition. We were entered in the competition by mistake thinking that it was a handicap scoring scheme. We ended up playing some low handicap serious golfers. My partner and I even managed to win a game and performed very well in the final at St Albans GC – the home of the founder of the biannual Ryder Cup competition between the US and Europe. We got a score of 19 which was better than several other teams. I have never got a hole in one but recently got an eagle on the par five on the third hole of our old course. At Essendon Country Club we are very fortunate to have two 18 hole courses. My best performance abroad was at Enniscrone links course on the west coast of Ireland. On a wet and windy day I got round with a stapleford score of 35. I was sober because we headed straight for the golf course once we touched down at Knock Airport. The next day at the famous Rossa's Point in Sligo I did not fare so well mainly because of our excesses the previous evening.

SAVING A MAN'S LIFE

One would not normally expect to save a man's life on a golf course apart from maybe giving resuscitation in the case of a heart attack – and they certainly do happen on golf courses, think of all that stress when the golfing goes wrong. In my case I saved a man from drowning.

It was a fairly warm June day and I was playing in a four ball. On the long par 5 third hole on the new course I hit my third shot into a large lake in front of the green. Two of my playing colleagues had already made there way across the bridge and I was left with Ron, a large man in his early 70s, who decided to try to fish my ball out of the lake. I told him that it was a waste of time as my ball had gone well out into the lake. I do not know what it is about some golfers but they love looking for golf balls, even if they are millionaires and maybe it is because they are millionaires. But Ron saw a ball deep down in the water and started to use his telescopic retriever – some golfers have everything on their trolleys and that is why they have large power batteries and even radio control to guide their heap of possessions around the course.

I saw Ron stepping on the slippery plastic pond liner and then slowing slipping down. Next, I saw the panic in his eyes as he realised that he was going in. He carried on down and just as his head was submerging I went in after him. Sliding underneath his body we both now went under. Ron managed to get a bit of grip with his spiked golf shoes on the slopping bottom and made a lunge for the bank but could not get a grip on the slimy plastic bank lining. As he was going under for the second time I came up underneath him and held him straight and luckily the depth of the lake was such that we could stand with our heads above the water. Ron was now in a state of real panic and I now realised that he could not swim. Even if he could, it would have been difficult because of the heavy multipocket army type jacket he was wearing. I shouted at him that I could swim and told him not to move as I held him upright. He still tried to make another lunge for the bank but I held him steady. He now had more confidence in me and started to relax a little. I shouted to the other two golfers on the distant green, who could not see us and wondered what had happened. Eventually they arrived and with great difficulty using two ball retriever sticks and my willingness to go deep under water to get a foothold on the lake floor, we managed to heave big Ron out of the lake. A golf buggy arrived from the clubhouse and took Ron and me, soaked to the skin, back to the clubhouse. Just before Ron went into the clubhouse for a hot shower and to recover from shock, he "fished" out a couple of miniature brandy bottles from one of his jacket pockets and insisted we down them to celebrate the fact that he was still with us – but only just. I then made my way home for an earlier bath than expected.

Later I told a fellow club member about the incident and when he rang Ron to find out how he was his wife answered the phone. She knew nothing about her husband's close encounter with the next world. No comment!

Ron soon entered my life again but this time in a golfing context. In the tough foursome competition I mentioned earlier, Ron was my partner for our first match at Letchworth GC. He was selected as his home overlooked the course and even though he was a high handicapper no doubt he would have local knowledge of the course. Ron drove off from the first tee, a distance all of 120 yards. Our opponent, handicap 3, drove 260 yards. I then drove Ron's ball from just off the fairway another 200 yards with a seven wood. Our second opponent landed their ball 160 yds to the middle of the green. Ron drove our ball all of 90 yards and we were still 10 yards short of the green. I then discovered that Ron had never played the course before. Needleless to state we lost the hole and the match. Again no comment! Still Ron was a very likeable senior citizen and sadly lost his young married and only daughter to cancer not long afterwards.

GOLF AND URBAN SPRAWL.

It is extraordinary to think that when my mother was a member of Mill Hill GC that her club was only about ten miles from Piccadilly Circus and yet the club is bounded by major roads like the A1 and M1. It is only because the club was established in the late 19C that it was saved from 20C urban development. This is repeated across London, with golf clubs like Dulwich, Hampstead, Highgate, South Finchley all well within ten miles of central London. The golf clubs, along with the many parks and squares give green lungs to London, making it one of the greenest capital cities in the World.

CHAPTER 13

I NEED TO WRITE ABOUT KEVIN – KEVIN WHELAN (1956 – 2006), ONE IN A MILLION

It is difficult to talk about my family gatherings, parties and other adventures without mentioning Kevin Whelan who was the life and soul of many of these events.

Kevin was taken away as a child from his mother and has no memories of her. He was put into an orphanage in the south of Ireland. Kevin had to leave the orphanage at 14 years and got a job on the railways serving in the catering carriage. The one thing he did get from the orphanage was the ability to play the violin. After a few years on the railways, Kevin came to England and worked at a petrol station in London. Kevin did go back to Ireland to try to find his mother and looked around the Cork area. Some years later with the encouragement of his daughter Lisa he traced a half Brother John living in Macroom, Cork and a cousin in the west of Ireland. Through John he found out that his mother had married and had more children. In fact, she was still alive when Kevin first went to searching for her in Cork. Kevin was very disappointed to get so near and fail to find his mother. His half-brother had a tough time surviving when he left the orphanage and he was taken advantage of by the farmer he was put to work for at the tender age of 14 years.

John got on well with Kevin and visited him in Gravesend and kept in contact until Kevin's death.

He became a very close friend of my sister Dorothy and her husband Pat when he lived in Maidstone, Kent. Kevin worked as an area manager for the Oil retailer Conoco and eventually had his own garage in Gravesend just off the A2. Pat was one of the first to encourage Kevin to develop his musical talents and after a few years, Kevin was an accomplished singer, violin and keyboard player especially in the realm of Irish folk music. Kevin had real charisma and was well liked by his large circle of eclectic friends

He was always one of the main players on our rugby and other outings. I am still indebted to Kevin and his band for their contribution to my 40th and 50th Birthday parties and to our silver anniversary party. Kevin was booked to play at my 60th Birthday bash but by then he was dying from cancer.

THE SNOWDEN CLIMB – BY ICE PICK.

On an early February morning in the late 1980s I was picked up from my school in Cheshunt by Kevin, Pat and Keith; we were off for a few days to Snowdonia. As we sped up the motorway to the country music sounds of Joe Sun we all knew that this adventure was going to be a bit different from our usual rugby outings and all night parties. This trip would be more physical with the aims of abseiling and climbing up Snowden's Pig Pass to its summit – ice pick axes required.

Kevin had befriended Kieran Jones who was ex army and a physical fitness fanatic. They were very opposite in character and political outlook but Kevin's charisma and Irish music were too much for Kieran to resist. The IRA campaign in England was at its height and Snowdonia was a training ground for several army units and in particular The Irish Rangers. This unit was not allowed to serve in Northern Ireland because of their predominately-Orange Order membership. Kieran Jones was well aware of Kevin and my republican sympathies and made it his mission to be our protector. He would also be our adviser and safety officer on all mountain climbing matters and he would lead from the front. It would be a nice comfortable hotel in Betsy Coed for us and a tent in the garden for Kieran and his like-minded mate. Betysy Coed is one of the wettest places in Wales but all we had to contend with was a few snow showers and some ice patches on the Snowden climb.

We did not stay up too late in the bar on our first night as Kevin got his violin and piano fingers warmed up for later evenings. Next morning we went to a mountain and hiking shop to get our equipment sorted out, not forgetting the vital ice axes. Then it was off for a bit of abseiling that went well until we saw the local Welsh speaking farmer speeding towards us in the distance in his 4x4. The army and English tourists trampling all over their farms did not over please the locals. A bit of quick thinking from Kieran Jones was required; send the Irishman down to meet the irate farmer. I walked about a hundred yards away from the abseilers before I encountered the farmer and heard a diatribe in Welsh before he reverted to English. He wanted to know why we were trespassing never mind abseiling on his land and where did we come from. I said that I was from Ireland and this really stopped him in his tracks; but immediately added that the other lot were from the London area and some of them were military people and this was my first time in this beautiful part of the world. He asked me where about in Ireland I was from and told me he always wanted to go there. But catching sight of the "English" abseiling on his rock outlets he told me that he wanted them off his land now. He then relented a bit: within two hours. We got a result but I did wish that Kieran Jones had asked permission in the first place.

Next day was climbing day. We would make our way up the shorter more difficult climb along the "Pig Pass". There was the longer easier way up along near the train track and of course we could have taken the train if it had been running. As we crossed the gentler lower slopes through open valleys, Kevin opened up to the tune from the Sound of Music. Further up we got more serious and I did not like the consequences of slipping in the wrong direction. Soon my ice axe was my best friend along with our leader Kieran Jones. We had one very brave climber who led us all the way up Lester, a social friend of Kevin's from Gravesend. A couple of climbers passed us on the way down, when one of them tripped and somersaulted. I thought he was a goner but the rucksack on his back acted as a brake and stopped him sliding down to his possible early demise. Note, going down a mountain can be even more dangerous than going up has been the case for many mountaineers on Everest. With a great sense of relief we reached the summit which was shrouded in cloud and very cold. I assumed that Lester who had led us up would lead us down but dear Lester panicked when we reached the first steep descent. We had to help him down. Lester was a university graduate in science and I was astonished that he did not think about how he was going to get down the mountain and that this time he would see all those valleys ahead that he could fall into as he descended.

Back in the hotel, we prepared to celebrate our successful climb and it was not long after dinner that Kevin was on the piano belting out some great rebel songs. Soon we noticed that we had other guests and Kieran Jones was now on full alert. We made a rousing chorus to some of Kevin's songs and thought nothing of it until I went to the toilet where one young man with a northern Irish accent threatened to kill me. My response was that I would report him to his commanding officer who I noticed earlier hovering close to Kevin. I did not have to go to him as the good Colonel found me instead and quizzed me on whom and where we came from. I said they were just a lot of garage owners, architects, dentists, post office workers, dentists and teachers (me) from the London area. This information put him at ease and I hoped he had his way of handling the Irish Rangers who were now in our presence. I noticed that there was one woman of certain looks and mature age in the bar. Later one surprising friendly and drunken soldier told me that he had woken up one morning in bed with her and was horrified to see her in full daylight. The previous evening with drink on board and in dim light he thought she was beautiful. The evening ended peacefully and I was left with the feeling that, apart from a few, the Irish Rangers actually enjoyed our company and even the rebel music; but it is still a big thank you to the good Colonel.

There is a sad postscript to this adventure involving Kieran Jones. Keiran had plans to explore the Amazon and other parts of the world. Kieran was attracted to Catholicism and under the guidance of Kevin, Pat and others converted. He had a lovely tolerant wife and two children.

He failed to get into the London Marathon on the ballot; but this did not stop him running the course loaded with a rucksack full of weights during the night before the marathon guided by a Spanish friend Arturo. One of his party pieces was to place his head one stool and, fully stretched, place his feet on another stool. He then invited people to sit on his stomach and see how long he could hold them up. Sadly, Kieran died suddenly in his mid 40s from a brain aneurism.

Kevin's musical prowess greatly improved over the years and it was not long before he had his own band. At our parties in Hertford – and in Maidstone and other places – Kevin and co would arrive mid evening and leave late morning. He could play all night with a few breaks and still enjoy his pints and cigars. At my 50th, the band got off to a great start but they were now using electrical amplification and keyboards. Kevin's keyboard was playing up and he got wind of the fact that I had done my own electrics for the extension. Well he gave me hell. I checked out the electrical sockets, the main fuses and still Kevin's keyboard was intermittent. After a couple of hours, I thought that maybe it was not my electrics but Kevin's. I happened to push in and hold the main keyboard cable and it sprung into life. Kevin had used and moved the keyboard around so much that some of the connecting cables were much worn. Now it was my turn to give him grief. The party went on even later to make up for lost time.

Kevin's DIY skills were not quiet on a par with his musical skills. Just after one Christmas when he lived in Maidstone, Pat and I on our way to the pub popped into see if Kevin would come with us. We found him in the upstairs bathroom with bits of pipes on the floor not to mention the washbasin and the toilet itself. We could see that Kevin's plumbing would need another plumber to put it right. No doubt, his wife may have been pleased with his good intentions but not the results. It did not take much persuading to get Kevin to join – after first a few large brandies with his wife. Many hours later, I thought it would be a good idea to use the newly fallen snow on his lawn as a bed. This was another unforgettable night of many with Kevin.

One of my favourite memories and event with Kevin was when we attended the Tricycle Theatre in Kilburn, London. My sister Avril from Canada along with Dorothy, Pat and my wife Alice were present. We had one very special guest "Apple Bill" (the star of one of my school assemblies) who joined us from his lodging in nearby Harlesden. He was happy to prop up the theatre bar while we were at the show. The show was a wedding comedy and the audience were invited on stage to be part of the wedding party. At the interval the cast invited us for the cutting of the wedding cake in the bar area. Kevin and I met up with Apple Bill and all the men got pints of Guinness. There was time for a second and as we progressed with the wedding party back to the theatre, pints in hand, we were told that we could not take our drinks into the theatre. We protested that we were at a wedding party but to no effect. Kevin and I had no intention of surrendering our pints and so we turned back to join Apple Bill at the bar. We joined the rest of the party later on at a restaurant outside the theatre. This was one unexpected wedding that we enjoyed. Whilst on the subject of weddings we were at Liam Horgan's wedding the photograph session was a very complicated and time-consuming affair. It was not long before Kevin and I decided that time went a bit quicker at the hotel bar and this was a preamble to another of Kevin's late night music sessions, this time joined by Liam's brother Adrian on his violin.

Kevin had some issues with Conoco and his garage contract with them. Things were not as promised and legal proceedings were taken. This caused a lot of stress for Kevin and his family. He eventually got some sort of agreement or compensation, I am not sure of the exact details. The case took a lot out of Kevin and he lost a little of his old fire. Sadly Kevin was taken ill with terminal colon cancer. Despite the fatal prognosis Kevin got back some of his old sparkle for the remaining three years of his life. He refused to prolong his life with chemotherapy, opting for a quality of life instead. I remember meeting up with Kvin and Pat to hear the US country singer Joe Sun (played on the car disc player on the way to our Snowden adventure). I was surprised how well Kevin looked and in later conversation with Joe Sun concluded that the singer was taking far more pills than Kevin to keep him going.

KEVIN'S DAY OUT IN LONDON TO THE TUNE OF HANDEL AND A MEETING WITH DR DEATH.

In 2007 I was back at The City of London Girls' School situated at the centre of the Barbican. I mentioned this to Kevin and we agreed that it might be a good idea to spend a day in the city. Kevin and his friend Paul Gannon arrived at my school earlier than expected and were show around the reception area where a lot of the girls work was on display until I arrived. They were astounded by the quality of work and the school's facilities and location. After a quick tour of Milton's church St Boltop's next door to the school and just outside the still visible Roman City Wall we went for a morning coffee and early cognac in a very nice pub overlooking the school. Kevin saw some of the girls walking past carrying their musical instruments and commented how lucky and privileged they were. Upon reflection, of course, he was right and they certainly did not have to start life in an Irish orphanage.

We looked around Spitalfield and at Wallace's memorial and made our way towards Bloomsbury where we had a good pub lunch and good banter with some post office technicians who had finished their shift. We stayed longer than anticipated so it was a taxi to my main destination for the day, The Coram Foundation.

Thomas Coram was a rather cantankerous early 18th century shipwright who spent some time in Taunton, Massachusetts shipbuilding – his clapperboard house still exists. On his return to London he was taken aback on his early morning walk to his office by the dung mounds and the dead infant babies that were put out on them overnight. He decided that he would seek Royal Patronage and support from well-known people of the day to set up an independent foundling hospital. This was unusual as most children's charities were church controlled at the time. Against the odds, Coram succeeded in building his Georgian style Foundling Hospital and playing fields near Bloomsbury which open in 1745mm. Handel donated the rights of his Messiah and Hogarth many of his paintings to the foundation. The Royals, the rich and the famous visited the Foundling Hospital on Sunday afternoons to hear music played by the foundlings and to view the works of art and attend Handel concerts. In fact, the Foundling Hospital became de facto the first institution to have an Art Gallery.

Not all mothers were successful in having their infants admitted. Admittance was down to chance and if they selected a black ball from the bag their child was not admitted in other words they were "black balled". Some of the Governors were Masons and this method of selection may have had something to do with Masonic practice. Surprisingly the Foundling Hospital survived the Victorian with its puritanical attitude to "fallen women, prostitution and orphans".

I did worry if this was the right place to take Kevin in view of his own experience in an orphanage but he was enthralled by the history and life of the foundlings over the centuries. I arranged for a personal guide – surprisingly from Sweden – to show us around. Kevin was moved by the glass cabinets with the trinkets left for the foundlings by their distraught mothers to remind them of a previous life that they would never know again. After a tour of the Art Gallery, we went to the top floor to the Handel Room where we sat in deep leather armchairs, put on headphones and individually selected our own excerpts from the works of Handel. After half an hour, we descended the stairs and left the building in silence.

It was now Guinness time with a difference. A taxi to Covent Garden for a quick pint and then to a restaurant for evening dinner. This was going to be a surprise for Kevin as we were going to Rules, London's oldest restaurant which sources its own food from its own estate in the north of England. The menu reflected the seasons and what type of Game from the estate was available. In the past Crown Princes dined here in private rooms upstairs along the Stars down the centuries. Before I arrived at the restaurant I told Kevin that he could still have a Guinness before the meal. Signed in and ushered to our seats I immediately ordered 3 pints of Guinness to Kevin's amazement. Five minutes later his Guinness arrived in a Silver Tankard. As we inspected the menu I knew that Kevin would like a good red wine and to his surprise I ordered from the wine waiter a magnum of Mouton Cadet from the French Rothschild Estate in Bordeaux. Apart from this being a good wine I had very tenuous link as far as I had visited the estate with my son Ragnar on a trip to Bordeaux and also taught a young De Rothschild at St Paul's Girls' school.

We were all pleased with our menu selections and the excellent service. As we were leaving we had a look at the rooms upstairs and when I went to the toilet I got talking to a regular customer from Essex. Without asking he showed me his gold credit card with the name "Dr Death" on it. Paul Gannon came over to have a look and as we were well oiled we thought that Kevin would see the funny side of meeting this customer who was so proud of his name. Dr Death came downstairs with us and was very forthcoming in introducing himself to Kevin and we all engaged in some deathly banter. It was agreed by all that Dr Death would be visiting all present eventually and on his terms.

It was a great day out and I think greatly appreciated by Kevin.

I did have another day out with Kevin, Pat and Paul visiting my old haunt Hampstead. This trip included a trip to Kenwood House and a walk on the Heath. Kevin did well to keep walking with us, especially up Fitzjohn's Avenue and on other hills around Hampstead. Our day out was memorable for its finale in the George, a well know Gay Pub. We entered full of "spirit" into the Pub Quiz and I got the feeling some of the ladies present were getting a little jealous of all the attention Kevin was receiving.

Kevin was a great friend of his local hospice. He entertained and played music for the patients. Paul Gannon and Kevin did have an extra incentive for attending the hospice – the drinks trolley was circulated around for everyone to help himself or herself.

Kevin lived to have a great 60th Birthday and managed to join his band to play some great tunes for all present. Only a couple of months before he died I got a phone call from him, still cheerful, but we both knew that this was his final farewell to me. Kevin died in the Hospice in December 2007 and my sister Dorothy and her husband Pat and his immediate family were with him to end.

His funeral mass and burial took place on a cold January day. His Guitar, painted in colours of the Irish Tricolour rested on his coffin.

CHAPTER 14

A LIFE IN AND AROUND POLITICS

Very few children escape the politics of their parents and I am no exception. My parents always voted Labour although in Irish politics my mother was Fine Gael that has its origins in the pro-treaty with Britain in 1921 and tends to be the party of small landowners and farmers. Fianna Fail was the party supported by my father in Ireland and has its origins in the anti-treaty and pro republican party founded by DeValera. Ireland had an agrarian economy up until modern times in contrast to Britain that has a large industrial working class. Added to the mix in Irish politics was the power of the Catholic Church, which was essentially conservative and supported the Irish establishment of the small middle class. When my parents moved to England in the 1950s, they viewed themselves as moderate Labour Party supporters and always voted Labour in elections.

My political awareness in England was raised by my involvement in student protest movement, the growing problems in Northern Ireland and membership of the university debating union.

Union Politics

I "inherited" the political beliefs of my parents and like them voted Labour. It is often said that if you are not a communist when you are young there is something wrong with your heart and if you are still one when you are older there is something wrong with you head. In the main people tend to get more conservative when they get older. During their life most people acquire property and possessions including family and inevitable are more protective and risk aversion. The British Conservative party is very pro home ownership and introduced schemes like 'the right to buy' your own council house and in 2015 the right to buy your own Housing Association home. They know that the more people own the more conservative they will become.

I have become more conservative as I got older and even voted Liberal Democrat in a recent General Election. However my political beliefs are based strongly on social and economic equality of opportunity. The wealth of the nation should be used for the benefit of all. That is why I could never support educational selection at age 11. This gave a minority a head start over the majority even though all pay taxes. I object to the 11+ on moral grounds as well. Supporters claim that selection allows social mobility – yes, it does for the select few.

During my teaching career I have always been a member of a teaching union or association although these have not been overtly political. Their main aims have been to provide legal aid, health and safety support, salary and pension rights and curriculum development. Unfortunately some unions are overtly political and are more a political party than a representative of their member's working interests.

When I was teaching in London I joined The National Association School Teachers (NAS) which supported a career pay structure for teachers. The majority union was the National Union of Teachers (NUS) that represented mostly primary school teachers and wanted equal pay rises across the board irrespective of any management structure, They also had a left wing activists section. After only two years of teaching I was called out on strike by the NAS and had 3 days off school without pay. Upon reflection, it seems odd that it was the more conservative union that was on strike while the left wing union stayed in. I am pleased that over the years the teaching profession now has a pay structure that reflects the experience, education and level of management responsibility.

At Finchley Grammar School I attended two NAS Easter conferences, one at Scarborough and one in Torquay. We gave up a week of our Easter holiday to attend but it was a great experience beside the seaside. When I went up to Scarborough I did not speak on any conference motions due to ignorance of the issues and lack of experience. I found the evening sessions in the bar stimulating in terms of debate and it was there that the real learning took place and agreement reached on the matters of the day. Things were very different later at Torquay where the Barnet delegation had a visit one evening at our dinner table from one no other than our constituency MP Margaret Thatcher. These were the days of "Thatcher the milk snatcher" resulting from her Education Department ending free school milk in primary schools. This acquired reputation had no effect on Thatcher, the thick skinned, determined and always right consummate politician. She still knew that all politics stems from local politics and made sure to cultivate her constituents – the fact that most of us at the table were Labour supporters made no difference to her.

This time I did speak in the hall to conference on the subject of raising the school leaving age from 15 to 16, which I strongly supported. I remember saying that it was better for 15 year olds to be at school than being unemployed and hearing the clicking of the heels of their hob nail boots on the cobbled streets of Newcastle. Later in the bar colleagues told me that part of my speech was televised on the evening TV Nationwide programme. Clearly I had hit on a good "sound bite" without realising it. Today political speeches contain key sound bites to catch the short attention span of Joe Public. I would have liked to move up the power echelons of my union, but growing family and promotions in my teaching career had to come first.

LOCAL POLITICS

I still had the political bug and when I moved to Reading, I joined the local branch of the Labour Party. Reading at that time was in the main conservative but there were some pockets of strong labour support in the older parts of the town. Unfortunately my branch of the party was based on the northern outskirts and was part of the South Oxfordshire parliamentary constituency which was strongly blue and included well to-do towns like Henley and Marlow in the constituency. Our local Labour Party had a lively membership with a traditional grass roots Welsh contingent. The Welsh have formed the core of the Labour party since its inception. As mostly Methodist in religion and non-conformist, they were not part of the established churches and thought outside the box. They have a strong moral and social compass for the needs of ordinary people and Welsh Labour MPs have played prominent roles in establishing the NHS and comprehensive education for all. One particular older Welsh member took a liking to me and after a few meetings of our branch suggested that I stand for parliament against the local conservative MP the well known Michael Heseltine. I would have no chance of overturning Heseltine's very large majority but he reasoned I could stand up to him in terms of debating and promoting labour policies. In order to insure my selection as a parliamentary candidate he put my name forward to attend the Annual Labour Party Conference at Blackpool. Party conferences are held in early autumn before the new session of parliament but unfortunately for me they were in school term time. I asked my Head teacher to support my application for a week off to attend the conference. He was not happy, pointing out that I had a Head of Science job to do. Also if granted it would be without pay, a problem because of our large mortgage and two preschool boys to support. After a lot of consideration, I decided that I could not go to the disappointment of my Welsh mentor and that was the end of my national political ambitions. It was upsetting to think that most of the delegates at the conference would be there on full pay and positively supported by their employers. Later the same Head teacher refused to support my application for a year sabbatical to study for a MEd degree which I had to do part time over two years travelling up to London twice a week for lectures. Most of the people on the course had been granted full sabbaticals. I was at a great disadvantage because the full timers got first access for all the books and articles recommended by the lecturers. Fortunately I managed to use the facilities of the Education Library at Reading University for some of my research projects. Sometimes in the lottery of life, those that have get even more and those that have little get even less.

HERTFORD COUNCIL

A few years later in 1981 when we moved to Hertford I joined the local Labour Party. The local party veteran was one Henry Sergeant, a town and county councillor for some years. Hertford and surrounds was and is solid blue. Henry asked me to stand in his own Sele ward for the town and East Herts councils. This was a generous offer as the area contained a large well-kept council estate and the only area in Hertford that regularly returned a Labour majority. Our election agent was the venerable Peter Wood. Peter was old middle class Labour. He went to Cambridge University in the 1930s and the university had a strong Socialist Club that invited nationally known speakers. The future PM Clement Attlee addressed the society on several occasions. No doubt Peter as a young socialist was greatly influenced by socialist philosophy and activities at Cambridge, so much so that today in 2016 in his 100th year, he and his wife are still committed Labour Party members. Over the years I helped Peter with party fund raising activities and at his behest put by name forward for election at town and county level with no hope of being elected. The first time I stood for election with Henry I had a real chance of holding on to the Labour seat that I was defending. Unfortunately Thatcherism was on the rise and her promise to support the sale of council houses helped win the day for the Tories and I lost the "safe seat" by a couple of hundred votes. Labour was wiped out at town and county level with Henry the only Labour councillor left on the town and East Herts councils. I have one pertinent memory when out canvassing. As I knocked on one door, a young woman rushed out, car keys in hand, apologised for not stopping but wished me luck and said, "I used to vote Labour but I am all right now".

Labour did have a revival under Tony Blair and even gained control of Hertford Town Council but by then my political flame had gone out. The recent council elections in 2015 saw Labour completely wiped out on Hertford and East Herts councils. I recently asked a long-standing conservative councillor "what's it like operating under a one party system – a bit like North Korea maybe?" It was clear that he would like to have some opposition councillors but our winner takes all system unfortunately leads to total party domination in some areas. Even our national elections are all about winning marginal seats and the safe seats are taken for granted. Not good politics in the long-term. My final flirt with politics was in 2014 when I met the former Labour leader Ed Miliband on a train from Oxford to London. On hearing that I was a former member of the party, he used my iphone to phone my daughter to ask her to get me to rejoin. We did not discuss issues and he was obsessed with party membership. He lost the subsequent General Election and at least I had a nice photo of the two of us that now has lost any value it might have had.

MY CURRENT POLITICAL STATE OF MIND.

As I approach my 70th year I have come to the conclusion that the poor will always be with us but their lot will be much better than in previous generations. The poor in the West today have relatively cheap technology – large flat interactive screen TV, iphones with advanced camera/video facilities, internet and access to all kinds of film and music – that even the very rich would not have had in the previous generation. They have some access to a large variety of cheap food from all over the world. Housing is a problem in the south of England but the quality of modern social housing in terms of heating insulation and household appliances is light years ahead of what it used to be. The rich and even richer will always be with us. One does not have to build factories and manufacture large quantities of goods to sell to get seriously rich today like the cotton and steel mill owners of yesterday. A clever iphone app can make you millions in a year or two with few overheads or large workforce to worry about. The founders of the social media Facebook were billionaires before they were thirty years old. Over fifty percent of young people go on to higher Education. By contrast I know some local pensioners in Hertfordshire who have never been outside the south east of England.

The main gripe of some young people today is that they cannot get on the housing ladder. My sister got on the housing ladder in 1964 with a council mortgage. They got a semi-detached house on a new estate in Maidstone and my brother in-law Pat had to get up at 5.30am to take the train for his Post Office work in north London. He was lucky if he was home by 8pm. The house they got had no central heating, no wall insulation, no double-glazing, no garage, no down stairs toilet and a back garden with not a single plant in it. Today they still live in the same house and over the years have made costly improvements to bring it up to the standard of a modern new build house. Their generation and mine are viewed by the next as the generation of baby boomers who have it all.

I have with age become more cynical about politics and politicians. The problem is that I cannot see an alternative. The extraordinary progress of China under a one party communist system and one that has taken capitalism and profit as its modus operandum was a great surprise to me. If you can put human rights to one side, then it is a model for success. Singapore is another one party state success. As for the Arab world, the removal of the dictators Gadaffi and Sadam Hussain has led to terrible civil wars and the failure of the "Arab springs".

In short, it would appear that the western democratic model is not a one fit all success. In Britain we find that with continuing economic and social development the gap in policies between the main political parties is narrowing. In previous times Britain had an Empire and a disadvantaged large working class to mange. Today government are micromanaging what we teach in schools and even down to what we can and cannot eat. We are urged to think cancer with every glass of wine we drink and to think diabetes with every spoonful of sugar in our tea!

I will always continue to support policies that promote equal social, educational and welfare opportunities and foreign cooperation, but I am no longer a diehard socialist and I never was a dyed in the wool Tory.

CHAPTER 15

ANOTHER RUNG ON THE HOUSING LADDER AND GERMANY CALLING

In 1975 I received a significant pay rise- back dated – after a long overdue review of teaches' salaries – which at last took account of school management structures and associated responsibilities. I had also taken on part-time evening lecturing to ONC level at Reading College of Technology. In the 1970s mortgage lending was strictly based on a fixed multiple of annual salary. We were interested in a new four-bed detached house in west Reading. The builder had gone bust as the housing market rapidly cooled off. We sold our house for about £10500 (bought at £6800) and we were able to put down a deposit of about 25% on the new house that was on the market for £ 16,500. We needed a mortgage broker to help us secure a mortgage. The broker visited the bursar at Reading College to check out my part-time earnings and my total earnings just about qualified for the new mortgage needed.

NEXT STEP GERMANY.

Alice did very well in her A 'Levels and got a place at Reading University to study German and Linguistics. She got a grade A in Economics in one year and she considered a degree in Economics. However, she wanted to be a teacher but

Economics was a minority sixth form subject and there were more teaching posts available for modern language subjects. I was keen on Alice studying German because she would have to study abroad for a year and this would help us to make contacts with Germans on a social, cultural and educational level. As it turned out, I was right.

In the summer of 1977 we travelled as a family to West Germany to find Alice and the boys a place to stay for the academic year that was a requirement of her university course. Reading University had links with the well-established Bonn University, and Bonn was now the capital of West Germany – the capital reverted to Berlin after reunification in 1989.

Just before we left for Germany my next door neighbour told me that Maidenhead, where I worked, was twinned with Bad Godesburg (partnerstadt), a well off suburb of Bonn along the Rhine. We loaded up our old Ford Cortina with camping gear and essential clothing and supplies for their yearlong stay. Somehow we managed to squeeze the two boys (now aged 8 and 6) onto the back seat. We found a campsite along the Rhine just south of Bonn where we set up our MFI frame tent and early next morning we woke up to what appeared to be an earthquake. The ground shook accompanied by a thundering noise. I rushed out of the tent to be greeting by several horses on a full gallop past our tent. In the days that followed on this campsite we did not need an early morning alarm clock we had our galloping four horses of the apocalypse instead. Maybe the appearance of these horses was sign of the trials and tribulations that lay ahead of us as we tried to find accommodation for Alice and the boys.

To find social accommodation in Germany you need to have a permanent address in the country and in the municipality where the accommodation is located – a campsite did not qualify. We managed to find the address of the person who organised the German side of the twin link with Maidenhead, one called Herr Ohm who was a senior teacher in the local gymnasium in Bad Godesburg. After we did some wining and dining, he agreed to let us use his address as our place of residence – a good start. We looked at some rooms to let but these were very unsuitable for a mother and two children and many of the neighbouring rooms were occupied by non-German speaking Turkish guest workers. Alice visited the student's union at the university and happened to get talking to a young couple with a baby daughter. It transpired that they had finished their studies and were moving out of their two bed council flat and thought that Alice as a foreign student with two children would have priority in getting the flat. They were wrong. The manager of the block of flats was from Saxony in East Germany and behaved as if he owned the place. The man at district council level that we had to deal with was no better. Both of them wanted stamped "papers" from all sorts of departments before they would even entertain our application. Council offices closed to the public at 3pm and that made it difficult for us to get the completed forms returned as we move from one office to another across Bonn. Eventually we collected all the forms needed and headed for the British Embassy.

At the British Embassy the person that we needed to speak with was away – no surprise there. Whilst the deputy showed some sympathy he would not stamp our papers of residence as supported by Herr Ohm. Next stop, the Norwegian Embassy. This was a very tearful meeting between now a desperate Alice and a very sympathetic Norwegian women official. Despite tears all round no agreement to sign our residency papers was forthcoming. Finally, I had enough and had a moment of inspiration – the Irish Embassy.

At the Embassy we met a smart young official who immediately understood our problem. First orange juice for our boys and coffee for us before he went to make some phone calls. On his return he stamped all the key documents needed. Job done.

We returned to the municipal council and the official was surprised that we had all the forms stamped and muttered something "like African Embassies". We choose to ignore him.

Equally surprised was the Saxon estate manager but German officials always act on officially stamped documents and the flat was hours. We gave him a carton of duty free cigarettes to keep him sweet in case Alice had any problems with the flat. Later we met up with the German couple who had told us about the flat for lunch and they formerly introduced us to their lovely blond baby daughter Christiania. The parent's names were Hannah and Ludwin. Nearly forty years later we are still in contact with the family. Sadly, Ludwin died at 46 from a congenital heart condition. Their marriage was one made in heaven and it took Hannah years to recover from her husband's sudden death. They have four children and three of them: Christina, Barbara and Mattie stayed as teenagers with us in Hertford and attended the local school sixth form. They have all obtained professional qualification; Christina is a Doctor of Psychology. I remember Christina watching a TV documentary in our house about the diary of Anne Frank, the young Jewish girl who died in the Bergen-Belsen concentration camp. As the programme progressed Christina curled more tightly up in her armchair and at the end of the programme told me "I hate being German". To think that I had held this lovely blond innocent baby in my arms 16 years earlier and now she had to suffer for the crimes of her forbears. Modern Germany has come a long way since 1945 and in 2015 Chancellor Angela Merkil was almost a lone figure in welcoming the desperate refugees from war torn Syria.

We now had the task of furnishing the flat and finding a school for our sons. When a flat is vacated in Germany you are expected to repaint the walls and ceilings, disconnect all light fittings and leave the place empty of all furniture including kitchen fittings. Alice bought a second hand bunk bed and got some kitchen furniture from Ilse, Hannah's sister and who would become a lifelong friend. At that time once a month in the locality people put out at designated locations on the streets any old furniture and electrical goods that they wanted to get rid of – called Sperrmull. We managed to find some a coffee table, chairs and a big chest freezer. I surprised myself by lifting the chest freezer on to the roof of the Cortina car and getting it back to the flat in one piece. Neighbours helped me take it up the stairs to the first floor flat. We bought a cooker advertised in a local paper and my neighbour was keen to help me connect it to the mains. After he received a couple of electric shocks his enthusiasm for the task rapidly diminished. I discovered that the Germans use an industrial three phase electrical system and eventually worked out how to connect it up. The area we lived in was a brand new development called St Augustine on the northern outskirts of Bonn. We had no problem getting our sons into the nearby school and I remember taking my eldest son Ragnar to school on his first day. As the classroom door opened his head bent a little and he gritted his teeth as he saw some thirty German kids looking at him. I really felt for him as he did not speak German and had the added difficulty of coping with a different writing system.

Soon I would have to return alone to Reading. Hannah had given her sister Ilse's address as a contact. Ilse was finishing her course training to teach English. She turned out to be a great help to Alice and the boys. When Alice had afternoon lectures she dropped the boys off at Ilse's flat where they could play with Ilse's young son Jan. German schools and nurseries finish early afternoon so without Ilse's support Alice would have to pay for a minder for the boys, although or next door neighbour helped out on occasion.

CHRISTMAS IN GERMANY

During Alice's stay in Germany I visited them for the autumn half-term week and two weeks at Christmas. Our neighbours had good reason to remember my Christmas visit. I arrived a few days before Christmas and was surprised to find no Christmas lights or Christmas trees lit up and set about putting it right at least for our flat. I bought a nice Norwegian Spruce- on

Alice's orders- and lighting decorations. When I carried the tree upstairs to our flat I had a following of local kids behind me. They sensed that this Englander was going to do things differently. As they waited outside the open door of the flat I fuelled their expectation by giving them sweets. They watched open eyed as we decorated the tree Norwegian style and their eyes nearly popped out of their heads when I turned all the Christmas lights on. Later my family and I walked around the area in the few days before Christmas and we could not help noticing that we had gained local celebrity status. The local kids had told their parents about the Englanders lighting up their flat and the lights were seen twinkling and flashing through the large windows of our second floor flat in the gloom of winter darkness throughout the estate. Even strangers were now bowing and wishing us Frohliche Weihnachten. The big mistake that I had made was not to wait until Christmas Eve morning to decorate and light the tree. In Germany and in most of northern Europe the main Christmas celebration is on Christmas Eve unlike Christmas Day in Britain and Ireland. I can only think that our neighbours concluded that these Englanders were so happy to be in Germany for Christmas that they could not wait until Christmas Eve to light up their tree. They were probably impressed how quick the Englander took up the custom of the German Prince Albert's gift of a Christmas tree to his beloved Queen Victoria and popularised by the carol "O Tannenbaum". It certainly kicked off an early Christmas to the delight of the local children. Just before New Year, Hannah and Ludwin invited us to a very grand house for a party. There I saw the ultimate in Christmas trees, one lit up by real candles delicately balanced on the branches with coloured paper napkins for extra affect. We left the party at 2am and I can only hope someone remembered to put out the candles!

In late August 1977 as I prepared for the long drive back to Reading, this time alone. It was not easy to leave my wife and children in a country that I was still getting to know but I felt that the key problems of accommodation and the boys schooling had been solved. Just days before I left I wondered why most of the neighbours were blasting out Elvis Presley songs on their record players and soon discovered that the King of Rock and Roll was dead. Elvis had been a big part of my late teenage years and memories came back of hearing him on the jukebox in a local cafe with Alice when I first visited Norway in 1967. Then, as now, I was leaving my beloved behind.

HOME ALONE WITH MY NEW LODGERS

When I got back to Reading I contacted local schools to see if I could find some newly qualified teachers to the area who needed rented accommodation and ended up with a Welsh Music teacher, a Welsh PE teacher and a female English Maths teacher and all were smokers. At times on a Sunday afternoon, it was difficult to see the TV screen through the cloud of smoke they produced. This was their peak smoking period and was probably due to worries about going back to school on Monday morning. The good news was that they liked to party and on one occasion we went to a real ale pub that served ten different ales. In the mid 1970s lager was then becoming the drink of choice driven by a big advertising campaign. CAMERA – the campaign for real ale – was set up to try to save the real ale business. At the pub the male teachers, large of body and belly, decided to pint their way in order down the list of ten real ales which ranged in strength from 3.8% to 5.5% alcohol by volume. I decided to go on half pints down the list and the female teacher would drive us home. I was surprised that after eight pints the larger of the two teachers had to stop to throw up outside before resuming. The other teacher Vernon, got through the list and I finished my five and one half pints, feeling very happy with the world. Later at our house Vernon managed to peel potatoes and make chips whilst almost comatose.

Vernon was also addicted to pub one-arm bandits and sex. He invited me to London to the cinema. It was only when

I got there and after he signed in under a false name to an underground club in Soho that I realised he was an addict for pornographic films. Later he went up to London, a ninety mile round trip, on his own. At weekends his girl friend from Wales would arrive and I would in effect have four lodgers in the house. I discovered that she was a tax inspector so had to keep her on board in case she reported me as an illegal landlord.

SCHOOL – THE DAY JOB

Back at school there were big changes. A block of eight new laboratories was built, new science staff were appointed for a growing school that was now 1100 pupils in total. As stated earlier, we made some good appointments. Geoff Cooper, a Cambridge graduate as the new Head of Chemistry became a close friend of mine. He was a county level squash player and I ended up joining his squash club in Maidenhead. I liked playing squash because you really got a real work out during the 45-minute session, much more so than tennis. It also helped with my football fitness, but one should never play squash to get fit, but should get fit to play squash and this I did by going for runs.

We had very good working and social relationship with our laboratory technicians. One of our technicians, Maureen was a very good cook and invited us to her house for dinner parties. She had already split up from her husband in rather acrimonious circumstances. Later Geoff graduated from a social to a more intimate relationship with Maureen.

The science curriculum was under a radical revision. There were new Nuffield and Schools Council supported courses that we put in place. Some people think that all classes in comprehensive schools are in mixed ability groups; but we had complete freedom on how we grouped the pupils. In science we started the first year in mixed ability groups and when we got to know the ability level of the pupils opted for two equal top ability, four middle ability groups and equal lower ability groups. The lower ability groups were smaller in number than the top ability groups in order to help to give them more support with their individual needs. In addition the school had special needs staff to give further support. It was possible for a pupil to be in a top set for English and French, middle sets for Physics and Geography and a lower set for Maths. Each year we reviewed every pupil's progress and set changes were made if appropriate. There was no one size fits all as often claimed by the supporters of Grammar schools.

I have always believed that good teachers should make every effort to keep their knowledge up to date and with this in mind I engaged on some research into Energy Analysis supported by Dr Pete Chapman of The Open University. In the early 1970s we had an international energy crisis when a middle east cartel restricted oil supplies. We had become not just petrol heads but energy junkies with the US the lead junkie. It was extraordinary to think that the US had one of the biggest oil and gas domestic supplies but had come to rely even more on oil from the Middle East. The heating insulation in most houses in the UK was no better than it was in Victorian times and most of our national grid energy came from coal. The price of goods did not reflect the energy needed to manufacture them and this was at the core of energy analysis. Just how much energy does it take to make a loaf of bread or a milk bottle? In the case of the milk bottle, progress had been made in so far as the milk bottle was a quarter of the weight and stronger than a decade previously and therefore took less energy to make it. It would make sound economic sense to have the fixed unit of energy "the Joule" as a guide to the value of goods rather than just the pound or the dollar. Linked to this energy research was the need to promote solar energy and reduce our dependence on nuclear energy. The latter because of safety and nuclear waste disposal issues. I wrote some articles for a national science education magazine but my life was too occupied to get time to do enough research for a PhD.

As a science department we got involved in writing and trialling new material for a GCE AS Level Science in Society project. The idea was to try and broader the knowledge of sixth form students. The leader of the project was John Lewis, Head of Science at Malvern College and an Officer in The Association for Science Education. Two university science departments in Scotland and England supported the project. We had many a pleasant weekends at Malvern College working on the project and never failed to dine well on Saturday evenings rounded off with the best malt whiskis – guided by the Scottish contingent and occasionally we did get to walk the beautiful Malvern Hills nearby.

THE GERMANS ARE COMING. THE 21-YEAR-OLD SIX-FOOT GERMAN GUNHILDA ENTERS INTO MY LIFE.

Early on at her course at Bonn University Alice met a German girl, Mechthild (Mekki) who wanted to spend some time at an English University studying English. Mekki wanted to improve her English as a matter of some urgency and found out about Alice through a flat mate of hers who was on the same course as Alice. Mekki, who was and still is a very outgoing person, went to see Alice at her flat in St Augustine, Menden. She remembers meeting our two boys and recalls Fingal always smiling and Ragnar prone to crying – news to me! Alice told her to contact Reading University for a temporary place on one of their English and History courses. It was not long before a six-foot tall blond German girl arrived on my doorstep. Her boyfriend Johannes – six foot six inches – drove her in a classic VW beetle from Bonn. He was studying History and Sport at Bonn University and hoping to become a teacher. They arrived in mid February at the end of the German semester and fortunately Alice and the boys were home for a short stay. Two of my lodgers had left but the third, Vernon and his weekend girlfriend would stay until the end of April. Alice, Johannes and the boys went back to Germany by train leaving Mekki and her VW Beetle in my care. As Mekki's circle of friends developed at the university my phone never stopped ringing- no mobiles in those days. Eventually Mekki and I could not cope with all the calls and it was her decision not to release the house number to any more men wanting to date her. After about two months with me she moved into Sibley Hall, one of the Universities halls of residence. Her social life escalated further and I can remember going with her along with my close friend Charles Bond to a dance at Sibley Hall. We were the only white people present. The music was all Reggae and I enjoyed the first hour or so. After another two hours of Reggae I never wanted to hear any more of it for at least ten years.

The ever enterprising Mekkie got a job in a local pub, that might not have improved her received English pronunciation but did improve her knowledge of real ale and her drinking capacity. The male customers wanted to buy her the ladies drink Babysham but were astonished when she said she wanted to go native and preferred a whisky or an ale. Back in Germany Johannes and Alice went to see The Dubliners- a very popular Irish folk music group at the Beethoven Halle in Bonn, named in honour of Beethoven's birthplace. Not many folk groups get to play in the national concert hall.

Mekkie is an only child born on a small farm near the Ruhr in north Germany. Her father Franz fought on the Russian front in the war and was lucky to get back to West Germany ahead of the Russian advance. Mekki's mother is a very extravert women and I was soon to discover this when her parents and Mekki's first cousin arrived on my doorstep in May 1977. They had never been to England before and they only came because of wanting to see their only daughter and to check that she was safe living in a house with a married Irishman and a strange lodger! They arrived in a Ford Granada and to my delight with 16 bottles of German wine. I had learnt some German at evening classes so we were able to communicate in basic German – noch ein Bier Bitte und kein Problem.

Soon after they arrived Franz heard a very loud noise over our house and looked a little nervous. Maybe it brought back events from the Russian front. I told him to look up eastwards and he saw a large swanlike object coming towards us and heading west. It was the supersonic aircraft Concorde heading for New York. Passenger supersonic flights had started only a year earlier in 1976 and this was the first time Franz had seen Concorde. I could see that he was taken back by this Franco-British development and probably realised just how much German aviation had fallen behind since the war. Franz had trouble with his car's engine overheating. My solution was to take the thermostat out as they did not need the car heater in the summer and stop water leakage by cutting out a cardboard gasket as a sealant. Franz recognised the adjustable Stanley made wrench that I used. The wrench was invented by the English engineer Richard Clyburn in 1842 and is know in Germany as an "English Key". Franz was a skilful handyman and my little bit of car mechanics impressed him, we were now best mates and it was soon time to visit the pub.

One evening we went to "The Jack of Both Sides" pub in east Reading mainly because it regularly featured live music. There was a bit of a problem, the pub had a large West Indian clientele and Maria and Franz had never met any black people before. Maria loved the music and loved to dance. One black customer often danced on his own – I had seen him many times before. Maria thought this strange that a man should have to dance on his own and immediately decided to change things. The man was astonished to find himself swept off his feet by a large white German woman. There was an almighty roar from all the other West Indians as they swirled around the dance floor. Franz was ashamed and shrank almost under the table. The more they danced the greater the cheering. Afterwards a host of colourful West Indians surrounded our table to kiss and congratulate Maria. Well Maria may not have met any black men in her life before but she made up for it at the Jack of Both Sides. I am not sure if Franz ever recovered or forgot that memorable evening. A few days later Mekki took them to a German Beer Keller inWindsor. I was fast asleep when they arrived home in very high spirits at 1am and had to get up and join them for a nightcap.

A few years later we visited Maria and Franz at their farm in north Germany and discovered that Maria had a way with the Boar pigs. Some Boars had difficulty with their love making after all it is not easy to direct a corkscrew shaped penis to its target. No problem, a quick helping hand from Maria guaranteed hitting the target. Franz gave the boys a run around on his tractor and later took us to a shooting festival with copious supplies of beer and sausages although I was not too sure about the shooting bit. The ever-generous Maria made sure that we all had large quantities of her homemade sausage for breakfast, dinner and supper and sometimes even in between. I am now on statins to reduce my cholesterol level!

IN THE FAST LANE

Fortified with sausages, Franz took the boys and me for a spin in his now fixed Ford Granada. A trip in a car with Franz on a German autobahn was the nearest one could get to experiencing what it was like to being in a Grand Prix only scarier as he competed with the Porsches for the outside lane of only two at well over 100mph. Later when Franz was over 80 years old and suffered from dementia, his daughter Mekki had to hide the car keys to stop him heading out on to the autobahns around Bonn. When I went back in the summer of 1977 to bring Alice and the boys home I decided to go and test out the world famous Nurnberg Ring Grand Prix circuit about 50 miles west of Bonn in the Eifel Hills. We paid our money and set off in our underpowered 1300cc Ford Cortina, with suitcases strapped to the roof and the boys sitting in the back with no safety belts on what I thought would be a lap of about 3 miles maximum. As we headed out into the countryside, I saw the circuit stretching miles into the hills in the distance. I got up to a speed of about 90mph on a downhill section only to be passed by motorbikes and cars going over 120mph. We could hear the cases on the roof shifting as we went round the bends, but we had to keep going in the hope that we were not hit from the rare by passing cars and motorbikes. I finished the twelve-mile circuit in a lather of sweat and never again would I venture on to a racing circuit. I cannot remember what our boys thought of the experience but they never forgot it and now as adults they are not petrol heads owning speedy cars- I wonder why not?

CHAPTER 16

OUR YEARS OF CAMPING BEGIN – 40 YEARS ON THE ROAD.

THE TENT PERIOD – IT STILL HAS NOT QUITE ENDED.

In the 1960s Ireland the idea of going camping was anathema to most people. A bit of weekend camping for boy scouts was acceptable, otherwise camping was the sole preserve of Gypsies or more generously "the travellers". The great famine in the mid 19C displaced hundreds of thousands of people from their homes. Most of them immigrated, died or ended up as homeless travellers. In the more prosperous 1970s, the life of the traveller was given a romantic touch to entice foreign tourists who could hire horse draw colourful caravans and meander around countryside along the bohareens. Compared to the UK and Europe there were very few private or municipal campsites and those that did exist were often owned by Dutch or Germans. Camping and Caravanning in England was as a middle class activity whereas in Ireland a caravan was the symbol of the traveller to be avoided at all costs. Camping in a tent was unthinkable.

After my grim tenting experience in France in 1962 I never ever contemplating going camping again, until that is I met my wife Alice. Camping and the outdoor life in Norway is part

209

of the national psyche. Alice as a small girl had many happy experiences of family boating, fishing and camping near her home in Hamar. Her father took every opportunity to get his beloved boat out and sail along the local lakeshore to find places for weekend family camping. Hamar had a wonderful lakeside town camping site that was frequently visited by Germans and Dutch.

We could not afford any holidays in the early years of our marriage, but when we got our first car, Alice was quick to realise that we could go camping in Devon and Cornwall. We bought a basic MFI frame tent with two internal curtained off bedrooms for the boys and ourselves along with a Primus stove and groundsheet and headed for sunny Cornwall. Usually we found farmers who reserve a field for campers and we could use their outdoor toilet and sometimes we had the added luxury of fresh cow's milk with our breakfast cereals. Our school holiday period at end of July and August was the only time that we could go camping. August can be a very variable month weather-wise. We encountered dense fog, gale force winds and daytime temperatures ranging from 10C to 30C+.

Our most testing camping experience was in August 14th 1979. We found a farm site that over looked the sea in south Cornwall and I decided to pitch our camp at the top of the sloping field to get a better view of the sea. This turned out to be a big mistake. As darkness fell the wind increased and torrential rain came down with bursts of thunder. I decided to park the car alongside the tent so that two of the car wheels were on the side flaps of the tent to make it more secure. We tried to sleep hoping that we had tied the tent down with enough stays. At about 3am we were woken up by howling storm force winds and the tent was lifted up and about to be blown away. We heard other campers shouting out instructions to secure their tents. I jumped out of bed half-naked and held on to the central roof bar just in time to stop the tent blowing away. Other campers came over to help and we were able to secure our severely battered tent with several of its supporting rods bent. The next morning the campsite looked as if it had been bombed. We went the local town Penzance to get some repair work done where we were joined by scores of other campers who also suffered tent damage in what turned out to be a force 10 gale.

However, we campers were very lucky because just off the south coast of Cornwall the yachtsman in the historic Fasnet race took the full force of the gale which caused the sinking and capsizing of several yachts with 15 yachtsman and 3 rescuers killed.

MY SISTER DOROTHY'S FIRST TENTING EXPERIENCE

When Alice was revising for her final degree exams I took the boys along with my sister's family for a camping experience to Devon during the summer half term holiday. My sister Dorothy and her husband Pat had won their mini car in their church draw and for several years the mini was their sole means of transport for them and their three sons. It was called into service for the Devon trip. I carried all the tenting gear in my newly acquire Austin Princess. Most of the week it was windy with intermittent rain clouds sweeping across the sky. I managed to get the now ageing frame tent erected and my sister who had never camped before was getting desperate for her pot of tea and cigarette. I set up the gas burners for the kettle and a camping chair and table in the middle of the bare tent floor. I had not set up the interior bedrooms yet. Soon the kettle was boiling and Dorothy finally got her cup of tea and cigarette. Meanwhile as the rain poured down Pat, I and the five boys headed into the village and nearest pub. I have an abiding memory of leaving a very happy Dorothy in the middle of the tent in a swirl of cigarette smoke and a cup of tea in her hand at complete peace with the world – maybe camping was not so bad after all.

Camping in the great outdoors can expose one to hidden dangers. Once when camping in Cornwall we spent a whole day on the beach on a warm but cloudy day. When we got back to our campsite I noticed that one of my legs was swollen and I felt feverish not to mention having a face that was turning beetroot red. It soon became clear that I had mild sunstroke and had failed to realise that in late July a lot of UV light is still transmitted through the clouds. Luckily the boys and my wife were not too badly sunburnt. On another occasion, again in Cornwall, I took the boys for a little fishing on a deserted cove on a warm, wet and windy day. In a moment of madness I decided to have a swim even though there were large waves breaking on a lovely sandy sloping beach. One wave completely turned me over and I was dragged out to sea by the backlash of the wave on the sloping beach. Disorientated and gasping for breath I thought that this could be the end of me. Fortunately I was strong of arm and body and managed to surface and swum in on the next wave and managed to not get dragged back under a second time which would have been the last time. My boys on the beach were unaware of what happened and it did not take me long to get them off the beach.

OUR FIRST CARAVAN

When we moved to Hertford in 1980 we got our first second-hand caravan – a heavy 4 berth glass windowed. Lunar. It came with a large awning and gas cooker plus a portable gas chest fridge. Camping from now on would be five star for us or so we thought.

Our first caravan trip was to Ireland in August 1981.On the way to Fishguard in West Wales we had a puncture in one of the Caravan wheels on a main A road with heavy traffic. I had never changed a caravan wheel before and had difficulty even knowing where to place the car jack under the caravan without it going through the floor of the caravan. Alice and the boys thought that our mishap was worth recording with our borrowed school camera but I was not amused with the added worry of possibly missing our ferry. After a lot of swearing and sweating I got the job done and we made our ferry on time. I was beginning to learn that towing a heavy loaded caravan was not that easy and I now began to worry about the overheating engine of our high mileage Austin Princess car. This Princess would not be as Royal as hoped. The boys got there first glimpse of Wexford and Ireland on a fine sunny afternoon from the top deck on the ferry. Soon we were in place on the local municipal campsite – on of the few in the Republic. Alice felt more at home when she discovered that Norwegian Vikings founded Wexford and we were all happy to discover that the famous Wexford Festival was in full swing. We saw a delightful play "The Matchmaker" by John B Keane and later headed for Kilkenny. On the way we passed several travellers caravans parked along the road and all of them gave us a big wave assuming that we were fellow travellers, which in a way we were. We could not help noticing that the local farmers that we passed did not seem too pleased and were probably thinking that we would try to camp in one of their fields.

In Kilkenny we found a campsite along the river Nore close to the Castle grounds. Kilkenny is the best-preserved Norman town in Ireland and near the main church is a classical round tower used to defend the local monasteries from marauders, especially the Vikings. The boys and I were keen to climb the tower and on the spiral staircase on the way up I was astonished to hear some people coming down speaking Norwegian. I seized the moment and spoke in Norwegian to the effect that I should be coming down and they as the Viking attackers should be trying to go up the stairs. I think that they will remember our interaction for the rest of their lives. Alice was able to explain to them in Norwegian the significance of the round tower in Irish history. My first cousins Patrick and Geradine Fitzsimons, along with Alice and I returned to Kilkenny in 2015 and once again I climbed up the tower; but no Vikings this time.

In 2009 my eldest son Ragnar and I had another surprise meeting with Norwegians when walking the Dingle Peninsula in Kerry. We had just left our B&B in Annascaul on a wet and windy morning and decided to visit the Polar Pub and the memorial to the Antarctic explorer and local man Tom Crean. Crean won three polar medals and was a key member of Captain Scott's 1911-13 Terra Nova Expedition that was beaten to the South Pole by the Norwegian Roald Amundsen. During this expedition, Crean walked nearly 60km across the Ross Ice Shelf to save the life of Michael Evans that led to him receiving the Albert Medal for Lifesaving. He went on to more heroics on his third and final Antarctic adventure when he joined fellow Irishman Ernest Shackleton's Trans- Antarctic Expedition. He was one of the open boat crew who sailed 800 nautical miles from Elephant Island to South Georgia to seek aid from for the stranded party. Crean opened his Polar Pub in 1920 and lived there until his death in 1938.

As we were just about to leave the road to rejoin the public footpath, a young couple in a hired car stopped and the lady passenger asked if we would like a lift. I immediately recognised her Norwegian accent and thanked her in Norwegian for the offer. They were astonished to find someone speaking Norwegian in such a remote location. I carried on in Norwegian and told them about Crean and how their hero Amundsen had beaten his team to the South Pole and that they should turn around and visit his memorial and pub up the road. Every Norwegian knows about Polar Exploration and by now the unfortunate couple were almost speechless. They wanted us to come to the pub later that evening in Tralee but by then we would be up somewhere in the mountains.

I cannot remember much about our stay in Cork except for all the black flags in the streets marking the death of 10th and last hunger striker Michael Devine (27) on 20th August after 60 days without food. That evening we were in a pub listening to Irish folk music and it is traditional to play the Irish National Anthem at the end of the evening. The owner thought otherwise and asked the customers to leave. His well intentioned effort to cool patriotic ardour could have back fired and caused a riot instead. Onwards to the ring of Kerry and the traditional Killorglin Puck Fair.

A wild buck goat from the local hills is captured and made king of the three day fair. He is placed on a secure platform high above the market square. The event attracts tourists and "the travellers" from wide and fair. The main event for the travellers is the horse fair and they normally camp in a local field, which is where we ended up in the absence of any official campsite. The local traveller kids showed a particular interest in our British registered car and concluded we needed looking after. One particularly forward young fellow suggested that for a couple of pounds he would look after our caravan when we went into town. I just knew that this was an offer that we could not refuse. The town was awash with inebriated people that was not a surprise as the pubs were open until 3am. We were relieved to get back to our caravan and paid our keeper who then had other suggestions as to how he might be of use to us. We were glad to get out of Killorglin early next morning while the camp was sleeping their excesses off. Next stop: the west of Ireland.

After a tour of Galway we headed out into the Connemara and the Gaeltacht (Irish speaking area). It was hard work towing the caravan along the narrow roads and eventually we got lost as all the road signs were in Irish. Soon we had a much bigger problem when the spare wheel that I put on in Wales collapsed and the caravan shuddered to a grinding halt helped by slamming on the car brakes before I ripped the bottom out of the caravan. With no spare wheel we were stuck along the roadside until morning. During the night the caravan would shake as the odd overloaded lorry passed by. In the morning I jacked the caravan up – knew how to do it now – and with the punctured wheel and the collapsed hub of the second wheel drove off to find a garage. I found a garage a few miles away and told the young mechanic my wheel problems. In conversation I mentioned that I had a great friend Joe Coyne from the Gaeltacht who was at school with me in Kells in the east of the country and had emigrated to America. It turned out that the mechanic was also a Coyne. The outcome was that he welded the hub of the damaged whee together and fixed the two punctures and refused to accept any payment no matter how hard I tried. Go raibh maith agat – thank you.

Next stop the O'Reilly homeland of Ballyjamesduff in County Cavan. Our boys were really looking forward to visiting Cavan, the homelands of Clan O'Reilly.As recounted earlier we did not find as many O'Reilly as expected, they used their first names on the pubs and shops to avoid confusion. Anyway the boys were delighted to know that the clan was still well represented in the town.

Back at the campsite we met a German couple with a very large new motor home who spent a lot of their time fishing with their son on the lake. There was no one else on the site. The Germans had driven all the way from Cologne to northern France and then took a ferry to Cork and then up to Virginia to stay on the campsite for four weeks and they had done this for the previous 3 years. Alice was able to speak German and they invited us to their home for a meal. They were highly qualified medical doctors who worked in a busy hospital in Cologne. They loved the emptiness, peace, scenery and people in Ireland. We felt a little guilty at disturbing their solitude but I think they welcomed our company – for a short time anyway.

BACK TO IRELAND 1992 – OUR DAUGHTER'S ASTRID'S HOMECOMING

It was ten years before we returned to Ireland with our caravan. This time we had my sister Avril from Canada with Astrid, our lovely 6 year-old daughter and us. We did a similar route to our 1981 trip. Some of the roads were in a worse condition than before because they were never designed to cope with the new heavy Lorries. On a very wet day in west

Cork Alice was towing the caravan along roads that were minor roller coasters when the inevitable happened. The Caravan came off the tow bar, the emergency caravan brake cable was activated and then broke leaving the caravan heading into a roadside ditch. End of holiday after only a couple of days we thought. A car of young local lads arrived and they helped to get the caravan out of the ditch. The front offside was badly damaged but the wheels were ok and we managed to hitch up the caravan onto the tow bar. We got to the nearest town and booked into a hotel. As AA members, we were able to hire a caravan to continue our journey – holiday back on course. We had a memorable stay on a campsite in Tralee, Kerry. We met up with Michael Horgan, Dorothy's brother-in-law, who had moved over to Ireland from London. Michael was fascinated by our life in a caravan, especially when I served him a large measure of his favourite Cognac. He had acquired the Irish belief that caravans were only for the Travellers but could see that there were advantages of using one on a tour round Ireland. One day we went with his family to the seaside and spent most of the day drinking in the local pub. The girls stayed on the beach while the men rotated their beech-pub visits. The amount of litter, including wine and beer bottles, strewn around the lovely sand dunes was a big surprise to my wife. Late that evening as we were leaving we suggested that we pick up our own rubbish but were over ruled by the majority view to leave it to someone else to do it. During the day, Michael bought some vegetables for the evening meal that he would cook back at his house. The vegetables remained on the bar top all day acquiring a smoked Guinness flavour. We arrived back at the house around 8pm, in time for a few more jars in the local pubs in Tralee. By midnight I was starving and we sat down to the most over cooked meat and vegetables that I had ever eaten, then it was back to our campsite where some of the campers were still socialising and celebrating the Irish boxer Michael Caruthers's Olympic Gold win earlier in the evening at the 1992 Barcelona Olympics.

MAYO AND CONNEMARA

Our next stop was Mayo along the west coast where we set up camp on a farmer's field on the edge of a beautiful empty beach in glorious weather. That evening in the local bar I met an American Irish girl, Mary Cunningham, who was back home from Chicago to claim her small farm left to her by her recently deceased father. She invited us to come out next evening to the pub in her local village. On our way to the pub I picked up a smartly dressed local farmer – in dark suit, white open necked shirt and well polished shoes – who thought nothing of walking the two or three miles to the pub. He reminded me of 1950s Irishmen in London going to Sunday Mass before the pub of course. We got to the pub to meet similarly dressed silent men and a few older women. The few that did speak were speaking in Irish while all were supping from their Guinness glasses. As the pub filled up and the Guinness went down one of the older women started to sing in Gaelic to the sound of silence. Then the first fiddler started up and the conversation grew, then Mary Cunningham arrived and introduced us to some of the locals and then more people started to sing and more fiddlers joined in and all hell broke loose. Four hours later, we left the pub still in full swing. I kept in contact with Mary for a while and remembered receiving a black rimmed St Patrick's Day card from "the desk of Mary Cunningham, Chicago, and Honour to the Hunger Strikers".

BACK TO CAVAN THE O'REILLY HOMELAND

As in 1981 we headed for the O'Reilly homelands of County Cavan. We stayed on the same campsite, little changed since 1981, along the lake in Virginia. This time, as stated at the start of this book, I had finally found the whereabouts of the farm where my father was born. I also found the address of a first cousin, Ann Perry O'Reilly who lived in Virginia, the town where our campsite was.

Ann's unmarried brother, John was living alone on the family farm. Later after his death, the farm was taken over by Ann's youngest son Robert who did a lot of renovation work. Ann eldest son Brendan had his own music group "The Dead can Dance" and was not interested in farm life. A few years later we saw Brendan perform his Gothic style music in Kentish Town London. As of 2016 I am still in close contact with Ann who is now 80 years old.

From Cavan we went to Kells, the birthplace of my mother and visited the farm in Cookstown, that was designed and built by her father Patrick in the 1920s. The present owner, Mr Cassidy (deceased) showed us around and gave us an extra large afternoon tea. We finished our Irish tour in Blackrock, Dundalk where we partied with my first cousin Patrick Fitzsimons and called on to meet his mother Phyllis nee Connelly, on her farm near Carrackmacross on the way back to our campsite in Virginia. A few weeks after we arrived home our battered caravan was deliver back from Ireland by the AA. I patched it up and managed to get a couple of more camping trips to Norfolk before sending it to the caravan graveyard.

THE FOUR-MAN TENT

For some of more exciting and cost effective camping experiences we used a small tent with lightweight portable cooking equipment, collapsible table and chairs. Towing a caravan in Norway was not really an option for us but we could use our 4-man tent to save on astronomical hotel costs.

One memorable trip was to my brother's Vincent's wedding in Visby, Sweden in 1983.We took the ferry from Newcastle to Bergen – no longer possible- and with our boys camped overnight along a fjord on the way to Hamar. From Hamar we drove to Stockholm, camping and swimming in lakes along the way and then took the ferry to Visby on the beautiful island of Gotland in the Baltic Sea. The wedding was a grand affair with guests from 61 countries – Vincent and Eva were very international in their outlook on life. My parents found their own way there and I still managed a drink with my father in the local pub at enormous expense. My one abiding memory is of Vincent taking my bed the night before the wedding leaving me to sleep on the floor. I can only conclude that he needed a nice soft bed to sleep in more than I did.

On the way back we decided to go to Denmark and take the ferry to Harwich. Our first camping stop was near Sweden's biggest Lake Vattern on an open patch of ground near a forest – difficult to avoid forests in Sweden. We had a nice meal and then settled down for the night in our tent. We then heard high pitch jet like sounds – the mosquito invasion had started. The battle lasted all night as we fired our anti mossie spray guns in all directions. BY morning the Mosquito army retreated leaving us covered in the scars of war. We had learnt a lesson- do not camp in Swedish forests even if it is free.

NEXT STOP: COPENHAGEN

As dusk approached, we decided to see the famous Mermaid before heading for our campsite. We drove along the seashore but no sight of any mermaid. It was only later that we learnt that the mermaid is a rather small statue sitting on an even smaller rock and we must have missed her in the gathering gloom. Next day we had a walk around the palace and saw the Danish version of the changing of the guards. The boys were happy as they were still into making armies of toy lead soldiers, but they really wanted to go to Legoland.

It was difficult to get our eldest son Ragnar out of Legoland, he had the caught the Lego bug. Now in his mid 40s he has a shed full of Lego models. One of his latest projects was to build a Lego model of the new Colchester United Football Stadium that was photographed for one of the match day programmes. The boys spent some hours building with the Lego and entered a competition. Later they would be able to take their own children to Legoland a lot closer to home near Winsor Castle.

Our next stop, Odense and the birth place of Hans Christian Anderson. This time we did see The Little Mermaid but she was encased in 2D in a book of fairy Tales written by the great man.

Anyone connected with Scandinavia is into Viking ships. The boys had already built Viking boats in Lego but now got to see real ships over 1000 years old at the Roskilde museum. As late 1997 the longest ever Viking warship at 36 metres was unearthed nearby. In 2014 the ship was flat-packed (IKEA style) and reconstructed at a special Viking Exhibition at the British Museum. Alice, Einar, her brother over from Norway, and I were impressed by the exhibition and I believe our son Ragnar also went. I assume that he is stilling building a 36-metre model of the Roskilde 6, in Lego of course.

A MILITARY EARLY MORNING WAKE UP CALL

Time to look for a free camping place and prospects looked promising as we drove through some open countryside near the coast with boarded up houses and not a human to be in sight.

I did notice what looked like some large tractor tracks around the site we picked to pith our bright blue tent. We had a very comfortable night and no mosquitoes to attack us. However around 6am we heard a buzz that turned into a scream above our tent. I jumped up and looked out to see the flames spurting out of the tail from the departing NATO jet. Awoken we decided to have breakfast and then I heard a rumbling noise in the distance. Soon the first forward army scout car arrived and an officer jumped out and asked why we were in the middle of a military restricted war practice zone. Alice asked him if there was time for breakfast not a good idea with the tanks approaching. He sent a radio message back to headquarters and escorted us out of the danger zone pronto.

The boys thought this was better than anything they read in their war comics.

ASTRID'S RABIES SCARE AND THE PATH TO ROME.

Our next caravan was a German make and was acquired under very tragic circumstances. As a thank you for hosting their daughter Christina, Ludwin and Hannah our long term German friends gave us the use of their caravan which was to be based on a lovely campsite about 40km north of Rome. Unfortunately, Ludwin died suddenly of a congenital heart condition at Easter 1996. The second hand caravan that they bought was still in Germany and Ludwin's distraught wife suggested that we come to Germany and tow the caravan to Rome taking two of her children Mattie and Barbara with us and this we did. She was to join us later in Rome. I always wanted to maybe bike or walk to Rome and I never anticipated that it would be this way. After our trip to Rome we bought the caravan from Hannah and towed it back to England.

Sometimes when we went to Italy we left the caravan over winter there and used our 4-man tent to stay at campsites on the way there and back. On one memorable trip we stopped off at a campsite in Alsace and as we were registering in the campsite office who walked in but our neighbours from Bramfield near Hertford who were on their way to Italy. We had met them a few days earlier at a BBQ and did not even know that they were campers, a small world as they say.

That evening there was a show put on for the campers and Astrid and I went along but Alice preferred to stay back in our tent. Astrid did an Irish Dance that was very well received, especially by one French man who spoke to me in French for the next two hours. The more wine he drank the more he spoke. My Francaise is minimal but I fed him a few French terms like "Vive La Republick", Charles De Gaul and this would set him off nonstop for several minutes. The embarrassment came next morning when he and his family walked past our tent and he greeted me in French like along lost friend. Fortunately, I was able to introduce Alice to him and as her French is much more fluent than mine she saved the day. I resolved there and there to learn a bit more French at evening class.

BIT BY A BELGIAN DOG IN GERMANY

We then moved on into Germany and camped near Titisee close to Switzerland. Camped just opposite our pitch was a heavily tattooed Scottish couple who were well into their cans of Scottish Special Brew and were anxious for some company. Unfortunately the man was a Glasgow Rangers FC fanatic and did not take any Catholic or Republican prisoners. I managed to hide my Celtic FC support and Republican sympathies from him. Upon hearing that Alice was Norwegian he told us about the Viking and German origins of the Scottish people. It was as if he was in some Wagnerian fantasy world that was uninhabited by Celts. Later I suggested to his girl friend that he was a little extreme with some of his views. She agreed with me but thought it best to leave him in his fantasy world – smart women.

Some of the campers had dogs with them that they were required to keep on a lead. Astrid went to play at the children's swings nearby when we heard her scream accompanied by a dog barking. A small terrier dog, off the leash, had taken a nip out of her leg and our first thoughts were "Rabies". The owners showed us the dog's vaccination certificate against Rabies but they left the campsite a few hours later and we decided to err on the safe side and take Astrid to the local hospital where all that was needed was a dab of iodine. The incident reminded me of the time in 1989 when I ran the Athens Marathon and got bitten by an Alsatian guard dog on the beach near Marathon and luckily for me despite all the wild dogs around, guard dogs are vaccinated for rabies, but the doctor also gave me the magic iodine dab to justify his fee no doubt.

In the nearby village Astrid and I got talking to a local German couple over a few beers. It was raining as we were leaving and they generously dropped us back at the campsite where they met Alice. They invited us to come to their house next evening for dinner and a grand occasion it was, helped as usual by Alice able to converse in fluent German. During our camping trips we have often met up and socialised with the locals which is one of the great advantages of camping.

SEE NAPLES AND EAT CAKE

It helps to get one noticed on campsites and restaurants when you have an attractive young blond daughter with you. I can remember when we decided to take our four-man tent from our campsite north of Rome to Naples to visit Mount Vesuvius and Pompeii. We camped close to Pompeii and had a lovely walk round the site and could not help noticing some of the phallic depictions on the walls in the ancient city's red light district. It was also the first time I realised how important the Alter was for sacrifices and how this was taken up by the early Christian church. In the evening decided to walk into the modern town and join the hundreds of Italians who like to turn the tree lined wide walking pavements into a sort of catwalk. We went into a restaurant where the owner was celebrating a young relative's birthday but few other outsiders were there except us. It did not take long before some little girls noticed Astrid and soon large slices of birthday cake were sent our way. A pity our Italian was poor but we did manage to communicate where we were from which encouraged the giving of more party goodies.

Our campsite was not far from the entrance to Pompeii and during the night the Italians nearly drove us mad buzzing around the nearby streets on their scooters. We were a bit tired when we drove up to the top of Vesuvius next day and walked close to the smoking sulphurous crater. A little bit farther down we spotted an ice cream bar and treated ourselves but in my case a wasp decided to land on my thumb and I instinctively squashed it with my index finger, not a good idea. I got an almighty sting, after all wasps have to be hardy to survive near the top of a volcano. Soon my hand and arm swelled up – might have been close to an anaphylaxis shock.

CHAPTER 17

LEAVING OF READING 1980 – LIFE AS A DEPUTY HEADTEACHER IN HERTFORDSHIRE.

M y parents were well settled now in Barnet and we never wanted to go too far from London. After nearly seven years as a Head of Science at Maidenhead I was more than ready to move on. The idea of being a LEA Science Adviser had some appeal and a Science Education Lecturer had more appeal. Jobs were few for Lecturers and not that well paid. I did manage to get interviews at Bath and Sheffield Universities but nothing came of it.

In early 1980 I applied for a Deputy Headship at Riversmead School in Cheshunt, Hertforshire, just north of London. To my surprise I got an interview and was one of six short-listed. I heard that Riversmead was built as a new Secondary Modern in the late 1940s to cope with a rising local population; many newcomers were from bombed out parts of Londoner. It had two former Grammar schools nearby so its intake was skewed to the more socially disadvantaged. What I did not realise then was that a 25% drop in school population was due within five years. Its most famous past pupil was Cliff Richards and his Drama teacher Jay was involved in the selection process. I found out later she really wanted her nephew, the Head of

English to be the new deputy head but he was not long at the school so was not interviewed for the post.

When I met some of the staff I was surprised to be asked by a member of staff what a well qualified person like me wanted to come to a school like Riversmead for? I was too keen and naive to investigate some of the hidden and not so hidden messages that were coming across. In those days the tour of the school and interviews were all done on a single day and the decision made by 6pm. I liked the Head teacher, Ian with his long side boards but did not pick up on the fact that he had many enemies in the school including the dodgy caretaker. At interview I struck a chord when I stated my position in support of comprehensive education. None of the candidates withdrew and later they offered me the post. A new stage in my life had begun.

A DIFFICULT START

At the end of the 1970s there was a lull in the housing market and it took nearly a year to sell our house. I had to start my new post at Easter, a very difficult and unusual time to start, with a timetable and curriculum to sort out. Alice would not complete her PGCE (teacher training course) until the end of June 1980 and the boys had to complete their summer term in primary school. The only option was for me to stay with my parents in Barnet and come back to Reading at weekends. My parents were delighted to have their 34-year-old son back home again to fill the gap left by my younger brother who moved home five years earlier to live in Sweden. My father had just retired from Barnet Council aged 66 years of age. He should have been retired at 65 but they his age muddled up. Over the years my father and I drank in every pub from: Baker Street, Swiss Cottage, Golders Green, Temple Fortune, East Finchley, Finchley Central, North Finchley, Wheatstone. Now we would have the chance to drink in all the pubs in Barnet. Before he died in 2002, we drank in all the pubs from Barnet to Hertford. More than a 100 pubs benefited from our largesse over the years not to mention our contribution to the government excise man. My presence at home was a bit of a relief for my mother because she get on with her golf and bridge without having to pay too much attention to my father's needs.

I was to embark on a steep learning curve at Riversmead School that had more to do with adult criminal and social behaviour than sadly with the teaching and learning of children. I visited the school before Easter and wondered why the tennis courts had wet carpets for nets. During the night a fire hose had been deliberately set off and flooded the library. It turned out that the caretaker was responsible and this was finally established after the library had been flooded on three more occasions during the summer term when I was in post. On one of the mornings that the library was flooded the caretaker arrived at my office and started to mend my door lock – odd as there was nothing wrong with in, but it gave him the chance to observe what was happening in the head's office next door to me. We eventually proved that he stole paint, cleaning materials and stationary materials, some of which were on sale at car boot markets – still the days before eBay. We had to sack the Head of Boys' PE after we discovered that he had falsified his department's accounts and had taken a job as a part-time fire fighter. He had also been involved in relationships with underage pupils.

TEMPORARY ACCOMMODATION IN HERTFORD (1980-81)

The LEA provided a council house – normally reserved for police officers – in Hertford where we stayed for a year on a reasonable rent. This was a lucky break for us because we had time to look around the area to find a new home. We loved Hertford, a small market medieval town and the County Town of Hertfordshire. The town was the venue for a Synod in 673 called by Theodore of Tarsus, Archbishop of Canterbury that fixed the holy day of Easter as the Sunday after the 14th day of the moon of the first month and banned divorce among other dictates. Its castle was for a time the home of the young Queen Elizabeth 1st and Parliament convened in Hertford in the time of the great plague in London. Alice liked the town because it reminded her of her hometown Hamar also a county town. We eventually sold our house in Reading for £39000 (bought for £16500 in 1975) and bought a house in Bengeo, Hertford for £53000. Hertford was a lot more expensive than Reading as it is only 25miles from central London and has two separate railway lines to Liverpool Street and Kings Cross/Moorgate. Our new house was only a 3- bed detached compared to our 4-bed with study detached house in Reading; but there was ample room to build extensions.

We now had the added difficulty of moving school for the boys, after the September intake deadline had passed and finding a first teaching post for Alice who completed her teacher training(PGCE) in June 1980. She got a job teaching German at the well established Hitchin Boys' School some 20 miles north of Hertford. Fingal started his last year of primary school at St Joseph's RC in Hertford but placing Ragnar in a secondary school was far more problematic. There was a good mixed secondary school across the road from where we lived in Hertford but this was full. The LEA offered him a place at Broxbourne about 7 miles south of Hertford but this would mean that all four of us would be located in four different towns. Eventually after keeping Ragnar at home for several days at the beginning of the autumn term, the LEA found him a place at Richard Hale Boys' School in Hertford.

HARD GRAFT AT SCHOOL FOR ME.

My main preoccupation in my new post was the motivation and disciplining of the varied group of staff that ranged from the: eccentric, the bone idle, the burnt out, the ambitious, the immovable, the innocent and the politically devious.

My most challenging department was the "Creative Arts" a misnomer if ever there was one. This mixed bag of subjects included: Pottery, Woodwork, Metalwork, Cooking (Home Economics!), TD and Art. The most intransigent member was Johnny the Potter. Pupils opted for subjects at the end of year (14+) and each year about eight boys and two girls would opt to take Pottery. Each year Johnny would argue for three groups – low, middle and high ability sets with special equipment facilities for the girls. Each year he demanded that his groups would need half-day sessions. Each year I would tell Johnny that he could have three groups if he could get 30+ pupils opting for his subject. At our weekly meetings, Johnny would puff on his pipe and complain about how I had it in for him. He would get and play on the sympathy other members in the Creative Arts Department who were all for stirring things up. The outcome was that Johnny never changed his teaching methods or adopted any modern changes to Pottery – and there were many exciting developments in pottery at that time. I was glad that only 10 odd pupils were exposed to his intransigence. I made sure to monitor their progress so that they did get a qualification in Pottery.

The Home Economics were not bad teachers but wanted cooking sessions to be three-hour lessons. I argued that few people could afford to spend three hours preparing an evening meal and that there were now more efficient cookers and the microwave oven would play a far greater role in the domestic futures of the pupils that they were now teaching. I managed to overcome some of their resistance to change and they had to settle for two-hour cooking lessons; but they had the satisfaction of joining the Pottery department on the list of hard done by departments.

We did have quite a talented woodwork teacher who managed to get the odd pupil through A'Level but at a great cost in terms of teaching time allocated to him. One of the metalwork teachers was a very gentle hippy type who could teach well when he was not on a high. The other one was more interested in the driving and mechanics of an old double deck London Bus that we used for school trips. He wore sunglasses in and out of class. Finally we did have two talented if demanding Art teachers who were at different ends of the Art spectrum and never agreed to cooperate on anything. What I really wanted to do was dismantle the Creative Arts department and start all over again, but there were other more pressing problems to deal with.

Our senior teacher Jay was a law onto herself and her great claim to fame was that she taught, mentored and later befriended the pop star Cliff Richard. He starred in her school play Romeo and Juliet and got an O'Level in Drama. At Jay's behest, Cliff gave several concerts in our school hall. I am not a great fan of Cliff who I viewed to be a poor copy of Elvis Presley but I was very impressed with one of his performance at our school. I got tickets to the sold out concert for my close friend Charles Bond – a keen Cliff fan, and my mother. At that time Cliff had a big number one chart topper with "We Don't Talk Anymore". He performed this song and his other hits with no backing group for two hours using only voice and his guitar – very impressive.

Most people are aware of Cliff's Christian Belief and one of his mentor's was the Head of RE at Riversmead who later left to join Cliff on his tours and lodged with him in his various homes. When Jay was due to retire she invited Cliff and his then girlfriend or friend the tennis player Sue Barker to her retirement party at the school. I found Sue a very attractive girl and wondered why they never tied the knot, but then Cliff never did marry.

Jay was a heavy smoker and always made sure to stub her cigarette out before filling up at the local petrol station. On one occasion, she wondered why it took so long to fill up her car's petrol tank and was very surprised that the bill was much more than usual. As she drove out of the station and just about to light up the petrol station manager banged furiously on the bonnet of the car and Jay stopped wondering why he was so frantic. The manager had seen petrol pouring out of the boot of her car as she started up the engine. It transpired that Jay had put the nozzle of the petrol pump straight through the concertina hosepipe leading through the boot to the tank and filled the boot up with petrol. One hates to think what would have happened if she had been able to light up her cigarette. When Jay retired she sold up and moved with her husband to Cambridge where she became a housing millionaire during the 1990s and easy lending. She bought a string of houses using the rise in value of each house to support the purchase of the next one. I often wondered what she did with all her money as her marriage was childless.

The job of a deputy head is very dependent on the leadership qualities and vision of the Headteacher. Unfortunately for me, Ian, the Head teacher could be a bit of a Walter Mitty character. He thought that headship was only for the precious few and did not give me the career guidance that I needed as he was a bit motivated by personal jealously. He was a man of small stature and needed to have his ego boosted by others. He loved using the term "we Heads" as if they were a separate special elite group. He fancied himself as a sailor and once I joined him, along with his wife, as crew on his 26-foot yacht in a race at Brightlingsea. It was quite windy and there was a bit of a sea swell. We just about finished the race but ended up with a bent mast. I was more impressed with his wife's judgement than with his. Later Ian decided to sail to the Azores and back in a biannual race with a friend. He got back three weeks later than planned claiming that he was becalmed for several days. His adventure was not very popular with the staff or me who had to run the school in his absence.

One story that did the rounds happened before I arrived. The pupils used to be able to take a subject called Rural Studies. Their teacher was wont to spend too long in the pub at lunchtime and was regularly late for his afternoon lesson.

One of his classes decided to play a joke on him. They dug a large hole outside the entrance to the hut and covered it with netting and a thin layer of turf – very inventive. They then hid and watched their teacher return and fall into the hole. I do not thing that he was ever late for a lesson again.

MANAGING A SCHOOL AMALGAMATION

I got on well with the Head of Science, Heddwyn who became a lifelong friend. Heddwyn a Biologist had to manage some difficult staff and was a bit disillusioned with the lack of progress and the uncertain future of the school. His and my problems were particularly acute when due to falling school roll we amalgamated with the Queen Eleanor School in Waltham Cross. It took two years to transfer the pupils to our site and the site was sold off for housing including some lovely playing fields. Most of the Queen Eleanor staff accepted the amalgamation and the fact that they would have to compete for their existing positions, face redeployment or redundancy. Who said teaching was a job for life?

One women deputy head transferred but did not cooperate in making the amalgamation a success, preferring to spend a lot of time on her golf course than at school. Her reason for being absent for months from school was to do with catching salmonella from a dodgy drink while holidaying abroad. Seemingly, she was a risk to the pupils for months afterwards! We did promote a colleague, an ex-police officer from Queen Eleanor to a Head of Year position. He broke his arm a few days before interview but managed to turn up for interview with the sleeve of his jacket cut off to make room for the sling holding his arm. The women staff were impressed and he got the job. We then did not see him for many weeks. I had great difficulty getting supply teachers in to cover his and other absent teachers' lessons in a time of work to rule by the teachers' unions. One evening I was running down Ware High

Street and whom did I meet running towards me, no other than our absent Head of Year. He was in at school the next day!

The work to rule by members of the NUT caused me a particular problem that came into the professional misconduct category when I employed a temporary teacher to cover for one particular subject. I had to give her a light timetable with the proviso that she did some extra cover lessons for absent staff and that she was happy to do. Unfortunately her Head of Department got her to join the NUT and marched into my office with his new recruit to inform me that she would not be taking any cover lessons. Not alone was I angry with the Department Head but I was very disappointed with the unprofessionalism of the women I had appointed and I would have had a strong legal case against her for breach of contract. I let it pass because I needed to conserve my energy for more important matters – like the education of the pupils.

A Pupil's success story.

Our pupils, unlike some of the staff, in the main were well behaved. Our intake was skewed to the less able and more socially disadvantaged and this allowed our neighbouring ex grammar schools to have greater success with public examinations and claim to be very good schools. I was doing some pioneering work with Durham University in developing value added measures to compare how pupils did when taking their socioeconomic status, cognitive ability and age into consideration. Our value added measure would also allow us to compare departmental and individual performance. I am pleased to say that in 2016 value added measure are in place in all schools.

I decided to completely revamp the traditional and somewhat boring school annual prize giving and organise it along the lines of the Academy Awards. Pupils were nominated for different categories that reflected the social, sporting, academic and cultural life and success of the school. Selected staff spoke on behave of each nominee. All were seated at tables around the large hall. The PTA served food, juices for the pupils and wine for the staff and guests.

The age of the microcomputer was beginning to impact on the school curriculum. I had already taught myself the Advance Basic Computer Programming Language at my previous school in Maidenhead. At Riversmead we had a modem link to a PDP11 main frame computer at Hatfield Polytechnic. I used this computer to help me sort out the pupil option choices for years 10 and 11. I had to directly access and programme files to get print outs of staff and pupil timetables. Sometimes, especially during a storm, some rubbish would come down the line and I would have to start all over again. I can remember my sister Avril giving us a surprise visit on a wet and windy March evening when I was using the modem from home and my wife was preparing her lessons for next day. We did not know that she was over from Canada. Avril had a Dictaphone to record our reactions when we opened the door and she certainly got a reaction – a much-unexpected one. Next day we both had difficult days at school due to lack of preparation. We are not keen on surprise visits, as they do not allow for looking forward to the visit and planning things to do – but of course we were delighted to see Avril.

At school I took responsibility for the design and construction of a class computer room of 16 stations and as my DIY skills were developing at this time and I personally installed and wired up the computers to the server – no job too small for this deputy head. We introduced GCSE Computer Studies as an option for Year 10 pupils. One outstanding pupil wanted to take an A 'Level in Computer Studies. His name was Kevin McDermott and I decided to give him two individual lessons a week. We had to use DOS and standard programming languages; we were just before the first Microsoft 1 came out in 1985. Kevin did a wonderful project that set up a computerised book search system for our school library. We also devised an automatic scoring and display system for our 10 round sports "It is a Knock Out" team contest at Waltham Abbey Sport Centre. The contestants could see their scores on the TV monitors around the hall as the competition progressed. adding greatly to the contestant and audience participation. Kevin got the school's first ever Computer Studies GCE A'Level (Grade B) and went to Newcastle University to study Electrical Engineering. I visited Kevin at Newcastle when I went up there as an external examiner for the Newcastle Polytechnic B.Ed degree. We went to a hotel bar for a few pints and I was pleased to hear that he was coping well with his degree work. As the evening progressed, we got into conversation with the middle-aged women in charge of the bar. I have never forgotten one statement she made – "there are major changes in most aspects of your life, including physical and emotional, every ten years". As I approach my eight decade I can personally vouch for the truth of this statement.

I have been lucky that throughout my teaching career I have been able to communicate, motivate and enjoy the company of the pupils, after all they are the bedrock of all schools. I would like to think that this also applied to my own children and I was about to again have the opportunity to hone and improve upon my infant raising parent shills.

A BEAUTIFUL SURPRISE – ASTRID COLLEEN ARRIVES

By 1985 our two boys were now well established at secondary school and Alice was getting on well as a German teacher at Hitchin Boys' School. We had been practising birth control in a relaxed manner. We were so busy since the boys were born that they arrived into their teenage years without Alice and I giving much thought to extending our family. If anything, we were beginning to think that we might have left it too late. In the summer of 1985 we went to Norfolk with our caravan. My sister Dorothy and her family came to stay in the caravan and we then went to Norway. We were a little shocked by how cold July that year was with some days not getting above 13C. The weather in Norway and later in Stockholm where we stayed with my brother, Vincent, and his wife, Eva, was quite pleasant. After our trip to Scandinavia we went back up to Norfolk in early September to join my mother and father who had taken over from Dorothy. One morning Alice was feeling a bit sick and a few days later realised that she maybe pregnant. We were a bit shocked but delighted. A week or two later as we had lunch in the kitchen and the boys were finishing their Spaghetti Bolognese, Alice told them that there were going to be some changes to the family. Ragnar cottoned on quickly to what was coming. Fingal, over two years younger, had no idea but when Alice said that she was going to have a baby he spluttered out some of his spaghetti in amazement. How could his mother be pregnant when she was so old? Old people do not do sex things after they have children. The sudden surprise induced in him an anxiety for the health and happiness of his mother. A further subliminal thought went through his mind; his friend's mothers were long since finished having babies and how could he explain to them that his middle-aged 35-year-old mother was having another baby when she had her first baby at 19 years of age.

Because of Alice's age it was though wise that she have an amniocentesis and we were delighted that all was ok. We were also especially delighted that the boys were going to have a sister. Fingal remembers a very happy mother coming up to his bedroom to give him the news. He recalls his mother smiling and admiring her bulging profile in the wall mounted mirror in his room. He was relieved to see that she was happy but he still had the worry of telling his friends.

During the evening of Tuesday 29th April Alice endured several vomiting sessions and her water broke around 1am. We woke up the boys to tell them the time had arrived and we were off to the QE2 hospital in Welwyn Garden City about eight miles away. As we got into the car, a chorus of song from the nightingales in the nearby trees regaled us in celebration of our impending new addition to our family. At the hospital Alice was put on a drip because she was dehydrated and endured several hours of labour and often I was the only person with her to help make her comfortable. At 6am we called for the maternity nurse and again to a chorus of song from the nightingales outside, our daughter arrived in this world at around 6.20am weighing in at 6lb 7oz. She made only a very mild squeak or two and I got worried as the nurse removed some mucus from her mouth because she was not breathing properly. I could not believe that here we were having the same problem as we had at our son Ragnar's birth. At the behest of the maternity nurse, a very relaxed male doctor arrived with bits of his breakfast still around his mouth. Seeing an agitated father, he got himself into gear and promptly got our daughter into a side room, gave her oxygen and placed her in an incubator to recover.

Somewhat relieved (but very tired) that daughter and mother were now being well looked after I headed off to work. There was no paternity leave in 1986 so the boys and I visited mother and daughter in the evening and found them both well. Fingal had to cancel his football training with Ware Lions and I am not sure whether he told the manager that his mother had had a baby!

Today many couples do not start families until their mid 30s. We had the advantage of starting early and then using our earlier experience to bring up our daughter. We were now more established in our respective careers and consequently I made a greater effort to record Astrid's development in diary and film formats. As a child I never had any fairy tales read to me and I decided that I would learn some fairy tales with my daughter. Alice was very good with reading Norwegian fairy tales to the boys and I too learnt from her. Today still, that big Troll waiting for me under the bridge haunts me and is certainly a match for the Irish Banshee on my nightmare list.

Almost every evening I read to Astrid some fairy tales and was delighted when I completed all the Narnia books for her.

Later on Astrid was able to read fairy tales and children's books for me – a bit of pay back perhaps.

A few excerpts from the diary I kept:

1/6/86 first smile noticed – 11/10/86 sat up unsupported – 6/1/87 Astrid cough and temperature, taken to Dr Stott-given Amoxil, evening temp 106.6F, stripped and sponged down, poor thing, penicillin slow to work, Friday temp down – 27/2/87 top two teeth appear, March 87 took Astrid to my school for Child Development class, girls love her – 24 22/5/87 walked four steps, hurray!; but does not need to walk because with her light body frame can crawl very fast – 28/7/87 has start making little sounds that indicates she wants things, the boys are having great fun with her – 6/10/87 Astrid still on breast, comes into our bed two or three times a night – 18/10/87 we had greatest storm for 200 years, Astrid and dad ill for a few days, noticed Astrid said "fisk" and "brest" and loves game Tit Tie.

INDUSTRY YEAR 1986 – A TASTE OF THE WORLD OUTSIDE SCHOOL

The amalgamation of our two schools was doomed to failure from the start mainly due to a continuing falling school population in London and the southeast of England. In our case, a third school should have been involved for a triple amalgamation, but politics and parental objections would never allow this to happen. Ironically it happened in the end. When the two amalgamated schools closed in 1989, the nearby Cheshunt school moved to our site and the Cheshunt site, including its playing fields, was sold to Tesco to build a giant supermarket. In the whole process two large school playing fields were lost to development.

As the school was wound down I had to think of my own future and jumped at the opportunity to take a four month secondment to study the world of engineering in industry. The programme that I joined was part of the government sponsored Industry Year 1986 and my secondment was sponsored by The Institution of Mechanical Engineers.

Our group of twenty seconded teachers had the aim of updating the school curriculum to include best management and engineering practice from industry. We started our programme with a stay in Nottingham to visit the headquarters of Boots and other industries. My one abiding memory was a visit to a cigarette factory. Nottingham then was known for having more available young women than men chiefly because local industry especially the cigarette and pharmaceutical manufacturers employed so many women. When we arrived at the cigarette factory we were asked how many of us were smokers and I was the only one in the group who admitted to being a smoker. I was an occasional social smoker of mostly other people's cigarettes. I never bought a packet of cigarettes in my life but I did have a predilection for the occasional Hamlet cigar when having a pint or six in the pub. In fact I did not give up on cigars until around 1998 and needed hypnosis to help me do it. I realised I was in trouble when I was smoking a whole Hamlet quicker than drinking a pint and then quickly finished off the pint so I could go up to the bar for another pint and more importantly another Hamlet cigar. Even worse after a few pints I inhaled more as well. During the night I would wake up with a throat as dry as a camel's arse and swear I would never touch another cigar. My sister Dorothy had tried hypnosis to help her give up cigarettes with only partial success. I discovered my local dentist was a member of The British Hypnotic Association and it was not long before I ended up in his dental chair for half an hour of hypnosis. He normally used his hypnotic skills for calming his dental patients. After the one half hour session I went to the pub and downed four pints of real ale and no cigars then or since. I had broken the connection between drinking and smoking. In 1986 I was still in cigar land and as "the smoker" I was treated as a VIP compared to my envious colleagues. I got taken to see the director suite and to sample their finest brands of cigarettes laid out on silver trays. When I met up with the rest of the group gift rapped boxes of cigarettes were waiting for me and of course the others got nothing as they were declared non-smokers.

We were all allocated different industries for work experience and study and at the end of the secondment we had to make a presentation at the Institution of Engineers at their headquarters in London. I was very pleased to be allocated to British Aerospace Civil Division at Hatfield. The site employed around 2000 people and manufactured the 125 executive jet, the 146 four engine short take off plane and the wings for the European Airbus. Formerly De Havilland, then Hawker Sidley, it is the birthplace of the first civil jet airline – The Comet and later The Trident.

My first placement was in the 146 modifications department. I had no idea just how many design modifications an aeroplane needs after its first inaugural flight. The four engine 146 is used mainly as a feeder airline for longer international flights. It is capable of taking off at high altitude airports and on short runways. As an example, one design modification was to cope with stones hitting the undercarriage when landing and taking off at airports in Alaska in the US. One does not expect to have stones on runways but then we are not coping with the weather and terrain of the wild lands of Alaska. Email had not taken off yet in 1986 but some memos were circulated to over fifty staff that needed to know about the modifications – a lot of typing and paper. One employee was an odd ball. He had not spoken or socialised with work colleagues for many years and he eat his lunch in his car in the car park. He could survive because everything in the aircraft manufacturing business has to be recorded and have a paper trail. Now he would have it easier by only contacting colleagues by email.

The 146 was one of the first planes to move towards fly by wire. The mechanical cables from the flight deck to the wings and other areas that contained moving parts were previously operated by pulleys and gearing mechanisms were replaced by electrical wires that carried an electronic signal to operate the remote moving parts. My time in the Electrical Systems Division was quite profitable. System development of any sort moves slowly in the aerospace and this is especially so with electrical systems. Think how long it took car electrics to modernise. Safety is of paramount importance here. I spoke to some Electronic Engineers and told them that they would be better off working in computer design, electrical monitoring and measurement and other fast moving electronic projects when they were young and then move to the aerospace industry later in life.

My next department was in Graphic Design. This department was by far the most silent, almost churchlike. Each designer was at their drawing boards working on design modifications. Occasionally some of them would go down to the factory floor to visit the mock up of the 146 to get a better visualisation of where the part they were working on fitted in the plane. Most of them use plasticine to shape the specific part into space needed. Next to the graphic design area there was a new computer design centre which went unused. The company even offered financial incentives to get the graphic designers to train on the CAD (Computer Aided Design) system but most of them were set in their ways. This meant that I had no problem in trying out the CAD computers myself. Nowadays it is all CAD.

The most surprising thing I noticed about this and other departments was that the heads of department were treated like an officer class and had their own canteen. It was a great surprise that most of the workers accepted this "class division". Soon this practice would disappear forever hastened by the new Japanese management structure employed in their car plants in the UK. I spent some time with the Chief Engineer and he and I went to the ordinary workers' canteen – he had no airs and graces but only a devotion to engineering and a love of the aerospace industry. Once in his office I commented how one of the plans of the 146 fuselage looked like a boat." It is a boat" he said, it just moves through air instead of water – stupid me I thought.

I did have a bit of fun in the Future Aerospace department which was involved in some futuristic if pie in the sky aerospace designs. I noticed in this department that there was some friction over the different rates of pay. There did not appear to be a published pay structure but one clever wit circulated anonymously a graph sheet with an X indicating his pay and years of experience and asked colleagues to do the same anonymously. The result caused a lot of consternation when some found out that others were earning far more than they were for doing the same job. British Aerospace also had a separate military division in Hatfield that was the envy of the civil division. They appeared to have few restrictions on their budgets and on what and how they paid their staff.

One of the high points of my stay was a trip on a luxury 125 Executive Jet. They were normally eight armchair seats with luxury bathroom and service facilities. Some of the finishing was gold plated and rich Arab states were the main customers. Today we can add the Russian and other Oligarchs to the list of purchasers. Twice a week key staff flew with the 125 jet to Bristol to link up with staff working on Concorde and then onto Chester and back to Hatfield. My kind man Ollie in Modifications wanted to give me a treat – see how the top staff lived as it were; but he had a problem to solve. The IRA was very active in 1986 and I held an Irish passport. BAe were in charge of all flights to do with the monarchy and maybe it was not a great idea to have an Irishman having a grand tour of BAe's top staff offices at three different sites. Ollie had to organise for a complete security check on me and I felt a bit guilty because he already had a lot of work and responsibility as it was without adding Irish security issues to his workload. Ollie got his way and soon I was sitting in a very comfortable armchair aboard the 125 Executive Jet early one morning, gin and tonic to hand heading for Bristol. It would be the first of many G&Ts I had on the round trip. BAe civil division was still organised on the military officer model. I drank and dined in the senior staff (officers) boardrooms and the only time I saw the workers was on a quick tour of the factory floor.

I noticed two very different working patterns to that which we have in schools and colleges. Firstly, there is no end of terms; the show in industry just carries on through the year. There is no end of year trauma when a whole group of pupils leave the school forever and another one starts. Staff did not retire or leave in large numbers like at the end of the academic year in education. It is a more gradual and continuous process in industry. From time to time we went down to one of the aircraft hangars to say good bye over drinks and speeches to a senior member of staff retiring or leaving for other reasons. Staff in this industry worked at a more relaxed pace and in a much quieter environment than schools or colleges where we are surrounded by loud energetic young people. Late on in my career I taught at two schools that did not ring bells signalling the start and finish of lessons in the hope of reducing the stampede and noise on corridors between lessons. It was a bit of a failure because some teachers went on too long and some pupils would arrive late for the next lesson. In fact, I noticed that some aerospace staff accumulated energy whilst sitting at a design board or computer all day. They could not wait to finish work and get on the Squash Court or travel to London to the theatre or some other event. In schools, we collapsed into chairs in the staffroom to recover away from the daily battlefield of the classroom. Of course, we had no choice but to win these battles in the interests of our pupil's education.

During my stay in the different departments I was looking for examples of the science and mathematics that might be useful to give practical relevance to the pure science and maths taught in secondary schools. I was also looking for examples of good methods of communication and management skills. It was not long before I had enough material to write up my report for presentation at The Institution of Mechanical Engineers in London.

My last department that I visited at BAe was the Technical Publications Division. The number of working manuals for just the 146 numbered forty and counting and scores of technical drawing people were employed because every part and its modification had to have a schematic diagram for it. Some of these people were quite talented but the Head of Department did not allow for scope for extra graphic arts skills – they would do it his way or not at all. Today CAD will have replaced most of these workers.

It took me about two weeks, with the help of the publications department, to draw up my report of 15000 words plus plans and drawings for presentation at the Institution of Mechanical Engineers towards the end of July 1986. It was nice to meet up with my fellow seconded teachers and to hear their presentations. We covered an impressive range of industries between us. My report was very favourable received by a panel of assessors from Glasgow University. In 1988 I moved to the post of deputy headship at Ashlyns Upper School, Berkhamstead in Hertfordshire and it was here that I would get the chance to impact the whole school curriculum with what I had learnt from my Industry Year 1986 secondment.

It is extraordinary to think that that only a few years after my secondment the Hatfield aerospace industry has completely disappeared. The Guided Missile Division closed in 1989 with the loss of 2000 jobs followed in 1993 with the closure of the Civil Division with the loss of 2500 jobs. Some of the employees got redeployed to BAe sites elsewhere. In 2016 an expanded Hertfordshire University, Industry Park and housing now occupy the sites. Few traces of 50 years of aircraft and missile manufacture remain.

Ragnar and me Hertford Half Marathon 1985

My First London Marathon 1984

Mum and Dad Finchley circa 1982 Golf on the Menu

Kevin left playing at my 50th Birthday Hertford 1996

Kevin Whealan red had Pat and me Snowdon circa 1987

Uncle Philip to my right Dorothy and Charles
Circa 1993 Silver Anniversary

Skiing Norway circa 1994

Cross Country Skiing Norway circa 1993

Cigar before I quit in 1998

Reading Narnia with Astrid 1992-93

Speech for my 50th Birthday Maria, dark
hair, to my right Ragnhild to my left

In my office Ashlyns's School Berkhampsted circa 1995

Vincent and Eva at my 50th Birthday

Interviewed by my students Ashlyns's School 1995

My Sixth Formers European Science Project 1997

Astrid with 1st cousin Liam Horgan 1993

CHAPTER 18

A DO IT YOURSELF ODYSSEY BEGINS – NECESSITY IS THE MOTHER OF INVENTION.

It is surprising how much of one's life is taken up with the challenges and stress of keeping your home and its contents in working order and in consequence I have allocated my DIY its own chapter. I have lost count of the number of times I have dismantled and tried to repair: washing machines, vacuum cleaners, lawn mowers and electrical gadgets over the years. My efforts delayed the day when we would have to buy replacements. Today thanks to China, the relative cost of electrical goods is much lower and it is not possible to repair most electrical items because they are modular designed. At best, one can have a faulty module replaced or just buy a new one.

By 1984 my farming skills that I had acquired in Ireland were a distant memory. The only practical skill that I used in my early years in London was gardening for my mainly Jewish clients. As a matter of necessity, and mentioned elsewhere, my car mechanics skills were developed in the 1970s. Our first two houses that we bought in Reading were new build and Alice did most of the painting and wallpapering – she is very good working up ladders. However the gardens needed to be dug out for new lawns, hedging and bedding plants and that was my main area of interest. I proved to be a good digger like my father. I can remember saying to my sister Avril as my our father was being lowered into his grave in Hertford in 2002 that that was one hole that he did not have to dig himself. However, our father was very practical and had to learn carpentry from scratch, helped by a few job sackings along the way, when he moved to England in 1954. As a symbol of his carpentry skills, I placed a steel set square and spirit level in his coffin to help him get a good start in the next world and avoid any heavenly sackings by the Lord.

When we moved into our new house in Hertford in 1981 it was only three bedroom with an ugly prefabricated garage and a large garden used as a chicken run. In other words, a lot of work had to be completed in and outside of the house. The house came with planning permission for a two-story extension and it was not until 1984 that we raised an extra mortgage to start on the extension.

We got started on the garden with the help of a woman designer who was a member of The British Association of Garden Architects. She was a bit old school but came up with a design that encapsulated our wishes and 35 years later her ideas are still baring fruit. Whilst digging to her new design I discovered an electric underground cable which supplied electricity for an old bungalow that once existed in our back garden. The serious digging began during my Easter holidays in 1984 when I worked on the foundations for our two storey extensions. We are fortunate to have gravel rather than a clay bed in our area that makes the risk of subsidence less. Nevertheless the planning authorities insist on a least a one meter dept for the foundations. Half a meter down the going got tough and from then on, every cm dept was only gained by liberal use of the pickaxe. At the same time I was in training for my first London marathon in mid May and I was running up to 50 miles a week which coupled to my digging activities was making me over tired and a bit irritable – sorry Alice. One could save on costs by mixing up my own concrete for the foundation but, wisely, I had the eight cubic meters of ready mix delivered. Through my squash club I met a bricklayer who with a mate agreed to do all the brickwork for me. I ordered 8000 bricks for the job. It would be a few years until I took on my own brickwork and plastering jobs. The next step was to brick up to damp proof course level. Whilst laying out the damp course roll I remembered again by mother telling me how she sat as a child on one end of the damp course roll to keep it in place for her father Patrick Fitzsimons when he was building the farm house at Cookstown, Kells in the 1920s.

I then developed my skills of connecting sewage piping to the main sewer, and laying another four cubic meters of ready mix concrete for the flooring. My dad was a great help in tapping and levelling the concrete floor and with the final screed cover. Fixing the joists for the first floor into the external house wall using an angle grinder was a new and dangerous task. My dad came to my aid again in laying the floorboards.

I had intended to have a professional plumber to connect the piping for the radiators and bathroom. One chap made a start but then disappeared – the recession was over and he wanted me to buy his overpriced radiators. I bought all the plumbing gear necessary and the important blowtorch. With pipes and solder to hand I started on my first solder joint. The blowtorch produced a large yellow fluttering flame that only served to heat the solder but not melt it. I noticed a piece of metal with a sharp needle at the end taped to the handle of the blowtorch. Then it all came back to me. When I was a scouting cub in Wicklow, Ireland we heated water for tea on Primus Stoves. Occasionally we only got a yellow flame and not a blue one. Solution, clean out the carbon with a sharp needle. Result, blue flame. With a little prodding of the needle my blowtorch roared into life and my plumbing career had begun.

With my Physics background, I felt a little more confident with the electrics. Unlike most modern houses that are built around a wooden frame with plasterboard interior walls with a brick external wall, my extension had concrete breeze block interior walls linked by steel pins across a 10 cm cavity to the external brick wall. I had to chisel out channels in the hard concrete blocks for the down and up electrical cables for the light and appliance switches and sockets. Separate lighting and appliance ring circuits were installed in the bedroom ceilings, lower floor ceilings and in the ground floor screed.

The roofing proved to be particularly troublesome, not least because of an error in the drawings. I had to submit new drawings because the existing ones were out of date for the original planning permission. This was advantageous because I added some changes, but unfortunately took the same roof pitch of 30 degrees from the original drawing assuming that it was correct. I had the roof rafters made to measure. In early July my bricklayers were putting the finishing touches to the wall plates to support the rafters. I hired a lorry to go to Norfolk to collect my readymade rafters. At this time I was extra busy with A 'Level Exam Board marking. One day when I came home from school with the intention of getting some marking done, I was confronted by my two worried bricklayers. They asked me to look up at the rafters on the extension and to my horror the rafters were higher than the roof on the main house. I realised then the error on the original drawing. The elevation should have been 22.5 and not 30 degrees. Therefore, it was back to Norfolk to collect a new set of rafters and accept a financial loss on the old ones.

All plumbers have to be able to handle lead, after all the word plumber comes from the Latin for lead-plumbum. There was a long gulley between the existing house and the extension that needed to be lead lined and I soon realised how heavy lead was and the need to use a wooden mallet for working it into shape. On this occasion I took the easy option and got a local tiler to finish off the roof. I had repaired a few broken windows in the past that gave me a little training as a glazier and this was of some help in putting over twenty pre-cut double glazed glass panels into the window frames, not to mention the problems I faced fitting the patio doors.

I spent many a happy hour with a pint to hand in pubs in front of an Inglenook fireplace and I was set on an Inglenook for our new lounge. I even convinced Alice to have similar wall lights that I admired in one of our local pubs. Inglenooks have a large supporting oak beam and I settled for a not so old oak beam from a shop in Bishops Stortford. I got special red antique style bricks for the surround and my local Blacksmith made the fireplace canopy with some nice brass edging. The fire grate came from a local antique shop. To finish the fireplace I developed my tiling skills and for a first attempt my efforts have stood the test of time.

Putting the ceilings and trap doors in was made a lot easier by using gypsum boards, even if a bit dusty. I left the plastering of the walls and ceilings to the professionals. The final challenging job was the building of a new bathroom with suitable cupboards. I was particularly proud of my new bidet – hardly ever used – and our powered shower pump. Even though I completely rebuilt the bathroom in 2003, the same power pump is still working in 2016, 32 years on!

I started this extension with some serious digging and finally finished it after a bit more trench digging for the rain soak ways.

It took eight months to complete the extension – quick even by professional building standards – and we celebrated with a party in early January 1985. It was a relatively warm evening and some of the guests were nearly overcome by the heat from the log fire in the Inglenook, but the fire did look really impressive.

After a two year rest from serious DIY I drew up plans for a new garage and study. We got planning permission in August 1987 and a mortgage extension of £12000. In November I got back to serious digging again. Trenches totalling 26 meters long and one meter dept were required. I can remember Alice calling me in for tea one day. She could not see me for all the piled up clay around the dugout trenches. As I looked up at the swirling grey clouds I momentarily thought of what it must have been like in the trenches of the first World War. I ordered tough concrete lintels to protect the main sewer going out of the property to the road from the weight of the garage walls. I was lucky to get my squash bricklayer friend to do the brickwork for me. He was delighted to get the job because he did not like the dusty interior job he was employed on in renovating the local magistrates' court. This time I decided to do the rafters and roofing myself. Ragnar did interrupt his studies for five minutes to hold the long roof ridge plank for me to nail it into place. I had fun learning how to bonnet tile the edges of the roof to match the existing roof on the main entrance porch. Inserting the spring-loaded large garage door was a testing problem and to my surprise the springs only lasted a few years. Alice did her usual painting and decorating of the study. In 2012 we gutted the study and put in a modern book shelving system along with a new electric heated wood floor and new patio door.

It was not long before I had to start digging again. A new Housing Association estate was built to the west side of our garden and we now had a cul de sac road right next to out privet hedge instead of neighbouring back gardens. We needed to raise another £3000 to build a 30-meter brick wall. Looking back I do not know why I did not rent a mechanical digger but I did gain some extra fitness in filling up a few skip loads with the heaps of clay and gravel that I dug out.

The British sometimes are behind their continental neighbours when it comes to interior design. Wooden floors have long been a feature of homes in Scandinavia and when in 1998 Alice inherited some money from her uncle Odd in New York, she decided to have wooden floors put in the lounge, dining room and hallway. She discovered a Danish company Junkers that made high quality oak inter locking composite floorboards. My wooden floorboard laying skills were about to be developed. The key piece of equipment was the jig saw along with a decent mobile workbench. We took great delight in getting rid of the carpets that despite regular hovering still collected a lot of ingrained dirt over the years. For a time relatives and friends admired our new wood floors and it was not long before nearly every house in Britain had wooden floors put in. At our Daughter's request in around 2000 we put in a new floor in her bedroom and as recently as 2015 we converted the small bedroom upstairs into a sewing and quilting workroom for Alice with a new wooden floor of course. Alice again did the decorating including sprucing up some bookshelves and cupboards.

I have always wanted a conservatory – where I am now typing this book. Surprisingly Alice was not convinced but now loves the extra light and opportunities for growing plants – including her beloved tomatoes and peppers – that a conservatory affords. I got my drawings approved by the planning department and soon got down to serious digging early in 2003. Sadly, my father who died in October 2002 would not be alive to see or advise me on my latest project. The footings and lower conservatory wall were strong enough to support a two-story extension if needed in the future. I went for a wooded upper structure rather than the dreaded ubiquitous PVC frameworks. A company from Cornwall called Baltic Pine provided all the wood and glass required based on a computerised analysis of my drawings. You could say it was the ultimate flat pack kit.

I had to move the downstairs boiler upstairs and relocate the outside boiler vent. Only then was it possible to start on the realigning of the sewage and kitchen wastewater outlets – a very testing job. I was particularly proud of my insulated under floor heating system and tiled floor. Levelling up the floor for the tiling was a bit of nightmare. I had to go to a building merchant in Ilford to get the right type of silvered under floor insulation boards. Another challenging problem was the lead flashing joining the pitched roof of the conservatory to the existing house and working the large lead lined gully between the external kitchen wall and the lower end of the conservatory roof. Thirteen years on the conservatory is in good shape as long as the external wood gets a regular coat of varnish.

It is surprising how quickly bathrooms and shower rooms become worn out and dated. In the last few years I have completely gutted both our bathrooms and put in new bath ware, lighting, tiled heated floors and storage units. Modern houses are sold with minimal fittings with a small shelf to hold your toothbrush if you are lucky. I am still astonished just how many different tools I had to use ranging from soldering iron to blow torch, tile cutters to Stanley knifes, wire cutters and hacksaws, cement mixers to polyfiller spatulas, electric multimeter, a whole range of wrenches, screwdrivers, pliers, hammers and much else.

Even now in my pension years, I still feel that there are many DIY jobs still to be done: including a new garage automatic door, new modern front garden gate – the original wooden one that I made has long since disappeared, new facia and guttering boards, new kitchen ceiling, tiling and LED lighting, improved external security system with video camera and new fencing. Any volunteers?

I am sure that my wife has a long list of jobs for me to do but I certainly will not ask her what they might be. I have come to realise just how many skills and thought processes are involved in good DIY work and, despite the frustrations along the way, how rewarding and cost effective it can be. As of April 2016 I have put in a new kitchen ceiling with new LED down lights and replaced the kitchen sink and surrounds. I still need to retile the floor.

CHAPTER 19

SKIING TAKES OFF

It was not until the late 1970s that our immediate family got into some serious skiing. Alice's sister, Ragnhild, had married Sverre, who was in charge of a mountain hotel in Hallingdal, some 40 km from the ski resort of Geilo. We tried to go to Norway every Easter and join the rest of the Norwegians as they rushed back to the mountains for the last of the cross country and to become Påske Brun (an Easter suntan). It might seem crazy that with spring in the air that people would leave the spring awakening in their gardens to go to the snow clad mountains but it can be very cold in January and February – minus 20 C in the daytime – so it does make sense to go at Easter when the days are much longer and warmer.

The area around the Hotel had prepared tracks for cross country skiing and we would go on ski tours for up to four hours with packed lunches and flasks of tea and juice for the kids. The better skiers would pull a pulk (a sled) for children under three years old. If the weather was good we would bring grilling equipment with pølser (sausages) on the main menu along with some baked potatoes in tin foil. The children would dig a hole in the snow and we would make a fire using mostly dry silver birch from the woods. Sometimes the snow conditions would change and we would have to stop and wax our skis to stop slipping back when going uphill and to stop wet snow clumping to the underside of the ski. In the 1970s our cross country skis were made of wood and could be quite heavy. The ski bindings rapped round the back of the ski boot. By the 1990s, the skis clipped on to the toe of the now much lighter ski boot and were made of light composite carbon material.

In 1980, a new ski lift opened near the hotel and Alpine skiing was possible for the first time. The lift was a single draglift T-Bar and a few years later the centre acquired a second drag lift higher up the mountain but even to this day the resort does not have a chair lift. Sverre had shares in the new ski centre and we could get a deal on ski passes. Extraordinarily, we were there on the first day the ski lift opened which was during the Christmas holiday. Even more extraordinarily, my brother Vincent, who had never been on skis, and his wife to be Eva joined us from Sweden. Still more extraordinary was the fact that this would be the first time my wife Alice – born on cross-country skis – would experience Alpine skiing.

It was a dull overcast day when we headed down to the ski centre to try on our rented alpine boots and skis. Vincent, being his usual self took longer than the rest of us to get sorted out and it was with great difficulty that we got him up the draglift and with even greater difficulty that we got him down the ski slope, even with the help of the local ski instructor who had taught in Colorado, USA. I think this was Vincent's first and last trip on skis. His talents were far more suited to the dance floor. Alice with her natural balance acquired when young coped well, as did Ragnar and Fingal. Memories of what I learnt on my first school Alpine ski trip to Austria in 1972 came back to help me get down without falling.

Over the years, we returned at Easter and tried to do both Alpine and cross-country. One of our favourite ski tours was to take the drag-lifts to the top and then cross-country ski on prepared tracks across the mountain plateau, descending beyond Myrland and then ski below the tree line back to the ski centre or back to the house – a round trip of about 20km. Sometimes at the top we could see a reindeer herd in the distance and on one occasion when we were having a quiet picnic the herd passed very close to us. Later, as our cross-country skiing skills improved we took the ski lifts to the top and then headed for Geilo taking about 3 to 4 hours of skiing. On reaching Geilo we had to cross-country down the alpine piste with skiers whizzing past us on all sides. I nearly always had a couple of great tumbles on the steeper slopes. Nevertheless, it was all worth it when we ended up in Dr Holmes Hotel. The hotel is one of the most famous mountain hotels in Norway and once welcomed Princess Margaret of the UK as a guest. I sweat more cross-country skiing than when I run marathons and the invention of the Helly Hansen vest was a great help in wicking the sweat away from the skin. But, it is still essential to get into dry clothing as soon as possible after skiing so, a Dr Holmes toilet cubicle was my first port of call, followed by a trip to the bar and a beer and aquavit as a reward (and never mind the cost). This was followed by a second beer and aquavit in front of a roaring fire, surrounded by some of Norway's top socialites enjoying the Après Ski. Flushed with the spirits of our exertions, the sober one in the group would drive us home for a fine Norwegian meal and plenty of wine. Easter Saturday was a very special day when we dined on the finest Norwegian mountain lamb. The lambs born in late spring spent the summer grazing on the finest grasses, herbs and berries on the mountain. They were slaughtered in the autumn when less than five months old. The maxim – an animal tastes like what it eats – works with this lamb. We always dined well at Ragnhild and Sverre's house and it helped that Sverre was a trained chef. He makes a brilliant fish soup and the finest sauce to go with local reindeer steaks.

In the 80s and 90s, we normally took the ferry to Norway from Newcastle or Harwich but with the advent of low cost airlines the ferries are no more. When we were able to bring the car we would load up wine and spirits which at that time were prohibitively expensive in Norway. On occasion, we brought hams, turkey and other foodstuffs. The easiest way to Hallingdal was to go via Gothenburg in Sweden, drive up to Oslo and then another four hours drive to the house. The Newcastle to Bergen route meant that we had to drive along the fjord to Aurland through tunnels and then a corkscrew tunnel up the mountain where we would sometimes have to put chains on the car wheels and follow a snow plough in convoy. On one occasion, our son Fingal drove in convoy in a blizzard and felt that he was going to the north pole. He was delayed several hours and lucky to arrive at all.

Norway was slow as a nation to excel in competitive international alpine skiing events. They failed to capitalise on the early success of Stein Eriksen who won the Giant Slalom and was second in the Slalom at the Oslo Winter Olympics in 1952. They excelled in Nordic Cross-Country, Biathlon, Ski Jumping and in Ice Skating. In the 1968 Olympics in Grenoble, France, they achieved first place in the medal table ahead of the Soviet Union – an outstanding achievement for a nation of under 5 million inhabitants. Even more surprisingly, they did it without achieving a single medal in any of the alpine events. By contrast, when we attended the Lillehammer Olympics in 1994, Norway won the most alpine medals, one more than Germany. They won the most medals overall but had one less gold medal than Russia. Alpine skiing had finally arrived in Norway.

AUSTRIA, AN ALPINE RUN OF 28 YEARS ON THE PISTE BEGINS AND WE ARE STILL GOING DOWNHILL.

Our first real experience of alpine skiing outside of Norway was in St Johann and nearby Kitzbuhel in the Austrian Tirol. Alice was teaching at Hitchin Boys' school and the school organised their annual ski trips themselves to Austria that was a lot cheaper for the pupils than using travel companies. Around 1989 Alice, Astrid, our son Fingal, my nephew Liam Horgan and I got overnight seats on the school coach to Austria driven by the school's Head of Technology (let us call him Alfred, as I will be mentioning him later). South of Calais we were able to convert the seats into bunk beds so could get to lie down horizontally. I have always found it very difficult to sleep sitting up. On occasion, I have managed to sleep in the aisle beneath the seats or on the floor of ferry lounges going to Norway. There was no room in the hotel for us so we rented an apartment up in the nearby hills. Austria was light-years ahead of Norway in terms of the quality and variety of alpine facilities. For starters, there were bars and restaurants on the slopes – alcohol was normally not available on any ski runs in Norway. I believe that our resort of St Johann in Tirol had and has more bars/restaurants per kilometre of piste than anywhere else has in the world. We also had the pleasure of going up a mountain on a gondola as well as three and four man chairlifts for the first time. We were in alpine heaven and 28 years later, we are still going to St Johann.

I can remember Fingal wearing a very noticeable 80s style speckled blue ski anorak but cannot remember much about Liam. Recently I contacted Liam and all he remembers is ducking under a sign to avoid been decapitated near a chair lift and ending up buried in the snow with a view only of the sky above and the people in the chairlifts looking down on him. He was not too happy about giving them some free entertainment. He also remembers mucking around with Fingal and meeting a fellow eighteen year old who was a model for the clothing chain Next. However, his main complaint was the lack of buxom Austrian blonds and English maidens. They did have to be back up in our apartment by 9pm as someone had to look after Astrid while Alice and I helped check the rooms of the Hitchin boys for cheap 80 proof rum purchased in the local supermarket and make sure the Hitchin staff had company in the hotel bar. I was surprised that Liam never went skiing again. I think he preferred to risk breaking a leg achieving his football dreams rather than break a leg skiing. Liam, it is not too late to return to the ski slopes, you can even try snowboarding, ski paragliding and even get to wear a ski helmet with a camera to record your adventures.

Compared to today there were few health and safety measures. For years, we skied in Austria without wearing helmets. The Hitchin staff took it upon themselves to give their pupils a few brief skiing lessons before letting them lose on the mountain. Initially we had one member of staff, a PE teacher who was a top skier and later two other staff acquired basic ski instructor qualifications. Accidents did happen but not always on the slopes. As the years progressed, we were able to name parts of the mountain after ski accidents or skiing mishaps that happened to staff. We named a tight turn on one slope 'Justin's elbow' because that was where Justin Thomas broke his elbow. 'Mather's tumble' after a member of staff did a complete summersault that put him out of action for a few days. 'Davis corner' was where our big Welsh Latin teacher and rugby player met his nemesis. He also had problems with sweaty feet and developed the biggest and deepest verrucas between his toes that I had ever seen. Often it was my job to pull his ski boots off without fainting. The more exotically named Velociraptor Junction after an incident involving two identical twins and our ski leader Alfred. True to form, Alfred had the pupils skiing difficult black runs after only a few days skiing. Alfred reached the junction first and waited for the first pupil to arrive. Twin 1 arrived and went straight past him into a ravine unable to control his speed. Alfred moved to the side of the piste to look down to see Twin 1 buried in the deep snow and very lucky to avoid hitting a tree. Twin 2 arrives and unable to control his speed crashes into Alfred and both end up in the ravine with Twin 1. The rest of the group arrive and most of them pass on down the mountain assuming their leader has skied on. Alfred with the advice of his fellow teachers selected the name Velociraptor from the two crazy Velociraptor chasing around the kitchen in the film Jurassic Park. It took some time to round up the group that afternoon.

If all else failed, staff and pupils knew where our favourite ski watering hole was. We called it Colorado Willy after the American eccentric barman who entertained us. All skiers had to pass this pub on the way down to the Gondola. Colorado Willy was easy to get to from the bottom – up a two-man chairlift then directly on to a three- man chairlift followed by a gentle ski run to the Colorado. One member of staff was not a very strong skier and was happy to spend most of the day enjoying the action from the bar at Colorado Willy. On many occasions, I joined him for discussions on the human predicament. Once I arranged to meet him there for lunch and found him in some discomfort and only on his second pint. He told me he had a fall on the way down to the bar but the discomfort in his chest would pass. It did not and we got him down to the hospital only to find that he had broken his collarbone. For the rest of the trip, heavily strapped up, he had to walk down the piste to Colorado Willy and Willy really did look after his favourite guest. After this incident, that part of the slope to the pub was called Eason's collarbone.

One of our favourite off-piste places we named 'Cherry Glade', which was a lovely undulating path through the pine forest. It was here that I had a lucky escape. After a heavy night on the booze, I was still feeling confident next morning on the slope and decided to take on Cherry Glade with my friend Andy Sloman. Whilst on the path I decided to go off the path following a very agile child down a steep U shaped dip (Andy, very wisely, did not). The kid made it up the other side. I did not. The upside of the U was a lot steeper than the downside and this was difficult to see from the edge, given the lack of definition on a very cloudy day. The young boy also had much shorter skis than I did. As a result, the top of my skis dug into the lower end of the upslope and my forward momentum drove me into the slope. As my helmeted head hit the snow I felt a sharp excruciating pain in my neck and down my arm. My mind was in slow motion as I thought my neck might be broken and I even thought of the resulting disability. I lay there motionless and waited, hoping I could move any part of my body. Soon I was able to move one of my hands and part of my back and relief came over me. Andy could see what had happened and was relieved when he finally saw some movement on my part. Eventually he got my skis off and helped me to stand up – more relief. I realised I had avoided the worse scenario. Two hours later I had my neck X-Rayed in the local hospital and was diagnosed with bruised neck muscles but my vertebrae looked undamaged. I had to wear a neck brace for several weeks and it took well over a year before I could turn my head without pain.

Alice, Fingal and I took turns to help our two and half year old daughter Astrid to ski between our legs down the mountain. Years later she would join the local ski school and we would all come to see her in her slalom race in the Ski School at the end of her week of lessons. Over the years Astrid became a fine skier and overtook Fingal as the best skier in the family. Ragnar was a competent skier but never wanted to be the equivalent to Toad of Toad Hall going down the ski slope (that role was reserved for Fingal). When Astrid finished school, she took a gap year before going to university. Her plan was to become a ski instructor in Austria for the winter season and then work in Disneyland, Paris to improve her French. In early November, she and I went to Cyprus to enjoy a bit of sunshine and run the marathon and half-marathon (Astrid) in Paphos. I ended up running the half-marathon with Astrid where she got home in 1hr 44 min, fourth overall out of the women, and a minute ahead of me! My marathon was cancelled on the morning of the event due to torrential rain and high winds overnight – it takes something very serious to happen before the Greek Cypriots cancel an event. My excuse for Astrid beating me was that mentally I had prepared for a full marathon. The following month we drove to St Johann to meet her ski school leader and set up her shared apartment. She had to complete and pass the tough Austrian Ski Federation Instructors' course before being allowed to teach at the Ski School. I bought her a microwave oven and Christmas tree with lights before I left. It would be the first time that our daughter would not be home for Christmas and it was a long drive back to England on my own. Astrid did pass her exam and had a very informative and eventful winter ski season. One highpoint I recall was when her ski school was interviewed with Irish RTE on St Patrick's Day. Her Ski School developed contact with the dry ski slope in Wicklow and Irish Travel Companies and one group brought over to have a ski experience was comprised of blind people, some of whom were terminally ill. Amazingly, despite having only partial or no sight at all, they were able to ski by listening to very precise instructions from their guide and "feeling" the snow. A very moving moment of that week was when one of the guests won a talent competition by singing, "Wonderful Tonight" by Eric Clapton. The prize was a free week's ski holiday for 2 back in St Johann the following year. Very sadly, the young man who had won said that he would give the prize to his parents, as he did not think he would survive to return a year later.

In 1990, we returned to Austria on the school coach and Fingal came with his school friend Darren. This time our close friends Debbie and Heddwyn Evans and their young children Gareth and Delyth joined us in renting an apartment. They drove to Austria – a long drive with two small children. For the next few years the Evans family went to ski in Italy with Debbie's school but then rejoined us in Austria until the present day – I think they have clocked up twenty years in total coming to St Johann. Fingal's friend Darren got a good Après Ski session in and we all knew not to go into the apartment bathroom until given the all clear.

In 1991, we finally got to stay in the Neuwirt Hotel with the Hitchin School staff even though we had to make do with a drafty room up in the loft of the hotel. We took the coach to get to the main Gondola in time for the 8.30am first run and often the best runs of the day. Sometimes the piste was a bed of frozen pebbles if the snow had melted a lot the previous day. After the piste was warmed up by the sun the snow would soften and you could get in a couple of hours of fine skiing before the crowds churned it up into small moguls. If the days and nights were below freezing then you would get perfect snow and the skiing was good all day. In later years snow machines and improved piste bashers helped to greatly improve the skiing experience.

Tuesday evening was bumpa music night in the Neuwirt or more correctly Tyrolean Abend, with lederhosen backside slapping and plenty of log chopping. After about three or four of these evenings we avoided the show like the plague and the Tyrolean bumpa music as well – familiarity breeds contempt I guess. In the early days once we got the kids to their rooms we settled down in the bar for card games and a continuous supply of Pilsen and Weizen Bier. As for me I occasionally "borrowed" some cigars from the front desk. Years later, I did admit to my cigar crime, but Herr Stoekl, the hotel owner forgave me in view of all the money we spent at the hotel over the years.

I also accidentally got involved in another crime. The school hired most of the ski equipment from a ski shop a few miles outside of St Johann. I hired a modern pair of Head skis and boots. During the week I had a little too much of the amber nectar at Colorado Willy and got into a session with an Englishman on a ski stop over on his way to do business in Hungary – way ahead of his time. Skiers were in the habit of leaving their skis on the ground because the ski racks were often full. Every day it was customary to get the last gondola of the day to the top where we all necked a double Williams schnapps and then set off down the mountain like the charge of the Light Brigade. Looking back on it now I am aghast at the speed we reached bearing in mind we were not on modern shorter carver skis. As I left Colorado Willy's to make my way down to the last lift I saw my Head skis lying on the ground and clipped my ski boots in as usual, perfect fit. When skiing down to the gondola I thought that my skis were longer than I expected them to be – too much beer can affect your visual perception. It was only when in the gondola on the way hope that I noticed that the rent stamp on the ski tips was a different renting company – the famous Christl Haas shop in St Johann. Christl was a local girl who won gold in the 1964 Olympics.

Later she had a sex change and called herself Eric. Sadly, 'he' died in a drowning accident at the age of only 58 years. It was just my luck that my boots fitted the skis and presumably the same applied to the person who took my skis. The problem arose when we had to give the skis back to the rental shop. A member of staff managed to tick me off the list of skis returned at the shop. I suppose I could have gone to Christl Haas with the skis but it all seemed a bit too complicated at the time. The Christl Haas skis are still in my loft and besides they were a challenge to ski on because they were really too long for my height.

School ski trips are insured for loss and damage to ski equipment. Some of the British school staff liked to have the latest fashion and advance technical development in ski equipment. Nearly every year they made claims for loss and damage to ski equipment. In the 80s and 90s, few people had any moral compass when it came to insurance claims. The thinking was that you were not affecting any individuals with an overrated or false claim. Ok, the premiums might go up but insurance companies and claimants were all winners. On some occasions coach drivers reversed 'accidentally' over skis or ski anoraks or had other inventive accidents to cameras or other equipment. The insurance companies paid up on all claims with minimal quibbling. On one occasion when we were away on a ski trip our house was virtually ransacked and we had to make a very genuine claim costing several thousand of pounds. We learnt a lesson, including our daughter Astrid, not to leave valuables lying around the house. I bought, for the first time, a secure safe box fixed into an upstairs external wall. Why did it take years for me to do it without having to learn the hard way?

Pupil discipline problems on ski trips were nearly always the consequence of drinking. Once we arrived early evening at Calais and stopped off to get some food and beer for the overnight trip to Austria for the staff. We told the pupils explicitly they could buy whatever they wanted except alcohol and cigarettes. About an hour later down the motorway I smelt some cigarette smoke and thought the pupils at the back of the coach were more lively than usual. A little later some of them were shouting about 'No Surrender to the IRA' and I could hear some talking about bombing. In the many years on the coach this was a first. They seemed to know that there was an Irish member of staff on board from another school and thought they would have some fun at my expense. I went into action and darted down to the back of the coach where there was a party in full swing. A nearly empty bottle of peach brandy was doing the rounds and several pupils were smoking. We have had some incidents like this in pupil rooms in Austria but never on the coach going there. I waved to our party leader to come and join the fun. We stopped the coach at the next motorway station and had all the pupils and staff off. We discovered cases of beer, several bottles of spirits and cartons of cigarettes. We dumped the stuff in the kerbside bins and waved to the parked up lorry drivers to help themselves. After a series of interviews, we identified two ringleaders. We would now stop off at Munich Airport and put them on a plane home. As we drove off, we could see some bemused but happy lorry drivers. On every ski trip there is a designated member of staff back at the school to liaise with parents in the event of any problems arising and on this occasion it was the deputy. Our leader asked him to book flights and contact the relevant parents. One of the parents was on holiday – some parents like to send their offspring on school trips as glorified baby sitters so they can holiday free of their children. Other pupils pleaded for the miscreants but to no avail. We stopped at the airport and escorted them to the check-in – they were on their way home. Later I heard that the parents refused to contribute to the airfares and contested our action.

Pupils who misbehaved at the ski resort were normally grounded for the day and stayed with a member of staff at Colorado Willy watching the staff and other pupils enjoying themselves – this was our equivalent to the naughty step. Each trip we took the pupils for a night out in nearby Kitzbuhel.

Some of the sixth formers often deliberately did not return at 10pm for the coach home, preferring to try out the nightclubs and come home early morning. They accepted the fact that they would be grounded but were probably too hung over to ski anyway.

LILLEHAMMER OLYMPICS 1994

One of the high points of our ski adventures was attending the Winter Olympics in Norway in February in 1994 and we cancelled our trip to Austria to do so – not a problem. I have one lasting memory of talking to a Canadian millionaire who made all his money from promoting his own ski wax. If I had not realised the importance of the right ski wax before I certainly did after my few drinks with him.

The previous year we had visited Lillehammer in the summer and stood right at the top of the awe-inspiring ski jump over looking the town and we also visited the new Viking Ship skating rink and the new Amphitheatre for figure skating and ice dancing in Hamar. It was very appropriate that Hamar should host the main ice skating events in view of the town's long history of ice skating in Norway and beyond. My wife remembers as a little girl getting the autographs at the Hamar ice-skating rink of some of her skating idols and meeting a lot of skaters from the Netherlands who came to train in the town. There were also opportunities to skate on the town's lake Mjøsa when it froze, which was most years.

The skating highpoint was Koss the Boss – winning three gold medals for Norway in the Viking Ship, and for British supporters, Torvil and Dean winning a bronze medal in figure skating at the Hamar Amphitheatre. The Amphitheatre Figure Skating Final gained worldwide attention when the two US skaters, Tonya Harding and Nancy Kerrigan competed for a medal. A few weeks prior to the Olympics Tonya Harding had arranged for her husband to have Kerrigan clubbed on the knee with a baseball bat. Kerry recovered in time for the final and won a silver medal. Harding ended up eighth and was, after an enquired, banned from skating.

We arrived for the first week of the Olympics and managed to see an ice hockey match and some Alpine skiing. Every day we had a clear blue sky but daytime temperatures were rarely above minus 15C. This made for great ice sculptures and I managed to get myself photographed draped over one of them for the local paper. The Olympics was a very special occasion for my brother who set up his own Northern Lights display overlooking the Olympic venue in Lillehammer. He had his equipment built in Sweden and delivered on a big transporter to Lillehammer. 3M and other companies sponsored his work. He erected eight pyramids lit up by computer-generated lights at their bases and using the colour properties of the 3M colour film covering the pyramids recreated an impressive simulation of the Northern Lights. His display featured every night on Japanese television and Hilary Clinton was an admirer in the nearby American team hotel. His team stayed in motor homes near to the site and when we visited one evening his display helped to overcome to some extent the intense cold we endured – I can only hope those staying in the motor homes did not freeze overnight. I think that his display should have been part of the Opening Ceremony itself, but the Norwegians wanted it to be an all-Norwegian creation.

BACK TO ST JOHAN, AUSTRIA.

In the late 1990s we started to organise our own trips to Austria and said good bye to the extra hassle of having to look after school ski parties. New health, safety and legal requirements placed far too many restrictions and responsibilities on school ski party leaders.

Some of the old Hitchin staff joined us and we often had nearly twenty people in our group and a lot more fun. Our core group was Heddwyn and Debbie Evans along with their children Delyth and Gareth, when available. They introduced their Bramfield neighbours Jill and Nick Savage with their two children, also when available. My old friend Andy Sloman from Ashlyns School also joined us and along with his wife Elaine when available. Recently we were presented with a certificate from hotel Kitzbuhler Alpen for twenty years attendance. I have watched the owner Gerti Stoeckl and her brother Christian progress over the years to taking over the business from their father who still runs his own farm in Oberndorf. The new gondola that replaced the single chair lift from Oberndorf (the little village adjacent to St Johann), up to the main St Johann ski runs has been a great boost to their business. We have also seen Gerti and Christian's respective marriage successes and failures over the years. Gerti fell in love with Paulo, a Portuguese waiter and chef, and they had two children together. We had great fun with Paulo but all could see that he had difficulty being accepted by the close-knit Stoeckl family. The father was not too keen on a foreigner getting a share of the inheritance. Gerti now has a more compliant partner from the old East Germany who even wears Tyrollean Lederhosen when requested.

SKI TOURING UP THE SLOPES

Over time we have seen ski technology and fashion change. New technology allows one to telemark ski that was once the reserve of experienced native Norwegians. In recent years ski touring up the slopes has taken off. In 2012, I was the first and only one in our immediate party so far to ski tour up the mountain in three and a half hours and a vertical height climb of over 1km.

The idea appealed to me because I liked to do strenuous exercise in addition to the more relaxing downhill skiing when in Austria. Often I would finish skiing early so that I could go for a run or a swim in the sports complex in St Johann and sometimes Astrid and others joined me on a run. The previous year, 2011, on a run with Astrid I was struggling to keep up with her and had to shorten my run. I thought it was due to running at high altitude but oddly, it never troubled me in previous years. I found that if I stopped and walked for a while I could get running again. Maybe it was age catching up with me. In April I managed to complete the Milan marathon in less than 4Hr25m but felt the going harder than normal – ok it was nearly 30C at the finish.

In 2012 I therefore felt I had a good chance of making it up the mountain. To my surprise, I had to stop for a rest after a few hundred meters and had to continue stopping at regular intervals all the way to the top. I also noticed some other ski tourers even older than me, could keep going and some even got past me – now that was serious. I was drenched in sweat but still kept going. At times I thought of giving up but somehow I made it.

A month later, I went into the Royal Brompton Hospital for a life saving double heart bypass operation. An angiogram showed I had what was termed in the medical profession a "widow maker". I had a 99% blockage at the junction of two of the three main coronary branches feeding red blood to power the heart. It was no wonder that I could not keep running and a miracle I did not have a heart attack going up the mountain – my first heart attack would have been my last.

A year later, now mended, I skied up the mountain again, still hard going, but in less than two and a half hours.

CHAPTER 20

ASHLYNS SCHOOL, THE CORAM FOUNDATION, OUR SONS TAKE WING, 1988-1999.

B efore I left my closing school at Cheshunt I was interviewed for two Headships, one at Enfield Boys' Grammar School and one at a school in Herefordshire. I had some big hurdles to overcome even to get to the interview stage. In the late 1980s managing amalgamations and school closures were not seen as a good career move unlike today. Staffs from stable and established schools were favoured. The establishment of the government school inspection service OFSTED and value added curriculum measures were not yet in place. Some of the perceived established and successful schools were in fact underachieving. County Halls and School Governors would soon learn the value of appointing Headteachers who had experience of the real world of redundancies, changing demographics and the social effects of rapid urbanisation. I also had the problem of anti-Irishness due to the IRA bombing campaign especially in the more rural shire counties. Added to this mix was a latent anti-Catholism. There were still strong Masonic influences in county councils throughout the land. My best chance of a Headship would have been in a Catholic school in an inner city area but I had not taught in Catholic school for many years and besides, I did not want Headship that much to disrupt my now established family. It did still irritate me to see less experienced and qualified colleagues in other schools in Hertfordshire getting interviews for Headships.

Hertfordshire LEA did recognise my contribution at Bishopslea, Cheshunt and I got redeployed to Ashlyns Upper School (13-18) in Berkhamsted in west Hertfordshire. It would involve a round trip commute of over fifty miles but we would not have to move house. The school was the only comprehensive school in the town so its future was fairly secure – a relief to me. The Headteacher was a nice chap but somewhat weak and withdrawn in publicising and promoting the image of the school and in improving and modernising the curriculum.

The interesting history of the school was a big factor for me agreeing to take the post. The buildings and grounds were originally The Thomas Coram Foundling Hospital that moved out of Bloomsbury, London in the 1920s. Some of the original Coram Fields and Main House are still preserved but the Foundling Hospital was demolished. With the sale of some of the site the Foundation was able to build a magnificent Foundling School, Chapel and parkland on a hill in Berkhamsted overlooking the town. The Foundlings would now have plenty of fresh air to breath.

With the establishment of the NHS, foundling hospitals were phased out and Herts LEA bought the site in Berkhamsted to set up a bilateral school (separate Grammar and Secondary Modern sections) served by three middle schools in the town. The Coram Foundation charity was set up to support children and young single pregnant girls in the London area and retained its links with its original benefactors including Handel and the painter Hogarth. Ashlyns School became comprehensive in the late 1960s and retained some links with the Coram Foundation in London. In 11 years at the school, I got The Coram Foundation involved with the London marathon and I raised several thousand pounds for them in three London marathons. The highpoint was when I ran the famous 100th Boston marathon in 1996 for the foundation under the heading

"Running the World's oldest modern Marathon for the World's oldest incorporated Charity".

As with most schools, Ashlyns had a few oddball staff and some that had been around for years. My fellow deputy head was promoted over the years from a trainee non-graduate PE teacher and way beyond his level of competence and had an influence in the school way beyond what he merited. I cannot understand how one can teach in the same school for 35 years or more without getting stale and out of touch with national developments. I always had the feeling that my fellow deputy was learning from me and even claiming my innovations as his. I can truly say I learnt nothing from him. He had far too much influence on the Head but the LEA had put me in this school to bring about change, which did happen I am pleased to record.

I remember another teacher called Lyn who served many years at the school and who was very set in his ways. The pupils did have great respect for him and his discipline was very sound. When he retired, he came back to the school a couple of years later to do some supply teaching for me. I was surprised when a pupil came to my office requesting me to come immediately to Lyn's classroom. I found Lyn red-faced cornering a girl up against the wall ready to almost throttle her. She was giving him some serious lip, something that never happened when he was a permanent teacher at the school. The girl did not know of Lyn and his previous reputation counted for nothing, he was just another teacher to her. Teachers who have experience of teaching in more than one school have a better chance of coping in different class room environments.

The school had a fair number of middle class parents who expected results that helped to put pressure on the staff to raise their game. Berkhamsted is an established Tory majority town but does have its social problems. I remember asking our local community police officer what life was like in the town in terms of social issues. He said that Berkhamsted was like a nice smooth crusty cowpat. When you stepped hard on it, the shit spurted out from underneath.

A few years later, I had to deal with one of the town's madams. Our Head of History was preparing her room for Open Evening with the help of some of her pupils. One of the pupils, who was sitting on top of a class table was not cooperating and was quite aggressive when asked to do a particular task. The teacher moved her hand to get her off the desk and the girl exploded. She accused the teacher of hitting her and stormed out of the classroom. She got her mother to go to the local police station to file a report of teacher assault against her daughter. Half an hour later a police patrol car arrived and the male and female officers were shown into the Head's study – he was at home sick avoiding the stress of the occasion and I, not for the first time, had to take charge, including giving the address to the Prospective Parents. The officers wanted to interview the teacher in my presence. The teacher was very distressed when accused of assaulting the pupil and was near to collapsing. I managed to assure them that we would solve this in house and I would deal directly with the mother and daughter. The mother was well known to the police as a madam in the town and they were more than happy for me to relieve them of the case. She arrived at my office dressed to kill in a mini leather outfit, boots and all. I realised quickly that she would be open to a bit of male charm. Tea and cake was ordered and I asked her daughter to stay outside while we discussed the incident. Of course I made sure to pay more attention to her mother's problems supported by admiring glances from me and I told her how I could not understand why I never had the pleasure of meeting her before. It was not long before she was complaining about her own daughter's behaviour and attitude to her and her 'boyfriends'. I never had any more problems again from mother or daughter.

The school was getting some British Asian pupils from Chesham in the next-door county of Buckinghamshire who failed the 11plus and saw our school as a better alternative to the local secondary school. In one of my bottom maths sets I had an Asian boy who I got on well with, who may not have been brilliant at mathematics but was very street wise. He confided in me that some weekends he went to Hounslow in west London where there is a large Asian community to meet up with some mates to take on some local white kids on nearby estates. At this time, there was a lot of prejudice against Asians who laid low and concentrated on their businesses and on the academic success for their children. It was clear to me now in the early 1990s that some British born Asians were ready to fight back. Unfortunately, today this young lad could end up being recruited by ISIS. I was also close to another British Asian student, Arslan, from Chesham who played youth county level cricket and he was greatly influenced by my marathon adventures. He was rejected for the London Marathon and he was delighted when I managed to get him an entry through The Thomas Coram Foundation and became the first ever student from Ashlyns School to run the London Marathon. Between us we raised a good sum of money for the Coram Foundation. No, he did not beat me but he was not too far behind. Arslan was yet another 11plus reject who went on to university.

SCHOOL ASSEMBLES

Many people remember school assembles as being a bit of a bore: hymns, bible readings, prayers, long lists of sports results. In recent years, there have been changes for the better. More pupil involvement, role-play, power point displays and outside speakers. Governments have legislated that there must be a strong Christian element in assemblies in state schools as well as faith schools, but have not be able or willing to put it into effect. We can get away with "Christian Light" assembles.

It is the pupils who are the backbone of any school and Ashlyns had some real characters. I taught some of the bottom sets and what they lacked academically they made up for in spades with character. I related well to three boys in particular whom I discovered liked to take on my accent particularly from my school assemblies. One of them could mimic me very well and was funny with it. Eventually I started to use their talents as props in some of my assemblies and it was not long before I asked them to organise their own assembly. Some staff thought I was going too far but as they did a good job, they had to shut up. For some assemblies I needed special lighting and could leave even this job to my three lads – one of them ended up a lighting engineer on a cruise ship. Another of these lads was a Dr Who fan with a large collection of Dr Who paraphernalia. Well, why not get him to set up an exhibition for Open Evening, which he did and the prospective pupils loved it.

My assemblies at Ashlyns were very varied and included topics that included: the Elephant Man, Graham Green, the preservation of the countryside, litter, health and safety, cycling hero-Lance Armstrong – that turned out to be a mistake, drugs and much else. As this book is biographic, I will only discuss two particular assemblies here.

THE HORGANS GO HOME TO IRELAND AFTER 60 YEARS IN ENGLAND

My brother- in- law Pat Horgan's parents Julie and Frank Horgan died at 97 and 90 years. They came to London in the 1930s and in 2007 decided to return to the place and country of their birth – Killarney, County Kerry, Ireland. Pat took them to Stansted airport for their Ryanair flight to Kerry. I was so moved by their decision to go back home after so many years that I thought their story was worth an assembly.

Frank had worked with his dad on the railways in Ireland and this work often involved bridge construction and repair. He and his many siblings were no mean golfers and in another era Frank may well have made a living on the professional golf circuit. Even at the age of ninety and partially blind Frank, with a little guidance, could hit a sweet seven iron to the golf green. When he moved to England he spent most of his working life with the Fairclough Construction Company. The company was started by the 30-year-old Leonard Fairclough in Lancashire in 1883. His son Leonard Jr became Director on the death of his father in 1927 and held this position until 1959. The work of the company expanded to include replacing antiquated sewage systems, dredging canals, maintaining Power Stations and building and repairing railway and later motorway bridges. The firm remained family and worker orientated and during WW2, Leonard was appointed regional leader under the Ministry of Works Emergency Organisation. In one operation alone, the firm remodelled 31 railway bridges near Manchester to cater for the system's conversion from steam to electric power. Frank worked for the firm all over the country and became a stalwart of the company so much so that when Frank suffered pleurisy after an accident to his chest at work – so serious that Frank was given the last rites – Leonard Fairclough came down from Lancashire to visit him in hospital. The combination of last rites and Leonard's presence had the right effect on Frank and soon he was back to his Herculean self on the job. Frank only needed about four hours solid sleep a night and got up for most of his life at 4.30am and hardly ever missed a day's work. Julie and Frank had two son's Michael (b1936) and Patrick (b1940). Their family remained in Kilburn, not far from several rail and tube lines throughout the WW2 and survived all the bombing raids – no child evacuation for this family. Many years later, Frank whilst waiting for a bus to take him to work was hit by a Post Office Mail van that came off the road and knocked him and the brick wall behind him over. Frank ended up in hospital for weeks but survived and went back to work again. Frank worked into his 70s and in his 80s collected up the beer glasses at his local pub in Kilburn. Free bottles of Guinness were his reward. I can remember meeting Frank just before he went back to Ireland and we shared our enjoyment for Hamlet Cigars. His wife Julie was also made of stern stuff. As well as looking after her sons, Frank often had to work long hours away from home, she took on part time jobs in local shops. She also had a domestic cleaning job for a very rich and generous Jewish family in Hampstead. The family, called Falk, ran an electrical supply company that was bought out by an even bigger national company called Osram and later GEC. Julie could not afford a baby sitter in those days and often brought her youngest son Pat with her to work. Pat had the time of his life at the house which had a heated swimming pool, gym and boxing ring. At times, Mr Falk would put his son in the ring with Pat so that Pat could toughen him up. Julie made a lifelong friend of another Irish women Peggy who cooked for the family. Peggy ended up marrying Gerald Horgan a first cousin of Julie's son Pat. As Peggy was about 15 years older and the fact that they married rather late in life they had no children. Peggy used to say that she was worried about who was going to look after Gerald when she died; but the good lord had other plans and Gerald stepped off this mortal coil many years before Peggy. Gerald was one of the best jokes tellers I ever met. I remember him regaling us, including my father, with hours of jokes at Pat's local Swan pub in Maidstone. Amazingly, Peggy and Gerald also returned to Ireland late in life and Peggy died in January 2016 at the advance age of 103 years. I have one abiding memory of Julie Horgan. After a session in the local pubs in Kilburn, my wife, mother, father, sister Dorothy and Pat went back to Julie and Frank's apartment for a nightcap or two. Pat decided to put on a 45disc on the record player. To my surprise, Julie watched him like a hawk and told him not to break the record player. Pat of course had his own record player and in his earlier uncompromising days would not let anyone else touch his prized possession. I could say son like mother here.

Julie and Frank were happy living in London; but Julie was finding it difficult to climb the external stairs up to their flat and would have preferred a transfer to a ground floor flat that turned out to be impossible to obtain. They decided that they would be better off going back home to Killarney where they would be near to relatives.

The pair cut a dashing couple at the airport, Julie in her famous high heels as they departed England for the last time. I can remember saying at my assembly that England had benefited from the most productive parts of their lives and owed them a lot. They never had to pay for their early education or any care at the end of their lives.

APPLE BILL – AKA WILLIAM HARVEY – THE GREAT TRAIN SET ROBBERY ASSEMBLY.

Until the digital age of the PlayStation arrived, every small boy's dream was to have a train set and William Harvey was no exception. William would have to wait fifty years to achieve his dream. William, to his friends Bill, was born poor in Peckham in South London. He served in Europe and North Africa in WW2, married and established a smallholding and house in Marden, Kent. Unfortunately, Bill's beloved wife died young and after a time Bill met another women who had a son by a previous marriage. She encouraged Bill to sell up and move in with her and her son at their smallholding. The holding had apple orchards and was near to Maidstone. Their relationship was not a happy one but Bill made a living by selling apples to locals. He delivered the apples in a van doing regular deliveries to his growing customer base and this is how he acquired the nickname "Apple Bill".

Bill made enough money to achieve his childhood dream to create a model train set collection. He built a wooden shed in the orchard well away from his wife's house and this became his own "King's Cross". He would enter the shed by a small door and sit on a stool with cigarette and cup of coffee surrounded by three levels of interlinking train tracks. He had nearly a hundred train engines, assorted carriages and sets of electrical operated signals and points. When I visited him we found him in his train shed surrounded by trains going in all directions, the smoke not coming from his steam engines but from his cigarette. He would spend hours in this train set world shielded from the stress of having to live in the house of his not very welcoming wife or son. Then, one-night tragedy struck.

Someone from a nearby traveller's site broke into Bill's train shed and stole most of his expensive engines. A distraught Bill told the locals at The Stile Bridge Pub what had happened. One of them informed the local paper and Bill's robbery was the front page story, "Local Pensioner's Train Sets Stolen after waiting a lifetime to achieve his dream hobby." It was not long after the robbery that I met Bill again and decided his story would make a good assembly for the pupils at my school. I borrowed one of his few remaining train engines, a modern 125 Diesel Locomotive, and a copy of the headline in the local paper. Before I gave my assembly there was good news for Bill. A local QC organised a collection for Bill and some of the newspaper readers responded to the story by donating some parts of their own train sets to help Bill put his train station back on track.

This very human story of loss and recovery went down very well with my pupils as I waved Bill's engine along with the newspaper headline above my head. I also recorded the assembly especially for Bill and he was delighted when I gave him the tape of the assembly and even more delighted when he got his new train engines.

A friend of my brother-in-law, Keith, had a house that he rented out to students in Harlesden in North London. I collected the rent for him for a year but was delighted to hand over to Apple Bill when he moved in. This allowed Bill to live out the last few years of his life in the company of young positive students well away from the cold exclusion of his wife's smallholding. Apple Bill was laid to rest at Kensal Green Cemetery in the company of quite a few famous departed. Amongst them, the great railway engineer Isambard Kingdom Brunel R.I.P.

SIXTH FORM CHRISTMAS DINNER AND DISCO

One of the highlights of the year for our sixth form was the Christmas Dinner and Disco. Formal dress was a strict requirement and for many it was their first time in formal dress. The girls were particularly excited by the formality of the occasion. However, there was a problem: a big one. The venue for the dinner was the local civic centre in the High Street and there was a midnight finishing time. Unfortunately, by then several of the students were drunk and continued their drunken antics out on the High Street and on many occasions the local residents called the police. The next morning back at school the Headteacher would make a fuss about how some sixth formers had let down the school. When I arrived at the school the passed the responsibility of organising this event on to me. After some enquiries, I soon realised that he had passed a poisoned chalice and that he and some of the other local "established staff" never attended these occasions. Some staff, who never attended any other school social occasion, only attended the event to enjoy seeing the drunken scenes and consequent embarrassment to the member of staff in charge. I only needed to attend on two occasions before I gave an ultimatum to the Head and Governors. The first occasion was to see what actually happened. Immediately I noticed that after the first course some students started throwing bread rolls around and half way through the main course half of them were out of their seats and moving to other tables. By the end they were all out of their seats and pigs would have left the dining area tidier – at least the pigs would have eaten the food off the floors instead of trampling it into the floor. The students were given two drink tokens but several of them arrived nearly drunk and smuggled in their own alcohol. During the disco they climbed into human pyramids and then collapsed across the dance floor. Conclusion: no wonder they enjoyed the occasion. On my second attendance and now fully in charge, I introduced strict alcohol control but the staff still found it difficult to "police" them. I had had enough and next morning informed the Head that I was not prepared to display our dirty linen in the centre of the town again. I could not understand why we had the dance in the Civic Centre when we had our own oak panelled dining room and magnificent hall. From now on, it would be held at school or not at all. I formed a sixth form committee to help with the organisation and I agreed with their suggestion that we employ three professional bouncers.

Our first Dinner and Dance at the school was an improvement but the sit down dinner was still a bit of a disaster. One drunken student who happened to be the Chairman of Governors' son ripped the satellite aerial costing around a £1000 off the roof. His father had to collect him later from the local police station. The occasion also attracted some outside visitors who kicked in one of the panels on the chapel door. As usual, the toilets were a mess and we had to get the cleaners in very early next morning to clean up. I did use the organising committee and extra helpers to clean up the mess in the Main Hall and Dining Room immediately after the event – some success here.

There was no doubt that the occasion was a great social learning experience for the students. Whilst in the toilet I noticed one young man looking at himself in the mirror. He did not like what he saw and punched the mirror so hard that he left a smear of blood all over it. I reassured the tearful fellow that he was actually a good-looking chap and he should put his action down to the effects of drink. Those who went over the top had the bouncers on their case. They were told to be on my bench outside my office next morning at 8am along with their parents. They would then plead with me not to tell their parents and I would agree but only for now. Result a very restless night for them as they started to sober up. The next morning I had some very tearful repentant sixth formers on my bench and as a soft hearted and forgiving teacher I always let them off. I even asked some of them to be on the organising committee for the following year's dance.

By the fourth Dinner and Dance, I had it sorted. Now I stayed overnight at the school, so I could enjoy a drink and a cigar at the dance and be seen to do so in front of the students. The Caretaker and I had a late night smoke and drink in the staffroom to celebrate after everyone had gone home and the alarms were on. I had no more sit down meals just a buffet and increased, at the request of the students, the number of bouncers to five. I even led the students on a dance to the great hit, "The Irish Rover" by the Pogues and the Dubliners.

Especially pleasing for me was the next morning when I greeted the Headteacher and his fellow shirkers who were expecting and hoping to find trouble. What Dinner and Dance? That is history now, we have a curriculum to deliver and pupils to teach would be my response.

SCHOOL NATIONAL CURRICULUM AWARD

During my eleven years at Ashlyns with primary responsibility for curriculum delivery, the situation was stable enough to establish some real lasting improvements. With some financial support from Wellcome, a major employer in the town, I was able to launch the new "Wellcome Computer Centre" providing hands on computer facilities for classes of 24 students at a time. Curriculum links were established with organisations throughout Hertfordshire and beyond. I was delighted to have the opportunity to put in place the lessons I learnt from my secondment to British Aerospace in Industry Year 1986.

Colour printing was becoming available, but it was still some time before desktop printers were available. Our links with Kodak in Hemel Hempstead gave me the opportunity to present our submission for the Curriculum Award in full colour. The colour printers we used were the size of a small car and cost almost as much. A large display of the links between all the school subjects with industry, environment, cultural centres and much else was put on in the school hall to be judged by external assessors. We were the only secondary school of many school submissions in Hertfordshire to gain the national award. The national presentations were made at The Barbican Centre in London.

TOSHIKO ARRIVES FROM JAPAN

I initially was reluctant to get involved directly with our modern language department's cultural link with Japan. Each year the Japanese government sponsored several one-year secondments for young professional Japanese nationals. The aim of the scheme was to promote awareness of Japanese culture and life in the UK. Our first hosted internship was very successful and as our curriculum award scheme was developing, I was keen to host a second internee but my Head of Modern Languages thought otherwise. She felt hosting foreigners was not her department's responsibility. Unfortunately, this is an ongoing problem in English state schools. The parents of pupils are happy to let their children go on school trips, especially ski trips, abroad but are reluctant to host foreign students in their own homes. I told her in no uncertain terms we were going to have a second Japanese intern and I would take direct responsibility.

As I waited at arrivals at Heathrow airport I wondered what I had let myself in for and my wife was even more concerned. Soon, I saw a petite Japanese woman with an enormous suitcase approaching me as I held a sign with the name, "Toshiko" printed on it above my head. She smiled and bowed several times in front of me and had won me over by the time we got to my car. Would she win my wife over so easily? Considering this was the first time she had left Japan her English was surprisingly good. She came from Kobe, that only nine months previously, in January 1995, had suffered Japan's worst earth quake in modern times – 6500 killed, most of them in the city of Kobe. We arrived back in Hertford mid-afternoon and in time for me to take her for a walk along the pastoral landscape of the river Lea. I could see that she was overwhelmed with how different England was from Japan, but I just knew that she liked what she was experiencing and seeing. Back at the house as my wife Alice prepared dinner, Toshiko noticed our piano and asked if she could play. As Mozart drifted through to the kitchen Alice came into the lounge not really believing what she was hearing. We had a concert level pianist in our midst. Now Alice was won over.

It took Toshiko and I longer to win over some of the staff at school and also some of our xenophobic students. Toshiko had spent several years working in Japan and had a lot to offer in addition her skills as free secretary. She performed a Japanese tea party for each department dressed in full kimono. The Home Economics department had free lessons in Japanese cooking and cuisine. The Art department had lessons in the history of Japanese Art and origami. There was no limit to Toshiko's talents and I even got her to help with my curriculum award display and much else. Soon the Staff ware talking about Sean and his Geisha girl – jealously gets you nowhere.

We hosted Toshiko for a few weeks at our house and then one of our part-time teachers agreed to host Toshiko in her house near to the school. This was much more convenient for her. On one occasion I took Toshiko to see our then ten-year-old daughter Astrid Irish dancing, a whole new experience for her. Many years later, I got an excited letter from Toshiko. She told me that she had been to see River Dance and her family and friends were all impressed that she had seen our daughter Irish dancing before River Dance became known across the globe.

Toshiko liked to go on school outings for the pupils and saved us from having to take an extra member of staff out of classes in the process. On one occasion, we visited the National History Museum in London. Half way through our guided tour some pupils rushed up to get me to come and comfort Toshiko who was crying. Well I know the National History Museum can be a little exciting but it is difficult to know how dinosaurs, stuffed whales and rock samples can draw tears of distress. How wrong I was. Unknown to me the museum had a special display simulating the Kobe and other earthquakes. They had a mock up of what happened to a supermarket in Kobe during the first few minutes of the earthquake. As one entered the supermarket the floor began to vibrate and you saw tins falling off the shelves and lights falling off the ceiling and then experienced severe floor shudders in total darkness. The kids loved it but it was a complete surprise to Toshiko when she stepped into the supermarket simulator and brought back horrible memories of that early January morning some months previously. Luckily none of Toshiko's immediate family were killed or injured in the earthquakes but some of her friends were. I managed to comfort Toshiko in the museum coffee bar and it was the first time that she was able to open up about the effects of the earthquake on her. Luckily she knew me well and forgave me for my oversight.

Soon Toshiko's year was nearly at an end and we attended a great friend of mine, Andy Sloman's 40th Birthday Party at Tring Cricket Club. I remember now that one of Andy's party tricks was to dance an Irish Jig on a small mat fortified by the amber nectar. Toshiko looked splendid in full kimono and I took her hand for the first dance. If they had not been convinced before some of the watching staff were now convinced that the rumours were right after all, Toshiko really was Sean's Sushi Girl. Arigato Toshiko, you gave us all a year to remember!

My last years at Ashlyns towards early retirement in 1999

Life at Ashlyns was in the main a positive experience. We were making progress with pupil exam results and my system of Value Added measures across all subjects was now established and ahead of the embryonic national scheme. The Head Teacher and I employed a professional PR company to promote the work of the school with a modest degree of success. It served to demonstrate just how much we were already achieving in terms of publications and events in-house already. We received a full Ofsted inspection in May 1997 and the curriculum and its management was judged to be a real strength, which pleased me. Some aspects of leadership were not as strong as they should be. No comment here from me on this one.

I got on well with our support staff, cleaners and caretaker. Dave Thompson our caretaker lived with his family in the house in the school grounds and always put the interests of the school first. His three children attended the school and I enjoyed attending the wedding of his lovely daughter, Lisa, in the school chapel. After his morning shift Dave liked to join his wife Maureen, who was also on the staff, for a full English breakfast at home. His work as am emergency fireman was a great asset in helping understand the safety issues of a school as big as Ashlyns, with hundreds of meters of underground tunnels. Soon after I left Dave died from a strokes when only in his late 50s.

We put our cleaning out to contract and our own regular Irish cleaners led by the good Mary from County Cavan were not happy. On one occasion, we found the manager from the contract company romping an employee in a cupboard. It was not long before we put all school cleaning back in-house with Mary in charge.

I continued to feel that I was a fish out of water when it came to our white middle class very conservative Board of Governors. Despite my success and popularity with the pupils and many of the parents, they felt I was not really accepted as one of them. As an example, I give the appointment of a British Asian to a language teaching post. Ramallah was a very attractive woman with a vibrant personality, well qualified in French. It was clear she would make an excellent contribution to our Modern Languages Department. It was obvious that she felt uncomfortable by the almost 100% white staff and the traditional and austere school buildings. The governors and head teacher sensed her unease. They came up with the idea, behind my back, that I should chair the interview panel. Their thinking was clear to me: Ramallah would feel less threatened and more comfortable with an Irishman in charge. It worked. When it came to considering me for headship their thinking was in reverse: O'Reilly great chap and popular with the pupils but the parents and residents of Berkhamsted were not yet ready to accept an Irishman as Head. Ironically, by the early 2000s the English attitude to the Irish had a complete turn around and this helped me later to secure posts in England's leading private schools.

After nearly twenty years of senior management in three very different schools I had been responsible for every possible area of school governance and often several times over. Exciting as it was I felt that I had had enough of school management and would like to step down. I had made sacrifices in terms of the opportunity to teach my subject in recent years and after the Labour election victory in 1997 the Grant Maintained status of our school was likely to revert to more LEA control. The door was closing on opportunities for early retirement and the head teacher and I took our chance to early retire. I got a tax-free lump sum and two years' enhancement to my pension that was indexed linked from the age of 55 years. I was quite happy with what came to be known as the gold plated pension compared to what was offered later in the private and public sectors in the light of an ageing working population.

On my last day at Ashlyns as I walked out the front gate I felt a great sense of freedom and the possibility of new opportunities. I knew that from now on I would be paid (not a large amount but enough) for the rest of my life.

The Graduates

Finn at O'Reilly Grave Ballyjamesduff 5 generations

Alice with her Great grandma 2012

With granddaughter Faye on her first day at Secondary School

Grandson Freddy with his prize art work Aged 8 years in 2015

Astrid and me ready to run 2015

Astrid completes London triathlon 2015

Finishing 100 mile Olympic Legacy Bike Ride 2nd August 2015

Caitlin wins Irish U 16 100meters Championship 2015

Avril with daughters and 2 of her Grandchildren Toronto circa 2006

Alice and brother Einar above the clouds Fieberbrunn Austria 2016

Returning to Colarado Willy Ski Bar after some years
and sober this time St Johann Austria 2016

Trying to get out of Pot Belly Bunker Prestwick Scotland 2015

With Dorothy and Pat at Christmas Ball
Essendon Country Club 2015

With Mekki Wagner and Alice At Samuel
Johnson's 18C house in London 2015

O'Reilly Coat of Arms

Rugby World Cup Cardiff 2015

CHAPTER 21

POST RETIREMENT YEARS 1999-2007 – BACK TO WORK WITH A DIFFERENCE

Work was not a priority and I was looking forward to a few months off before thinking of doing any sort of paid employment. However, work came looking for me when my friend and my former Head of Science, Heddwyn Evans, asked if I could join his department for the summer term to replace a Physics/Science teacher who had left. This was a tempting offer as I would get the full six-week summer holiday pay for only working the relatively short summer term. There was a down side. His school Mount Grace in Potters Bar was a challenging place with scores of pupils coming up from the council estates of Islington to add to the mix of working class whites from the council estates of Potters Bar. Mount Grace was considered a step up from the schools in Inner London and the London pupils helped to keep the school open in a time of falling school population. The experiment worked in the early years when the more motivated pupils from London came up, but soon some real problem children joined them.

The site and name of the school was a gift from Roger Fenton upon his death. Fenton was the first modern war photographer making his money from photographing action from the Crimean War in the 1850s. The school grounds still had many of the trees and gardens from Fenton's time. These were greatly appreciated by the urban London kids who made it their first task on arriving up on the fast train from Kings Cross to climb up as many trees as possible. The London kids never talked amongst themselves, preferring to shout at each other and even at the teachers. This was not the type of school in which I wanted to teach; but it was fun and a challenge that got me back into the classroom. The teaching staff had no time for internal strife; they were too busy using most of their energy and knowhow to survive the warfare in the classroom. The staffroom was the place for recovery and support for and from colleagues. I can remember consoling a young distraught female Art teacher and escorting her to her art room and letting the more brash pupils in her class know that I would be waiting outside to sort out anyone who stepped out of line. Some of the pupils were real characters. One black lad from London, Kyle Kid, was a superb athlete but would never write anything down on paper. Once I told him to forget my science lesson and just write anything he liked down for me on paper with the offer a small financial reward. He astonished me with the quality and length of the story he wrote. Over the next couple of months, he did some more work for me when not shouting at his mates. I guessed at the time that Kyle knew some drug dealers and this was confirmed over a year later when when I met him on a train coming out of Moorgate Station. He was on his way to training and in conversation he told me how much money he was making. He was able to divide one packet of cocaine into many one line fixes and increase his initial payment fivefold. I could not argue with his arithmetic or the splendid profit margin but I told him he was still wasting his talents. I still wonder whatever happened to Kyle out there on the streets of inner London.

The school was attached to a small sports centre and on Fridays a group of us would play squash and later in the bar compare our survival stories for the week.

During my stay at the school there was a derailment on the main line railway near to the school and several passengers were killed. At first I thought that maybe some of our pupils had thrown something on the line to derail the high speed train but was relieved later to hear the accident was due to poor maintenance of the track. I enjoyed my time at Mount Grace but was happy to move on to the next challenge.

My next post was a one-year contract as a part-time Mathematics and Physics teacher at Stanborough School in Welwyn Garden City. At last I had a chance to teach some A Level Physics but the Head of Maths loaded some of her lower ability maths sets on to me. Her background was in special needs and she should never have been allowed to teach higher ability sets. Her friendship with the cold and austere head teacher and the fact that she had taught in the school for years helped her to cover her tracks.

The government had recently introduced a requirement for all sixth formers to take a mathematics course in the sixth form that introduced them to application of mathematics in business, commerce and industry. My Head of Maths was more than happy to pass this on to me in the knowledge that she might be seriously exposed by some of the brighter students. I was delighted to take up the challenge and decided to use the world of stocks and shares as the main area of interest. Each student was given an imaginary sum of £50,000 to invest and we would see how much money they would make or lose over a six month period. They were all to use the FTSE 100 and draw up spreadsheets detailing their investments. They were lucky because in 1999-2000 the FTSE 100 was a very bullish market and rose to over 6,000 before the dot.com crash and went down to 3,500 a few years later while surprisingly house prices rose rapidly, aided by cheap and reckless lending, until the banking crisis in 2008. Most of the students made a profit but I did warn them that the market could be very volatile and the Bears often got the better of the Bulls. This subject was close to my heart because I had just invested most of my pension lump sum in shares and with profits bonds.

One of my Physics sixth form practical lessons was inspected by the County Science Adviser who questioned me as to why I was doing such basic practical work on the extension of springs. She failed to understand that the experiment was to do with the relationship between magnet force and distance that strongly depended on the inverse cube of the distance – quite an advanced concept for the students to prove from the graphs they had to plot. Perhaps she should have joined our Head of Mathematics in sharing their blissful ignorance and their promotions way beyond their level of competence.

I had the time to join staff to play five-a-side football in the new sports hall and the high point for me was when we played my former school Mount Grace in an eleven-a-side match. This was going to be a challenge for me since I had not played a full game for about 15 years. I opted for a midfield role and my marathon fitness got me through, although I did feel a bit stiff a couple of days later. On some days when I finished early I had golf lessons at a nearby sports centre with the intention of maybe joining a golf club – when I got older!

PRIVATE EDUCATION – A NEW BEGINNING

My maths-teaching contract at Stanborough School put me in a strong position to apply for maths and/or science posts. I saw a position at Mill Hill School for a two-term maternity leave maths post that would give me the summer term off –just what I wanted. I had never considered teaching in the private sector before mainly because of my commitment to state comprehensive education and politically I was not happy with the domination of the British Establishment by a public school educated elite. As mentioned earlier, I did have a taste of what it might have been like to teach science in the private sector when I got involved in the Science in Society Project for sixth formers initiated by the Head of Science, John Lewis, at Malvern Public School. I realised then the important role public schools had in developing innovative science teaching schemes. For example, Rugby School played a big part in establishing the Nuffield Physics developments in the 1970s. If I could have put some of my qualms about private education aside, I would have had a very rewarding experience educationally and socially, not to mention remuneration, in the private sector. My experience of the shenanigans and favouritism displayed by state school governing bodies only served to mellow my attitude towards public schools. I also found it difficult to fault poorer parents who made tremendous financial sacrifices to give their children a better education, especially in urban areas where the state alternative was often poor.

Mill Hill School has a great hill top location in North West London. One of its more famous pupils was Francis Crick of Crick and Watson DNA fame. It is also home to the well know Murray Library and Scriptorium. James Murray, a master at the school founded The Oxford Dictionary.

My interview with the Head Master went well and the salary offered was commensurate with that of a Deputy Head in the state sector – not bad for a maths classroom teacher. I was somewhat surprised when the Head Master told me that I could go out to do some shopping when I had a free period. It was only later that I realised I would be teaching a six-day week timetable. Friday night pub sessions would have to be curtailed until further notice.

The pupil intake had quite a broad ability spectrum, but the less academically able were still well motivated and were given extra tutoring. The school had a strong Jewish contingent and I found the Jewish teachers and pupils very stimulating to work with. One incident comes to mind. It was a Saturday morning and many of the pupils in my bottom maths set were tired and so was I. One rather challenging Jewish madam thought that it would be better to engage me with her own moody teenage self than to attend to her mathematics work. This was not the first time she was off target and I cracked telling her, "Just because you Jews have had 2000 years of persecution and we Irish have only had 800 years, do not push your luck on me Madam!" Once spurted out I immediately thought I had gone over the top. A few days later, I saw her dropped off at school from her father's Rolls Royce and she and her father greeted me with big smiles. I never had any problems from this young madam again; in fact, she became one of my biggest fans. In my experience meeting many Jewish people over the years, they like a good argument and people to call a spade a spade.

Whilst on the subject of the Jewish people I had a very likeable Jewish boy in another of my lower maths sets who always sat up front. I did not realise how much he enjoyed my lessons until I ticked him off rather harshly in retrospect for some perceived misdemeanour. I could see that he was very upset and when he saw me after the lesson he told me how much he looked forward to my lessons. I was mortified. I had no problem in apologising to him and put my action down to being overtired. I still have the lovely set of green wine glasses that he gave me as a leaving present. As teachers we do not always realise the impact and influence that we have in shaping the delicate, vulnerable and precious young lives in our charge. Our appreciation of our qualities is not enhanced by the vitriolic attacks on our profession from some irresponsible politicians and others who should know better.

One of my Saturday sixth form maths lessons was enlivened by a Russian pupil who took a very keen interest in my lesson on the motion of projectiles in a gravitational field. Later, as I walked around the class checking pupil work, I noticed that he had a book that was a lot bigger than the class maths textbook. It turned out to be a detailed manual of handguns and their firing capabilities. It made me think about how his father got the money to send his son to an expensive London boarding school. Later he, along with the son of the Chinese Ambassador were expelled. They got into a fight and the Chinese lad ended up with a broken leg. Apparently it was not the first time that the Ambassador's son had been expelled from a school.

I made close friends with members of the Art Department (although I'm not sure how this happened) and one young female teacher called Anne in particular. Mill Hill has two great cross country courses and at interview I offered to help out with school cross country runs as my extra curricular contribution. All staff were expected to participate in extra curricular activities and this is a policy I have always approved with. Some lunchtimes Anne and I would go for a run on the longer course of the two courses which included two steep hills. We were well matched and one of us, depending on who was in form, would pull away at the end to come home first. Anne began to confide in me and expressed her unhappiness with her salary and contract. I soon realised I was paid a lot more than she was but private schools were not restricted by government state regulations on pay. While sympathising with her I supported the principle of paying teachers their market value. Top Physics and Maths teachers had a far higher market value that was reflected in salaries in the private sector but not the state sector.

The autumn term in 2000 was one of the wettest I can remember until 2015. I was preparing for the Lisbon marathon at the end of November so had to up my mileage. I volunteered to act as the "hare" or pacemaker for the junior North London Girls' Cross Country Championship and was surprised when the muddy 13-year-old leader floated past me up the second big hill. I had to point to her the direction to keep going in. Later with Anne, I pulled my Achilles tendon running across a swampy cricket field, an injury I failed to shake off before I had to run in Lisbon. Lessons finished at 4pm and on Tuesdays and Thursdays I took the pupils on the shorter cross country course. In December and January, we finished almost in total darkness and sometimes I had to run back and collect, and find, the stragglers. The school experimented with having sport activities from 2pm to 4pm in winter and then resuming lessons from 4pm to 6pm but most of the pupils were too tired to pay attention.

One of the outstanding features of Mill Hill and other leading private schools are the facilities available for study, cultural and sporting activities. I played a staff hockey match against the students on a state of the art all-weather floodlit hockey pitch, which was a stark contrast to the muddy grass fields I played on in the state sector. The school had Eton Fives and Squash Courts, well maintained Rugby pitches and a lovely cricket pavilion as well as a new theatre and state of the art library. By contrast, I spent eleven years when I was Deputy Head at Ashlyns School trying to get the Governors and Local Authority to build a Sports Hall and an all weather pitch without success.

After my successful stint at Mill Hill my chances of finding a post at other private schools were now much greater – I had broken the public school glass ceiling. Public Schools leaders had come to realise that they recruit teachers from the state sector who were more experienced and better trained.

THE GIRLS IN THE CITY

I never thought that I would ever teach in a girls' school, never mind the number one school in the national league table – The City of London School for Girls. My application was motivated by the fact that we had a 14-year-old daughter, Astrid, and understandably my wife and I were very interested in the education of girls.

The school had a very highly qualified Russian Head of Physics who just could not win over the girls and resignation was her only option and at short notice. Private education does not come cheap and parents expect the highest standards of teaching and facilities. My task was to take over her post for two terms until the Governors appointed a new Head of Physics. I loved the opportunity to teach again at the highest level in a wonderful location and to make a difference. The City of London Girls' and the separate Boys' schools have a joint Governing Body under the Direction of the Cooperation of the City of London. The Girls' school is located at the heart of the Barbican and the Boys' school near the millennium bridge by St Paul's Cathedral overlooking the Thames.

Until they could set up my bank account, I got an initial forward payment by cheque. This was no ordinary cheque but was from the Bank of England in red ink and with the Cross of St George and emblem of the City of London. I was tempted to keep it as a souvenir but its cash value was too great. I did take it to my local pub to tease my fellow drinkers that they should change from their banks and use a proper bank. Little did I realise how near the bone I was with the banking crisis of 2008, when I wished that my account were with the Bank of England, but this privilege is only for employees of The Cooperation of the City of London.

My first day at the school was a sad one. At morning assembly, the Head Mistress announced that one of the girls was killed in an accident on a school trip to South Africa. The girl had finished abseiling down a rock face and had taken her helmet off and stood some yards back from the rock face. Another girl descending dislodged a small piece of rock that then deflected off a ledge and hit the girl standing below directly on the head, and killed her. The girl had her identical twin sister on the trip with her who was at the assembly. Both girls had performed with distinction in their GCSE examinations before the summer vacation. The twins' father Lord Justice Ward decided that this was a very unfortunate accident and did not hold the school or organisers responsible.

A year later Lord Justice Ward, along with two other judges, made a judgment in the High Court on the case of the Maltese conjoined babies Jodie (real name Gracie) and Mary (Rosie). Mary was alive because she was drawing on Jodie's lifeblood and if the twins were separated she would die. The parents were Catholics so taking a life to save another one was a big moral dilemma. Lord Justice Ward stated that, "Though Mary has the right to life she has little right to be alive". The judges gave permission for the 20-hour operation to proceed. Today Gracie is a healthy 15 year old who is determined to become a doctor.

Nearly every girl in the school played one or more musical instruments. I counted 15 grand pianos in the music department and several of the girls were involved with The Guild Hall School of Music that was also situated in the Barbican. Prize day was a grand affair. Staff in gowns and all the girls walked in procession to the Guild Hall. The girls provided a full orchestra and the school was honoured by the presence of the Lord Mayor of the City of London and other dignitaries. I particularly enjoyed the food and wine available.

On the subject of food, staff were invited to meet the Governors and members of the City Guilds over good wine and canapés. I was surprised to meet a Governor who told me the City still had links with the Guild of the City of Londonderry (Derry). I kept my republican views to myself.

In 2007 I returned to take on a short contract at the school – same problem, another Head of Physics not getting on with the girls. It was great to be back again and this time round I taught the younger age groups, which I loved. I gave one whole school assembly on my marathon adventures to promote the marathon I ran in Cornwall on behalf of the charity elected by the school.

ALLEYN'S SCHOOL DULWICH.

This was my first time teaching south of the river and I took on two contracts over two years. It was a long journey but it was worth it. The first contract I took over from a very good female teacher who was seriously ill with cancer and the second contract to stand in for the Head of Physics who had discipline issues.

I left home at 6.45 and biked to Hertford North, took the train to Old Street, then the tube to London Bridge, then grabed a Costa coffee whilst waiting for the 8.30 train to Dulwich East and finally a brisk 15-minute walk to the school. Surprisingly I quite enjoyed the commute that gave me time to read The Times, mark and prepare student work and improved my fitness by cycling, walking and climbing up long staircases. The downside was that I borrowed my wife's bike that was stolen from the station and the new replacement was stolen. She is still complaining about the increased insurance premium and the fact that I did not use my own bike. Sorry Alice, it is, I hope, never too late to apologise.

The physical demands of the commute and the chance to use the school's swimming pool and gym allowed me to get fit enough to run the Budapest Marathon in September 2002 for the school's nominated charity, The Delmelza Children's' Hospice and to give a school assembly to raise funding. I find the Motto for this charity very pertinent: "The Hospice focuses on adding life to days when days cannot be added to life"

The school has an unusual motto, "God's Gift" and was established in 1619 as part of the Edward Alleyn's College of God's Gift, although it separated from Dulwich College in 1882. The polar explorer Shackleton attended Dulwich College and he gifted the boat he used to get to South Georgia to seek help for the crew of his icebound wrecked ship in Antarctica to the college.

I came into contact with one interesting pupil, Pixie Geldof, youngest of Bob Geldof's three daughters. Bob, I believe, had tried to get one of his other daughter's in Alleyn's but Pixie managed to pass the entrance exam and I was part of a team marking the test paper's. I think Bob failed to turn up for his interview with the Head Master but then again he is a very busy man. She was a very likeable person. I remember taking a maths substitute class with her and I let it be known that I was also born in Dun Laoghaire, Dublin, like her dad. She paid me full attention for the rest of the lesson. She did miss plot a few points on one of her graphs but together we put it right. Today Pixie is a successful model and musician and no doubt can afford an accountant to plot any graphs displaying her income stream.

On the topic of income, Alleyn's School was the first and only place where I ever received a financial bonus. The school received a favourable OFSTED inspection and the Governing Body voted to give all teaching and non-teaching staff a pro rata bonus of £500. An action like this in the state sector would be anathema and viewed as wasting public funding.

One sunny mid-October autumnal day I invited our long standing German friend Ilse, a teacher at a Gymnasium school, to come and view the modern language teaching and facilities at Alleyn's. As I made a cup of coffee for her in the staffroom, the school secretary told me that my mother wanted to speak to me urgently. When I answered, she told me my father had died during the night at Barnet Hospital.

THE DEATH OF MY FATHER JOHN FRANCIS O'REILLY (1914-2002)

My father had retired from Barnet Council in 1980 at the age of 66 years. He got a small index linked pension and along with the state pension and his savings he had more than enough to pay the rent and enjoy his regular pub visits. I remember buying him a model clay kit to make chess pieces but it remained unused. The rest of the family were all giving him advice on how to use his time in retirement. What we did not realise was that he had more than enough physical work in his long working life and he surprised us all by starting a new hobby – reading books. He left school at 11 years of age but he was well versed in the 3Rs. My mother collected several books from the library each week and cowboy and detective stories were his favourites. During his working life he was tired and had too little time to read. I estimate that during his 22 years in retirement he read more than 2500 books. By contrast my mother took up Golf and Bridge in her retirement. They both visited Canada, Spain, Italy, Sweden and Ireland during retirement. I can still remember the shock on my father's face at the price of a round of drinks in a pub at my brother Vincent's wedding in Visby, Sweden. We were privileged to have them visit us in Hertford and almost on a weekly basis over the years I cycled out to meet them half way from their home in Finchley to pubs in Essendon or Potters Bar for a Friday night session. Alas, looking back now the years have gone so quick. So sad.

In 1984 we organised my father's first and only birthday party for his 70[th.] He was a bit embarrassed to let people know his real age because he looked relatively young and fit. I think his reticence came from working with younger fit men on building sites who thought he was younger than he was and this gave him a certain amount of job security and kudos. We gave him a quality garden reclining chair as a present and of course his favourite Bell's Whisky – several bottles. It was a great party and I was, for once, sober because I had to run my first ever London Marathon the next day.

Our father in his later years was always loving to his family and his wife, even though she was not always appreciative of this. He became a little more emotional and was easily moved to tears. He cooked regularly for our mother when she was golfing and made some super soups – like me he was a soup man rather than a dessert man.

He remained very fit well into his 70s. Only a few times did he complain about not keeping up with the Horgans and my sons as we raced up the hill to the Grey Hound Pub on Boxing Days. His hearing was going a bit and he started to prefer more whisky than too many pints. Every Christmas and on his birthdays we gave him bottles of whisky, which over the year he managed to consume at his own pace. He always preferred consumables as gifts.

It was in his early 80s that he confided in me that he had some blood in his semen and he was well aware of the possibility of prostate cancer. However, a consultant he saw was not too concerned. A year or so later during the Christmas vacation and when my mother was visiting my brother Vincent in Sweden, dad and I had a few pints in my local pub. At about 6am the following morning he knocked on my bedroom door fully dressed and with a packed holdall and asked me to drive him to the hospital, he was unable to urinate and was desperate to do so. I thought of his beer intake and without hesitation and within minutes, we were in the car and on our way. The poor man held on as long as he could in order to let me get some sleep. In A&E at the QE2 hospital I was surprised to see so many people waiting so early in the morning but the duty doctor reacted quickly and had my father into a cubicle immediately. It took some time to get a tube up his penis into his enlarged bladder to relieve the pressure but when they did, my dad was mightily relieved. It was clear that he had a much enlarged prostate and needed a catheter before they could arrange an operation to enlarge his urinary tract, drugs were not enough. We decided not to tell my mother in Sweden until she came home.

My dad had an exploratory examination performed by Mr Van Weningburg, a Belgian Urologist at the QE2. They discovered that he had a slow growing prostrate cancer, very common in men of his age; but not one that would necessarily kill him. The doctor put him on hormone therapy and it was not long before he got his first hot flushes, but he could live with that as a long as he still had his whisky and soda.

THE BIG FIGHT

As he got into his mid 80s, he liked to lie on his chair in the garden and watch the airplanes circling above in readiness to land at Heathrow. He also began to like his bed more. Once, when I visited in the afternoon I found him in bed and decided to lie down beside him and he was very happy for me to do. He told me that he spent time thinking of the past, which I knew because when we went to the local pub he was happy to tell me about his fights outside dance halls in Ireland and the problems he had with people at work – don't we all. He had one of his most memorable fights in the Cruel Sea Pub in Hampstead. Whilst he was in the toilet my mother, sitting at the bar, became the centre of attention, at first of another woman who came to sit beside her. She soon realised that my mother was not like-minded and moved on. The second time my dad went to the toilet – all those pints – she was approached by a young soldier in full military uniform. When my dad returned he was surprised to find the inebriated soldier sitting on his stool – maybe my mother liked his company more than that of the woman. He duly told my dad to clear off. dad duly invited the soldier to step outside if that was how he felt. The soldier laughed at him and stood up and landed a full punch on dad's chin and he felt his whole jaw move backwards but he had not reckoned on my dad's speed of reaction. He saw the punch coming and went low and hard with a right hook into his midriff. The soldier crumbled up in a pile on the floor. The pub Landlord arrived along with the soldier's mates and all the soldiers were ejected from the pub. Many of the customers came over to congratulate dad and even my mother was secretly proud of him. He had a very sore swollen jaw for days after the fight.

The Hospital Admissions Officer postponed the operation on dad's prostrate three times, once due to a urinary infection caused by the catheter and twice because of bed unavailability. My mother was a tower of strength in looking after all dad's needs short of doing the operation herself. His urologist was unhappy about the shortage of beds because it meant that he was underemployed. He even suggested that I complain in writing to the Secretary of State for Health, which I did. Dad and I were all ready to go to the hospital yet that morning they phoned to postpone the operation for the third time. I could see his head drop in disappointment and I went ballistic. I asked to speak directly to the CEO of the Lister Hospital and said I was still coming to the hospital and would chain my dad to the railings and then contact the local and national press. I would wait until 11 am before leaving for the hospital. At 10.45am the CEO's secretary phoned to inform me that they had managed to find a bed for him, we were on our way.

Dad was very spiritual and attended Mass regularly. He never forced his beliefs on us and took great solace from reading his prayer book. In his last years, he seemed content and tended to let matters pass over his head, especially as his hearing deteriorated. I never could get him to manage his hearing aid properly though he did manage to keep on reading. Two of his later aims in life were to see in the millennium and live as long as his mother (85 years). He was also happy to be able to attend his three grandsons' weddings.

His end came unexpectedly as they often do. Dad had the usual constipation problems and his kidney function was not too good. The GP was very concerned and thought it best he were admitted to hospital. My mother phoned me and I drove over to Barnet Hospital. I thought dad looked very frail and as my mother and I were leaving he put his arms around her and told her that he loved her. He had only eyes for her. I drove my mother home and thought that he might recover.

Back at Alleyn's School Ilse said that we should go straight away to Barnet Hospital. The Head Master was very understanding. He told me that he had recently lost his aged father but because he was around for all the main events in his life it made the loss even harder to bear. How right he was.

We met my mother at the bedside and I was shocked to see my father dead in the same bed that I had seen him alive in some hours earlier. It was comforting to have Ilse there because she had already gone through the pain of losing her parents. As usual my mother was calm, collected and action orientated. She was not one for displaying her emotions in public.

The head nurse told me that my dad had fallen out of bed during the night but that this was not the immediate cause of his death. She asked me to sign a disclaimer letter. I had great difficulty understanding how a frail man could have fallen out of a special designed hospital with movable side protection rails. I expressed my concern and signed the disclaimer. In retrospect, I should not have signed but I was not thinking straight.

The Funeral

We had already agreed with our mother and father that they would be interned in Hertford Cemetery rather than back home in Ireland. There was time for Vincent and Avril along with their families to come from Sweden and Canada for the funeral. Avril was very moved by the finality of seeing her dad lying in the hospital mortuary, stone cold to the touch. We all had a final viewing at the undertakers in Hertford just before the funeral mass. Our sixteen-year-old daughter shed a tear knowing she would never see her Grandfather alive again. There were many nice letters of condolence and a very touching one from Grant Hexamer, Avril's ex-husband.

At the time of the funeral my brother-in-law, Pat Horgan and his friend Keith were well into their Santiago de Compostela walk and my dad would have been delighted by their walk and prayers.

In the local church graveyard there were several graves belonging to an O'Reilly family of medics who lived in the locality in the 19th Century. One headstone had the inscription "I fought the great fight, I completed the course and I kept the faith. I was pleased to be able to quote this at the funeral ceremony. Not alone did he keep the faith but he passed on some of his beliefs and values and decency to his offspring. Now he has, with the Grace of God, made his final voyage to join the eternal family and, like the Irish Voyager St Brendan, suffered many trials and tribulations on his way through this life helped by his family, friends and strangers and above all his faith in God. Go raibh maith'. RIP

Life's Lessons Learnt

THE GIRLS OF ST PAUL'S SCHOOL – THE ACADEMIC ST TRINIANS.

In April 2005 I visited my cousin Angela McKeever, a nun, in Santiago, Chile where I ran a marathon in aid of her charitable work in support of the poor (ref: Marathon Adventures Across Europe and Beyond). I then moved on to Buenos Aires and it was here that I discovered an advertisement for a full time one-year post at St Paul's. I was 59 years old and the idea of a full time contract was not on my agenda, but then it was St Paul's and then the academically number one school in England. I knew I had a chance because of my successful stint at the City of London School for Girls. I fired off an email attaching my CV and expressing my interest but did wonder what they would think of an applicant who was enjoying the Dolce Vitae in Argentina.

Back in Hertford and to my surprise I received a telephone call directly from the High Mistress inviting me for interview. At the interviews the quality of the candidates, including a professor and candidates with PhDs, came as a big surprise to me. I reassured myself that this was a teaching post not a research post and it required personality and sound teaching experience. The Senior Science teacher and Deputy Head a Physicist selected an upper sixth form class of girls for me to teach. Several of the girls had already been offered places at Oxbridge and my task was to move them forward on their current topic "Quantum Theory of Black Body Radiation Emission". Later at home that evening, I got a phone call from the High Mistress that Astrid answered. I indicated to Astrid to pass on the message that I would be back in an hour. It is good to make things not too easy and not to appear over keen. She rang back again and offered me the post.

St Paul's Girls' School was founded in 1904 many years after the Boys' School. The founders made no apologies for the creation of an out and out academic school and one that promoted independently minded girls. This I found still to be the case today, the girls questioned almost everything I said and

322

I learned quickly that they were nearly always right. It did not take long for the school to catch up with their Boys' counterpart. The year I taught there, 2005-2006, they occupied the number one spot in the national academic league table. The Boys were several places below them. The school has never had a school uniform and preferred to award its own internal certificates for Music and Art. One of their outstanding teachers and Director of Music was the Composer Gustav Holst who composed most of his music, including The Planets, whilst at St Paul's. Of the many outstanding pupils, I single out Rosalind Franklin who provided the vital X-Rays for Crick and Watson to discover the Double Helix model of DNA. All the girls studied Latin and Greek and I remember putting my tutor group subject reports in alphabetical order. I had the problem of where to put their Greek reports there was no G and I asked a colleague who said "my dear it goes under A". How can Greek be under A I replied. "My dear, Ancient Greek", she replied.

CHOCOLATE HEAVEN

The school's privatised canteen supplied free coffee/tea and a big box of biscuits plus large jam doughnuts and flapjacks at morning and afternoon break times. The predominately-female staff normally consumed all these up by the end of the day. One can also add to this sweet fest the two or three birthday cakes that were placed on the table each week. Towards half terms and especially Christmas, Easter and the end of the summer term, the table was loaded with extra boxes of expensive chocolates of all possible sorts. As special thank you from some parents, several luxury large boxes of chocolates arrived from Harrods. No doubt, the parents wanted to keep the staff extra sweet. Amazingly, the voracious collective appetite of the school's 60 plus staff almost succeeded in devouring this mountain of chocolate by the end of each day.

Now knowing that chocolates were a girl's best friend, I decided to reward some of the girls in my classes chocolates for excellent work. I bought bags of mini Mars bars, boxes of Quality Street and mini Cadbury bars. I remember in one class I rewarded all the girls a chocolate of their choice from my collection, because I was feeling particularly generous, on a first come first served bases. They rushed up en mass to the front of the class led by Theodora Cadbury and she grabbed a Mars bar. Lizzy de Rothschild and Emma de Beers closely followed her. In the case of Emma, she was still of an age when chocolates were still her best friend rather than the diamonds produced by the de Beers.

The lack of testing class laboratory Physics experiments for the girls came as a surprise to me. There was an over reliance on teacher demonstrations supported by very good IT simulations of experiments. It was not the first school where I found class sets of equipment underused and one day I decided that all my year 9 girls would make their own electrical motors. The work required the stripping of wires and winding coils and other fiddly bits. It was hard work but greatly rewarded when I saw the joy on the girls' faces when their motors started to rotate augmented by sparks and all. I had my scary moments especially when I caught a girl carry a thin plastic beaker of boiling water back to her work bench and dropping it just short of the laptop and attached electronic measuring equipment. I had supplied each group with electric kettles but she had not noticed or listened to my instructions. I had some other scary moments as I circulated around the lab surrounded by very scantily clad young ladies, especially in the summer months. I have heard of men pinching women's bottoms but of course, it never happens the other way round, does it?

Like all schools, St Paul's had its fair share of odd pupils. I had a girl who joined the school in the sixth form from a RC convent school. This was a step up for her but unfortunately she thought the world owed her a living. During my A Level Physics class she sat aloof with arms folded and never wrote anything down. She would do the same when we had a class experiment and I would like to have strangled her. I also had problems with a girl called Cressida who went ballistic when I mispronounced her name. This should have been a warning sign. When I did my class rounds to looking at the girls' workbooks, Cressida would completely clam and tense up – a real odd ball. Thankfully all was revealed when I met her mother at a parents' evening. She asked me how did I "find" her daughter. I replied that I found her difficult and uncooperative. The mother told me that her daughter was a bxxxh and she gets it from her former husband. I think I would have preferred to teach Cressida's mother instead.

GIRLS A SCREAMING

The Head of Mathematics warned me in advance of the staff versus girls volleyball match in the hall: wear a set of earplugs was his advice, but I knew better. As a kid in Ireland I was never afraid of the screams of the Banshees on a dark windy late November evening alone with my granny in our big empty farm house. In two Boston marathons I had to run through a long channel of screaming female students from Wellesley College at the top of heartbreak hill. Yes, my ears were hurting but other parts of my body were hurting more. Some of the staff kitted themselves out in fancy dress plus earplugs and as we entered the packed hall it kicked off. "No, they cannot keep this crescendo of noise up" I thought. How wrong I was! Drunk from the noise it was my turn to serve and astonishingly I hit a winner. As I looked towards the side-lines all I could see were sets of vibrating tongues, tonsils and cheeks – a scene from Munch's "The Scream" multiplied a hundred fold. I cannot remember how the game finished but it seemed to take an eternity. The next day the girls told me that I played well. I think that is what they said anyway. My ears were still ringing.

St Paul's Cathedral Organs a bellowing.

Each year St Paul's Cathedral is given over to the Girl's and Boy's schools to commemorate their founding. It is a grand occasion attended by the Lord Mayor of the City of London, the Bishop of London, the Mercers' Company and other dignitaries. The schools provide a combined choir of over 200 pupils. We travelled up to the city in hired London double deck buses and entered the cathedral to the choir in full voice. I had a wonderful seat situated under the great dome, or so I thought. From this location one could hear with great clarity the opening anthem and hymns sung by the choir, until the organ started up. The noise nearly blew my eardrums out and drowned out the choir and I felt sorry for them after days of practice. I made up my mind there and then I would never have an organ played at my funeral, give me the sweet tuneful sounds of the human voice any day.

The Assembly – musical start and finish.

Each year the girls elected a local and national charity to raise funds and I thought that it would be a good idea to run a marathon to raise funds for their elected charities – microloan business projects in Africa and a local nursery school.

Friday morning assembly was given over to the girls to organise their own whole school assembly. I was a bit surprised that I was allocated a Wednesday which was a Church of England slot in the main hall with the High Mistress present. There would be fewer girls present because a lot of them would be attending their own religious assemblies –Jewish, Muslim etc. This was not a good day for me because I wanted all the girls present to help me raise as much money as possible and my suggestion to the School Chaplin, a Vicar, that a Friday was better as my assembly had nothing to do with religion was to no avail. Maybe the High Mistress wanted to keep an eye on me as I had a bit of history on the radical front but I went to work on the girls in my classes to spread the word that my assembly was for their elected charity, was not religious and I would reveal the marathon that I would run at the end of the assembly. It worked and I had a full house and the teachers involved with the religious meeting sat in empty rooms. Any wavering girls were persuaded to come when they saw all by marathon tops hung out on a washing line across the hall, the giant screen displaying moving pictures of my marathon destinations across the world and accompanied by the rousing music of Handel's Messiah. I had four senior students reading out extracts from my marathon adventures and charities supported, including The Coram Foundation hence the reason for Handel's Messiah that he gave the rights of to Coram Foundling Hospital. The assembly concluded by revealing the marathon that I was going to run in support of their elected charities to a rousing piece of music by Mozart – **The Vienna 250th Mozart Birthday Marathon.**

At the end of each academic year, the School Leavers put on a stage show that in the main lambasted the staff and other aspects of school life. They were free now from any retribution and dear me did they let rip. At the show I attended St Paul was depicted as a misogynist and they made fun of the people who named a girls' school in his honour. The High Mistress had a reputation for strictness and she was single, although it was known that she did have a close woman friend. She was tall, slim and always very smartly dressed. These traits were what the girls focused on when portraying her. A tall senior girl marched into the hall in Hitler style military uniform and up onto the stage where she shouted out discipline orders in the manner of the High Mistress to members of the audience. Soon to be joined by a subservient "girl friend". It was tough to watch and even tougher for the High Mistress to watch. I imagine she was just grateful that this lot would not be coming back next year. I suppose we could blame or thank the protected tradition of the Court Jester for giving us the freedom to lambast our superiors.

On my final day at St Paul's I took part in the staff talent show where with the help of two great sporting girls, I displayed some of my football, rugby handling and foot skills to the music of River Dance. That was conclusion to my year at St Paul's and the start of my state pension years.

The High Mistress, the same age as I was, also retired and as a reward for services to St Paul's and education could look forward to be conferred a Baroness. Sadly, a few months later I read her obituary in The Times. She died from a recurrence of breast cancer.

St Edmunds College, Ware

My final teaching contract was at St Edmund's College, the oldest Catholic school in England. I never thought that I would finish my teaching career in a Catholic school and a private one at that. It was in 1971 that I left Finchley Catholic Boys' School and here I was 36 years later back.

I had already had contact at St Edmund's because our daughter Astrid was a pupil there from 1997-2004 and ended up as Head Girl. My old friend Heddwyn Evans, rampant atheist, was now their Head of Science and he had a serious problem with his Head of Physics who was on sick leave. I was quite happy to help him out and was very well paid for doing so. Compared to other private schools I though some of the staff and especially a few of the senior laboratory technicians who were Catholics thought that they were deserving of extra favouritism. Heddwyn had told me about his problems and it was not long before I took direct action. At morning, lunch and afternoon breaks, the technicians left ten minutes before and came back ten minutes after each break. This meant they were not there to help clear away the equipment at the end of lessons or help prepare put the equipment out for the start of lessons. Furthermore, they were first to the staffroom and canteen and got to select the best cakes and lunch dishes as well as the best seats. Well I was always keen to make sure my technicians were treated the same as the teaching staff but not the other way round as was the case, more by default, at St Edmunds. It was not long before I was in the Head Teacher's office letting him know my views on the matter. It took some weeks to get the changes I wanted and as luck would have it, the lab technicians earned themselves a formal discipline warning along the way. One day there was a school emergency and the technicians stayed in the staffroom enjoying their coffee and cakes when the school was evacuated in what turned out to be a false alarm and the absence of the lab technicians was discovered during the whole school roll call. We could say that they were hung by their own petard.

As was the case with some other schools that I thought – private and state – there was an underuse and shortage of key science equipment. The Physics department was an Aladdin's cave of old and some new equipment. Sophie was a young, keen, inexperienced Physics teacher who was not given the opportunity to learn how to use some key science equipment in a demonstration or class practical context. We spent many happy hours bringing back to life equipment that had not seen the light of day for years and it was fun to relive my early life as a Physics teacher. It was a pleasure to help and guide a young teacher at a key point in her career.

There was a sizeable minority of pupils and staff at St Edmunds who were not Catholic but all bought into the school's moral ethos and values which I thought gave the school that bit extra, which was often lacking in less faith orientated schools. All pupils during the week attended I assembly in the wonderful Gothic Pugin designed Chapel. The majority of pupils in my sixth form Physics classes were from China and I often wondered what they thought of the English educational system. I think their culture fitted well in terms of discipline, morality and family values.

CHAPTER 22

THE DEATH OF MY MOTHER – MARY OLIVIA O'REILLY (NEE FITZSIMONS) 1921-2013

If it were not for my mother's knowledge and pride in her family history I probably would never have written this memoir. She was happy to recall her childhood memories and had a great memory of past events in the wider family. There were occasions when she knew more about my father's family than he did. Sadly, the O'Reilly family (with the exception of my first cousin Ann Perry O'Reilly in Ireland) for various reasons have not maintained family contact or tradition as much as they might have – and they do have an interesting family history.

My mother was a doer as well as practical, quick, energetic and a social climber. She had advice to give on all subjects. I inherited some of the latter trait and it was only in middle age that I stopped trying to advise people on what to do and felt better for it.

She had a few health problems in her life: hospitalised for weeks with glandular fever in her early 20s, hysterectomy and gall stones in her 50s and heart problems – mitral valve (pace maker inserted) in her 60s. She was very forward when it came to her medical care and prided herself in maintaining contact with Professor Fox at the Royal Brompton for many years. Despite her medical problems she continued playing golf at Mill Hill

GC into her 60s and was a member of two Bridge Clubs until her 90th Birthday. At her funeral I recalled the time she asked me to take her to see an old Bridge friend in Highgate. When we arrived at her friend's privately rented senior protected flat, the door was opened by a smartly dressed women who turned out to be 104 years old – the Queen's Birthday Telegrams on the side board by way of proof. We enjoyed a sherry together and I could not help but notice the nearly completed Daly Telegraph cryptic crossword on the table nearby. This woman only retired from Highgate Bridge Club when she got to 100 years old – too big a hill to walk to get there. She also had another friend Olga in her late 80s who was her bridge partner. Olga was a Hungarian Jew who spoke several languages and was still teaching French and Russian to business clients. My mother liked the company of other strong ambitious women.

She was very practical and hands on particularly when it came to dress making and the high point of her dress making was when she fitted out the actress Elizabeth Taylor when she worked at Chic Boutique in Hampstead, London. Needless to state that she was always immaculately dressed for special occasions that included the weddings and graduations of her grandchildren. It was the academic ceremonies that were her favourite outing as she was mightily ambitious and supportive of academic success for her offspring, some might say too much so.

We held a special family 90th Birthday Party for in January 2011 and she was the star of the party and looked more like 60 than 90. A year later she felt that matters were not right with her bowels and a colonoscopy at Barnet Hospital revealed a cancerous tumour in the upper colon. When I visited the consultant I was concerned that maybe my mother was too old to undergo an operation and that it might be better for nature to take its course. The consultant took one look at my mother, immaculately turned out as usual, and had no hesitation about performing the operation. She survived the operation but there was the added complication of her warfarin medication for her mitral valve problem. Unfortunately, when my sister Dorothy was there she had a stroke and ended up in the UCL stroke unit. It took a long time for her to get back to near normal but her drive and determination, not to mention the wear and tear on Dorothy and me got her through. She recognised that she could no longer manage on her own in her flat in Finchley and was very fortunate to get a place at Maidstone Care Centre where she had her own en suite and medical nursing care and my sister Dorothy to attend to her needs. We did look at a good care home in Ware in the town where her grandson Fingal is a partner in The Dolphin GP Practice but I was a bit worn out by this time because she was a very demanding and self centred mother at times and I had my own problems recovering from a heart bypass.

In 2012 we spent four weeks with our caravan in the south of France. We had not seen mother for five weeks and when we were leaving Dover we rang her to say we would call in to see her around 7pm before she settled down for the night. Well she gave me short shrift. She would be far too busy with putting on night pads and taking medication to have any time to see us. I ignored her anyway and after a very stressful tour of Maidstone finally managed to park the caravan in almost total darkness at the Care Centre. As we walked into her room she was sitting in her chair happily watching television, the care assistants had finished their work under her direct instructions of course. She was pleased to see us, but we knew we were secondary in the great order of events that she was undertaking in keeping her life going. Alice concluded that I need not feel guilty ever again of not going to see her at her command.

My mother was an enigma, very independent but still cable of making demands for family attention and was quick to let me and other family members know that we did not give her enough attention. In my case: "You're spending too much time in Norway instead of looking after your mother". This was somewhat ironic as my father and mother never spent much time with their own parents even when they were in old age.

Thanks to my brother Vincent she had Falun Gong – a Chinese practice of exercises and meditation. This completed the triumvirate of Golf and Bridge and was the one she kept going right to the end. I am convinced that Falun Gong added extra years to her life and she was always at pains to emphasise that it was complementary to her Christianity.

Towards the beginning of November 2013 mother was having problems with water in the lungs and swollen legs due to chronic heart failure, the end was near, but she was a great fighter to the end. She was now confined to bed and on my last visit to see her before she died, it was moving that "little Alice" – not so little now- her great grand daughter was with us. In the days leading up to her death Avril and Dorothy were constant companions and mother died peacefully on the evening of November 2013.

Her funeral in Hertford was attended by all her family including her 14 great grandchildren. She was laid to rest with her husband John who died in 2002. As a family we agreed on the inscription "I did my best" RIP

THE UNEXPECTED DEATH OF MY BROTHER VINCENT 2014

Six years was a big age gap between Vincent and me. It was even more pertinent as I never saw him growing up from the age of two to eight years of age as I was in Ireland. Vincent grew up in the rapidly changing big city urban environment that was post-war London. His parents and two sisters were all newcomers to the city and all had to learn quickly not only to adjust but also to survive. He had one incident in his teenage years that thankfully, he survived and this was to do with drug taking.

I am not clear on the exact circumstances but Vincent and some friends of his were high on Cannabis and were arrested by the police messing around in a Launderette in Hampstead. I remember visiting my brother in a prison like detention centre in South London. He was in a state of shock and was afraid of some of his aggressive fellow inmates. Later he appeared in court in Hampstead and my wife appeared as a witness – my parents and I were at work. We were expecting a possible prison sentence but surprisingly the magistrate dismissed the case. Vincent had learnt his lesson and stayed clear of the world of drugs. It helped that he was not a smoker and only drank on special occasions. He was quite capable of entering the spiritual and mystical world without the help of LSD and developed a fascination for eastern mysticism and philosophy, which he retained throughout his life. In his late 20s he spent time in Indian living the frugal and contemplative life in remote monasteries but he never did give up on his Christian up bring and saw eastern and western philosophies as complementary to each other.

He was drawn to the physical manifestation of the oriental way of life and regularly engaged in the practice of Yoga and the Martial Arts. One particular eastern philosophy came to dominate his life, Falun Gong. This suited his personality because the Chinese spiritual practice combined meditation with gigong exercises and with a moral philosophy based on the tenets of truthfulness, Compassion and Forbearance. Their teaching draws from qigong practice of the Buddhist school and also Taoist traditions. Practitioners of Falun Gong aspire to better health and ultimately spiritual enlightenment.

Falun Gong is organised in open and free group practices and because of this was seen as a threat to the state and banned by the Communist Chinese government in 1999. Vincent's big gift to my mother was Falun Gong that she practised with real commitment and spent many an hour practising in Regents Park with fellow adherents.

Vincent was fortunate to meet a lovely Swedish girl, Eva, from Gotland, Sweden. She brought tranquillity, financial stability and love into his life. They met at the Purple Pussy Cat a few hundred meters away from the Europa Club in Finchley Road where Alice ad I met. Small world and one could say Vincent followed his brother's example. They have two wonderful children Clarissa and Ossian. Family support and tolerance allowed Vincent to pursue his artistic and musical ambitions. We were all impressed with his Northern Lights exhibition at the Winter Olympics in Lillehammer, Norway in 1994 and his "Stonehenge light structures" and Prism Experience in Stockholm. Vincent often had difficulty controlling and focusing his creative energies with projects ranging from: furniture and jewellery design, 2D and 3D paintings, crystal and lighting design, Hair Fashions, house building, music composition and performance and much else. Even at the time of his death he was promoting a music group in Gotland, putting forward a proposal for a spectacular lighting display to the Stonehenge Heritage site in England and pursuing his efforts for peace through his membership and website "signforpeace".

Vincent's death came just eight months after that of his mother and was a great shock to all of us. He had excellent health throughout his life and he was looking very fit, if a little over weight, at our mother's ninetieth birthday here in Hertford in 2011. However, we did notice that he had an enlarged stomach when he attended mother's funeral in late November in 2013. This was odd as he was not a big beer drinker like his brother but he did say that he had difficulty trying to reduce his waistline despite doing a lot of power walking.

He phoned me in February 2014 to tell me he had just come out o f the local hospital after two weeks in the emergency care ward. Earlier he had severe pains in his chest and was breathless walking the few hundred yards to the hospital and on the final uphill path collapsed. In his own words he was a "dead man walking". Sadly, this turned out to be all too true. It later transpired that he had cancer of the peritoneum that had advanced beyond the operable stage. Dorothy, Pat and I visited him in early May and it was pleasing that his children Ossian (over from California) and Clarissa were there as well. His wife Eva, as ever, was a great support to him in his hour of need. Vincent knew about my heart bypass – a widow maker- in 2012 but he was right when he said that I did at least get a second chance. One evening when we were dining and pubbing in Visby, Clarissa and her boyfriend Calum spent the evening in the hospital watching the Eurovision Song Contest. Right to the end he kept his fervour for Art and Music going. Like his mother he had a penchant for watching football matches and one evening he enjoyed watching a friendly Sweden match that ended goalless. From his ward Vincent could look out westwards to the sea and in the evening witness some magnificent sunsets.

Before we left Gotland we went to mass at the local Catholic Church where each Sunday the presiding priest was flown in from Stockholm. The service brought back memories of the very happy occasion when I attended the wedding of Vincent and Eva in the same church over thirty years before. I had great difficulty and disbelief coming to terms with the circumstances that now brought me to the church. After mass we asked the priest if he could come to the hospital and give Vincent the last rites – the sacrament of the sick. He was very obliging but needed time to check out and translate the rites into English for our convenience. As we stood round Vincent's bed, he was calm, reassured and much taken with the words spoken by the priest. We were all moved by this very special spiritual occasion and knew that we could leave Visby knowing that Vincent was at one with God in all his manifestations.

During the following weeks the retired resident priest was a great source to Vincent and Eva. On June 21st 2014 Vincent died peacefully with his ever loving wife by his side. My wife Alice, son Fingal, sister Avril from Canada, Dorothy and Pat, and Vincent's great friend Philip Ng from London attended his funeral on a beautiful sunny day in Visby. After a moving funeral mass in the Catholic Church, we waved a final farewell to Vincent as the hearse departed into the distance.

The next morning still in a state of disbelief, I went for a run along the beach, past the hospital and a few kilometres along the coast to Vincent's favourite spot. Sometime later, the immediate family spread Vincent's ashes just off the coast. May his spirit always be with us. RIP.

CHAPTER 23

WHAT THIS LIFE HAS TAUGHT ME – REFLECTIONS ON THE FUTURE.

In May 2011 Alice was able to complete her dream 13-day coastal cruise with Hurtigruten from Bergen along the Norwegian coast up to Kirkenes on the Russian border and back – 34 ports visited in total. It was extraordinary to think that she had never been north of Trondheim and this city is still two-thirds the length of Norway from Kirkenes. As we sailed north the climate and terrain changed from early summer to early spring, still it was nice to see daffodils again. The company has several ships of different sizes and all are still working ships delivering and picking up goods and locals at each port. They are still the main method of transport where there are no roads or railways north of Narvik. We were a little disappointed with the fog we encountered at the North Cape but meeting the colourful Sami and their reindeers nearby was some compensation. I also enjoyed watching Alice having ice put down the back of her neck to testify that she had crossed the Arctic Circle. It had taken 61 years for her to do so.

Later we went on a 7-day Mediterranean Cruise where we were able to visit Jerusalem, the Dead Sea, the Pyramids and Antalya in Turkey that was very good value for money. A two-week cruise out of Miami around the north Caribbean in December 2014 was very enjoyable. Alice and I managed to swim and snorkel at every island we visited and I did not object to having Guinness and Oysters at an outside restaurant in Miami in 27C sunshine on 20th December before heading home to a dark freezing London.

As teachers, we could only go on holiday in high summer or half terms and had to pay the highest tariffs. After all our years in the teaching profession it was great, and cheaper, to see foreign lands that were not over crowded with tourists. We had wonderful trips to China and Sri Lanka. China was interesting mainly because of its long cultural isolation from the West and the varied landscape. Our week long boat trip up the Yangzi through the Great Gorge with 19th Century style coal power stations belching out black smoke and flames every 30 miles along the river was a once in a lifetime experience. It was not surprising that the famous Chinese fresh water dolphins were almost extinct. I would not like to live there and the trip served to demonstrate how fortunate we are to live in Europe.

Sri Lanka was worth the visit despite not being able to visit the north of the island because of the civil war. Apart from the Tamil problem, people of different religions lived in relatively harmony. On behalf of our travel group, I had the honour of thanking our Sri Lankan guide at the end of our trip and the group agreed with me when I said that he had explained the island's religious traditions with real understanding and empathy. This was quite an achievement in a country where over 90% of the population are religious and where Buddhism, Hinduism, Islam and Christianity are well represented. There were two high points literally on this trip. We visited tea plantations high up in Kandy, staying in an old colonial gentleman's' lodge. I saw some of the finest leeks and cabbages growing in this very temperate climate. There were some very poor people but no starvation that I could detect. The Buddhist temple of the Tooth in Kandy with its wonderful perfume smells and relaxed religious observance was quite an experience and contrasted greatly with the atmosphere in Christian places of worship.

The hilltop 5th century pleasure palace of Sigiriya was the "high point" of our tour. It forms an apex in Sri Lanka's Cultural Triangle. Half way up the 180m hill there is an extraordinary set of frescoes depicting a series of graceful and elegant women. The last bit of the climb to the palace at the top is exhilarating or terrifying depending on your perspective. We had a guide with us who not only carried our rucksacks but also climbed like a mountain goat.

We visited our daughter Astrid in Singapore in January 2013 and despite its autocratic government we liked it very much. From there we flew to Vietnam and Cambodia for an individual guided tour. It was extraordinary that our two first destinations in both countries were to visit the Viet Cong tunnels in Vietnam and "The Killing Fields" in Cambodian involving the death and murder of millions of civilians. The miles of narrow tunnels and the death traps built to trap the US infantry soldiers were both impressive and gruesome. I had cause to remember my Irish school friend Joe Coyne who helped me to do my Gaelic homework – he was a Gaelic native speaker from Connemara – when looking at the mantraps. Joe immigrated to America at 18 years old and ended up fighting with the American infantry in the very area where we now were. He saw some horrible war scenes that affected him for life.

REFLECTIONS ON LIFE

Some of my favourite short sayings that I tended to repeat over the years included; "What is it all about?", "Where do we go from here?", "No problem" or "Kein Problem" to my German friends and "That is that" – that one I picked up from my dad. I have always been very aware as Goethe said that "time waits for no man" or that a lifetime is but a "glint of light off a beetle's wing". I have to admit that people who act and think their life is never going to end irritate me big time. They will work beyond retirement because their pension will be that little bit more and they assume of course that their life will continue for years after retirement and that they will have the energy and drive that they had (or imagined they did) in their twenties.

The awareness of the passage of time and of one's own mortality has been my constant companions throughout my life. It is a paradox that the busier you are, the more you can do – give the job to a busy person if you want it done quick – and also the quicker time appears to fly. When I had my greatest challenges and busiest periods at work I seemed to live from one-week end to the next wondering what happened to the five days in between. Sometimes it pays to be bored because it gives you time to think about "what is life all about" and to feel the passage of time.

In my mature years four questions come to mind:

1. Could I have done more with my life?
2. What would I do different if I could live my life again?
3. Is there an end to the remorseless suffering and constant ethnic and religious conflicts of humanity?
4. Can science and technology save the world from over population and global destruction?

There is no clear-cut answer to these questions and besides the first two are hypothetical. We like to think that we are individuals with freedom to operate and to control our way through life but we are all very much products of our cultural, national and economic environments. Given favourable family and economic support everyone can achieve more in life and I am no exception. In a way I am glad that I was not too driven to achieve at the highest level because of the sacrifices necessary to be successful. Besides, I did not have the necessary brainpower or touch of genius to achieve at the highest level.

As a minor scientist I marvel at the Second Law of Thermodynamics and its relevance to human behaviour. In short, all systems tend to maximum disorder and you need to put energy into a system to get some order back – think of having the seemingly endless task of tidying up your house or the falling apart of family dynasties or empires. Related to this is the keeping of a system in equilibrium. If all the energy coming into the earth equals all the energy going out of the earth, then it is in thermal balance so no global warming. Also related to this law is that things keep on changing and in the context of human nature we often use the expression or cliché that one has to "change with the times" or one "cannot afford to stand still". Of course we also have the expression "what comes round goes round" which happens but it is not exactly as it was before and one hopes that this kind of change is on a spiral that directs us to betterment.

I have been excited by scientific, educational and social developments in the last two hundred years, far more than in the previous total history of humanity: evolutions, nuclear power, DNA, space travel, relativity and penicillin all come to mind. Science and education have helped to prolong life and relieve disease and famine. Of course, more needs to be done. I believe with education and better worldwide communication, people will be less likely to engage in warfare inspired by religious hatred and outmoded nationalism.

I marvel at the human ability to be conscious of self and of others. Even more astounding is the evolution of the human brain's ability to be conscious of consciousness itself. I am also surprised by the way our concepts acquired in our own macroscopic world: waves, particles, lattices, vibration allow us to come up with models for what is happening on the microscopic (atomic) scale.

However, our brain has its limitations. We only perceive part of what is actually out there and have to use previously built up images in our brain to operate. I am mindful of this limitation in writing this book and can only hope that my family and extended family will at least have a partial shared perception of the events described in the book.

One of my biggest disappoints with science is that we have not been able to discover anything, including information, that travels faster than the speed of light (em) – 186,000 miles per second. As we try to make an object move faster and faster we put more and more energy into increasing its mass instead of its speed – think of the increasing energy needed to keep rolling an expanding snowball along the ground covered in snow. To send a light signal to our nearest star and wait for its reflection off the star to come back would take eight years! We really seem to be isolated and alone in our part of the universe. Sometimes I think that humanity is like a goldfish in a bowel that has no idea of the world outside the bowl.

We may be limited in space and time but there are still many exciting discoveries to come that will help towards the eradication of disease, social deprivation and human conflict. I have been very fortunate to have lived in a period of great discoveries and change for the better. I have been even more fortunate to be part of a great family and circle of friends.

No, I would not have changed anything. Slainte